Ontologies of Sex

Reframing the Boundaries:
Thinking the Political

Series Editors: Alison Assiter and Evert van der Zweerde

This series aims to mine the rich resources of philosophers in the "continental" tradition for their contributions to thinking the political. It fills a gap in the literature by suggesting that the work of a wider range of philosophers than those normally associated with this sphere of work can be of relevance to the political.

Titles in the Series

Kierkegaard and the Matter of Philosophy, Michael O'Neill Burns
Arendt, Levinas, and a Politics of Relationality, Anya Topolski
The Risk of Freedom: Ethics, Phenomenology, and Politics in Jan Patocka, Francesco Tava, translated by Jane Ledlie
Nietzsche's Death of God and Italian Philosophy, Emilio Carlo Corriero, translated by Vanessa Di Stefano
Lotman's Cultural Semiotics and the Political, Andrey Makarychev and Alexandra Yatsyk
Axel Honneth: Reconceiving Social Philosophy, Dagmar Wilhelm
Sartre, Imagination, and Dialectical Reason: Creating Society as a Work of Art, Austin Hayden Smidt
Ontologies of Sex: Philosophy in Sexual Politics, Zeynep Direk

Ontologies of Sex

Philosophy in Sexual Politics

Zeynep Direk

ROWMAN & LITTLEFIELD
INTERNATIONAL

London • New York

Published by Rowman & Littlefield International, Ltd.
6 Tinworth Street, London SE11 5AL
www.rowmaninternational.com

Rowman & Littlefield International, Ltd. is an affiliate of
Rowman & Littlefield
4501 Forbes Boulevard, Suite 200, Lanham, Maryland 20706, USA
With additional offices in Boulder, New York, Toronto (Canada), and London (UK)
www.rowman.com

British Library Cataloguing in Publication Information
A catalogue record for this book is available from the British Library

ISBN: HB 978-1-78660-663-1

Library of Congress Cataloging-in-Publication Data

Library of Congress Control Number: 2020933468

ISBN: 978-1-78660-663-1 (cloth)
ISBN: 978-1-5381-4819-8 (pbk)
ISBN: 978-1-78660-664-8 (electronic)

Contents

Introduction

This book explores various ontologies of sex, in a philosophical field of research in which there is a multiplicity of theories. The field is animated by several metaphysical questions: What is the being of the body? What does it mean for the body to be sexed? How should we understand the process of sexuation? What is the ontological status of sexual difference? What is an erotic experience? What is an intimate sexual relation? What do the problems of ipseity (selfhood), authenticity, and identity, and the "truth" that accompanies them, have to do with sex and gender?

My book does not claim to be exhaustive and inclusive of all the theories that should be considered in this field. I consider only some important theoretical approaches in feminist theory and contemporary continental philosophy. In the field of feminist philosophy, ontologies of sex critically engage and compete with each other. In this book, I lay out what I consider to be philosophically important approaches to the leading questions I enumerated above, to compare them with each other and to see what kind of sexual ethics and politics they lead to. Such an overview of different positions helps us to determine and revise our own ontological and political commitments in the midst of ongoing heated debate.

To make an ontology of sex, one needs to think about problems such as the body's relation to the forces of nature, its environing world, the lived experience of the body, the body's situatedness in the world, the body's relation to others, and the materialization of the body in the midst of intersecting and interacting axes of power, norms, culture, and history. These issues are hardly separable from the metaphysical problems of freedom and determinism, the nature of subjectivity, and the role that ethical agency and political action play in processes of subjectivation. In different types of feminist philosophy, divergent ontological commitments are made. Not all feminist ontologies are ontologies of individual freedom. Some refuse to partake in metaphysics of subjectivity, draw from the natural forces, or appeal to the performativity of power to explain what it is to be gendered. There are relational ontologies and ontologies about processes of subjectivation.

Feminism's highly critical, dynamic, and interdisciplinary field is inhabited by a multiplicity of gender theories and theories of sexual difference. The philosophical debate over sexual difference versus gender is not yet resolved. In the early '90s, the debate over sex/gender was very much at the foreground of feminist theorizing. Despite the lack of resolution since then, feminist theory has rapidly become part of social and political philosophy. It has transformed the philosophical corpus of ethics, epistemology, and philosophy of science, even though ontology remains relatively undertheorized as a philosophical discipline. This is probably because, in the analytic strand of philosophy, the ontological question is exclusively framed as an explication of the objectivity of the objects. Nonetheless, the question of the body as an ontological question is the key for the transformation of "metaphysics" as another domain inclusive of feminist philosophical issues.

It is also true that in the last two decades feminist philosophers have been more interested in ontological questions. This is visible in Simone de Beauvoir studies and the field of naturalist feminism. The most remarkable example is Elizabeth Grosz, who uses the term "onto-ethics" to describe her own philosophical theory (Grosz 2017b). Carrie Hull's *The Ontology of Sex: A Critical Inquiry into the Deconstruction and Reconstruction of Categories* (Hull 2006) discusses the ontological implications of Michel Foucault and Judith Butler's attack on the natural categories of sex and situates the debates between realism and nominalism.

The novelty of my approach can be found in my strategy to discuss the ontological positions taken in the feminist field on the body as sexed being alongside the ontologies of Eros that are part of the contemporary French philosophy. My survey does not only include feminist philosophers and queer theorists—it also explores philosophical theories of sexual difference and erotic experience construed by Georges Bataille, Jacques Derrida, Jacques Lacan, Paul Ricoeur, and Jean-Luc Nancy, male philosophers some of which have not engaged with feminism at all, or who criticized either feminism of equality or feminism of difference, or perhaps both. For the most part, an ontology of sex can be formulated as a question of sexual difference because any account of sexual difference is underscored by an ontology that has already made some philosophical commitments. Luce Irigaray implies that when she argues that we cannot think sexual difference without developing a new ontological account of time and space. A different attitude toward nature, the transformation of the spiritual and cultural fields, would be required to make sexual difference appear. In other words, sexual difference would come with a new ontology. Different accounts of sexual difference imply different understandings of being, and rest on different ontological models. Nonetheless, many ontologies of sex focus on the nature and dynamics of erotic experience without paying special attention to the question of sexual difference. I believe that to broadly classify the existing ontologies of sex by making a distinction between naturalist accounts of sexual difference and constructivist approaches that prefer to talk about gender would be reductive. Some ontologies of sex that I consider in this book are less concerned with sexual difference than with the ontological question of Eros. They focus on Eros as an irreducible ontological dimension of our Being, which calls for a new way of thinking the relation between nature and culture.

The last fifty years of feminist thinking in France and in the English-speaking world has created a rich philosophical field, in which theoretical problems meet with concrete experiences and rightful concerns, which send us back to ethical questions of a good life and how we ought to live. Philosophical theories of gender and sexual difference are fundamental to the feminist task of bringing about political change that leads to a world in which there are no hierarchies created by gender. However, their ontological problematic is often insufficiently understood. I intend to show that different characterizations of erotic experience offer ontologies, as do accounts of sexual difference. This is why I concentrate on thinkers as diverse as Simone de Beauvoir, Georges Bataille, Luce Irigaray, Sigmund Freud, Jacques Lacan, Judith Butler, Elizabeth Grosz, Claire Colebrook, Jacques Derrida, Jean-Luc Nancy, and Paul Ricoeur to talk about what they have contributed to our understanding of what it means to be sexuated and in erotic relation with the other.

My first chapter, "Simone de Beauvoir: An Ontology and Ethics of Freedom," is devoted to an analysis of Beauvoir's ontology of sex. I begin with Simone de Beauvoir because she is the first philosopher who analyzes sexual difference in terms of sexual oppression in an ontological and phenomenological account of freedom. In other words, her phenomenological and existentialist ontology of freedom offers an ontology of sex. First, I argue that *The Second Sex* must be read in the light of the controversy over the problem of freedom between Sartre and Merleau-Ponty. As a response to that controversy, *The Ethics of Ambiguity* offers a new understanding of freedom, which leads to moral freedom and paves the way for *The Second Sex*, in which the question of sexual oppression is addressed. I show how her conception of freedom differs from Sartre's and argue that the ethical injunction to care for the others' freedom conveys her to the problematization of sexual oppression. The originality of this ontology lies in the analysis of sexual oppression as formative of sexual difference. Although Beauvoir argues that women are not free in their subjection to the realm of immanence, she leaves open the possibility of emancipation through what I would call "subjectivation." The possibility of subjectivation lies in the ambiguity of the "body in situation," which is lived under conditions of oppression. This phenomenological, existential ontology of sex calls for political action to render incarnated freedom possible. Although I did not develop that, I agree with the view that Beauvoir offers a feminist phenomenology of Eros on ontological and political grounds. Fashioning an ontological understanding of human being as both immanence and transcendence, she argues that erotic experience, when it is unimpeded by the patriarchal oppression, can be reciprocal recognition, the ground of free love and generosity.

Ontologies of sex can often be reformulated as ontologies of sexual difference; however, not all such ontologies view the question of sexual difference as the prominent problem. In Georges Bataille, for example, Eros plays an indispensable role in philosophical anthropology. Indeed, it becomes impossible to explain what it means to be human without an explanation of the ontological significance of erotic experience. This is very different from the limited role assigned to Eros in ancient epistemology and ontology. *Symposium* and *Phaedrus* considered Eros in the role it played in the acquisition of philosophical knowledge. They make clear that Eros belonged to philosophy, alongside *philia* (friendship), and had a role to play alongside the intellect in accounting for the philosopher's relation to truth; it set the soul in the movement of ascendance in the course of which forms are comprehended. In Neo-Platonism and Sufism, love has been the grounding effect of a relation to God. Eros disappeared from the philosophical scene in modern philosophy, to come back as a philosophical problem in Bataille, who reconsidered it by taking seriously Nietzsche's concept of life as play of forces and the teachings of the structuralist anthropologists, notably, Claude Lévi-Strauss.

In the second chapter, "Georges Bataille: Erotic Experience," I explore Bataille's economy of erotic experience. *The Accursed Share* describes the erotic experience as the expenditure of bioenergy and describes sovereignty with reference to the general economy of life. Bataille's economy of living being takes its departure from an understanding of the body as part of the global flow of energy and offers a reflection on the ontological significance of the erotic experience. I show how the question of human sexuality is related to the problem of the constitution of the profane world and how central it is to the sacred world. I argue that Bataille neglected the question of sexual oppression even though his theory makes room for a sovereign feminine sexuality and allows for an expansion of sexual difference via the queer pleasures attached to different drives. Throughout this chapter, I navigate significant differences between Beauvoir and Bataille by pointing to their common sources, philosophical problems, and concepts.

The contemporaneity of Bataille's ontology of sex with Beauvoir's attests to an intellectual movement that questions sex in a radical, philosophical manner. Foucault in *The History of Sexuality* shows how the historical transformation of the human attitudes toward sex in the late modernity might signal the production of subject by discourse/power regimes, which he contrasted with the ways in which the self was problematized by the usage of pleasures in antiquity. Both Foucault and Lacan put in question the political discourse of sexual emancipation of 1968. Foucault offered an historical analysis while Lacan highlighted the impasses of human sexuality in a re-reading of Freud's account of sexual difference.

In the third chapter, "The Problem of Phallocentrism," I turn to the psychoanalytical account of sexual difference and Luce Irigaray's critique of Freud and Lacan in *Speculum of the Other Woman* and *This Sex Which Is Not One*. I discuss Lacan's reinterpretation of Freud's "Feminine Sexuality" and his theory of sexual difference in "The Signification of the Phallus," and his explanation of female sexual enjoyment in Seminar Book XX *Encore*. Tina Chanter shows in her *The Ethics of Eros* how Irigaray's question of sexual difference is linked to an ethics of Eros (Chanter 1991). I explain Irigaray's argument that both Freud's and Lacan's theories of sexual difference are phallocentric and why phallocentrism makes an ethics of Eros impossible. In order to make room for the possibility of ethical relations between the sexes, Irigaray needed a new ontology. In my inquiry on her critique of phallocentrism, I show how this critique rests on a conception of the imaginary body as a condition of the materialization of the real body through the cultivation of its own natural forces in accordance with its own norms. Irigaray starts with the natural, biological existence of the two sexes, and she shows that patriarchy ensnares the feminine in phallocentric logic. Admittedly, both biological realism and the ontologies that difference feminism created, including Irigaray's, have to face the risk of essentialism. The burden of being born in a female body in a patriarchal culture, the historical oppression of women by men because of their sex, Irigaray thinks, should not lead us to dismiss sex as construction. By accentuating the role of the imaginary body in early texts, I attempt to explain why Irigaray's ontology of sex is not an essentialist ontology. Irigaray is stressing that we cannot understand patriarchy if we do not reflect on its symbolic system. The question remains if the disadvantages that the symbolic system creates for women would be annihilated by the new symbolic modifications, which open it to self-identification in the name of equality and inclusion.

The fourth chapter, "Different Ontologies in Queer Theory," compares Butler's ontology of the body as embedded in her queer theory with the naturalist accounts of sexual difference of Elizabeth Grosz and Claire Colebrook. First, I focus on Judith Butler's ontological understanding of the body, in *Gender Trouble*, which dates from 1990, and *Bodies that Matter*, which responds to objections in 1993. In *Gender Trouble*, sexuality is said to give rise to the construction of sexual difference, and gender identity is explained as an outcome of a gendering process. Butler transforms the idea of social construction, by showing how the gendered body is materialized in a relation to juridical systems of power. For Butler there is no sex without relation to law. Gender identity is acquired by the encounter of the body with the norms by means of which power regulates bodies. This is the theory of the performativity of power, which is *par excellence* an ontological account of the constitution of bodies. This theory of performativity is conjoined with an account of bodies' assumption and performance of gender norms. In this view, the body is conceived as capable of acquiring habits through the performance of gender norms that are socially, culturally, and historically produced. For Butler, in Western culture, gender is power that functions to produce and regulate bodies in a regime of compulsory heterosexuality. This gives rise to gender identity, which is inseparable from having an intelligible personal identity.

Butler sees the body as a schema of sedimented habits, always capable of rematerialization at the face of the law of gender. The psychic is only a second-order expression of the mechanisms of gendering. The law of its materialization is not given to the body from within its psychic interiority; it is received from the cultural world and gives rise to lived experiences of an interiority. Hence, the natural forces, whether they are physical or psychical, do not contribute anything to the body's becoming. They are simply irrelevant. Butler maintains that the existence of a natural sex is the grounding presupposition of the cultural process of gendering that brings a body into being, by engendering it. Body's capacity to take a shape through the repetition of the gender norms gives rise to a body that would be intelligible or unintelligible within certain gender regimes. In opposing the mind-body dualism of the metaphysics of subjectivity, Butler redefines the body as nothing else than an outcome of its encounter with culture. There is no free subject that shapes its body by freely choosing the gender norms that are already available to it in culture, for the corporeal being is always already produced by gender. The question arises if the body is not, therefore, entirely submerged in a cultural determinism in which its possibility of being otherwise is foreclosed. Butler finds the possibility of resistance and change by the coming into being of agency and through its performances that play with gender norms.

Contesting this ontology that focuses on how power materializes bodies and denies the relevance of a biological sex as separate from the gendering process, naturalism goes back to the notion of life in order to rethink the question of sexual difference. Elizabeth Grosz's naturalist ontology of sex, inspired by Irigaray, rejects the view that sex is socially constructed and projects to explore its reality. Naturalist ontologies challenge social constructivism and return to nature as productive of sexual differences that are not limited by two. The problem with making gender an umbrella concept is that it cuts the possibility of speaking of nature as productive of difference that can rise to culture. Naturalism disagrees with Butler's view, in *Gender Trouble*, that sexual difference is irrelevant to queer theory. Even if nature is conceived as producing sexual differences that are not limited by two, it is not clear if these differences can appear as what they are and be accessible in culture. My own position is that we should not erase sex and reduce everything to gender, but the account of sexual difference(s) must not be divorced of a critique of cultural oppression that opens a space for the negotiation of the different needs and interests of the oppressed groups.

In this difficult debate over gender, I think that a return to the existentialist and phenomenological feminist ontology is the best strategy. Neither ontologies of gender nor of sexual difference give us a good account of subjectivation cast in terms of political phenomenology. Simone de Beauvoir and Paul Ricoeur leave open the way for thinking subjectivation of a sexed being, in its vulnerability and capacity for emancipation. This political subjectivity is not divorced from ethical agency. And it is so much more promising than the politics of mobilization opted by some versions of naturalist queer theory and the politics of affects associated with it. Capitalism can also capture the desires, sadness, and fury of the sexually oppressed people and manipulate them as a cultural group to fulfill its neoliberal interests in opening new markets for biopower.

In the fifth chapter, "Jean-Luc Nancy: An Ontology of Sex," I discuss Jean-Luc Nancy's ontology of sex by comparing it with Derrida's. In *Positions*, which dates from 1972, Derrida argued that the pair of opposites, man and woman, is metaphysical and needs to be deconstructed. Derrida is a thinker of sexual difference. Since *Glas*, which is first published in 1974, he inquires into sexual difference that is not limited by the heteronormative binary; he ontologically conceives sexual difference as "dispersion," "dissemination," without grounding his view on a naturalist concept of life or on a phenomenology of the lived body. This is not to say that Derrida does not philosophize about the body. Taking his distance to Hegel's, Freud's, and Lacan's accounts of subjectivity as desire, he prefers in *Geschlecht I*, a text written in 1983, to discuss sexual difference by going back to Heidegger's existential analysis in *Being and Time*. In *Geschlecht I*, in a defense of Heidegger, he gives an ontological account of sexual difference beyond the binary division into male and female. *Geschlecht* is a term that signifies at the intersection of race, ethnicity, kind, sex, social position, and gender. Derrida's account sexual difference enables a reflection on sex as intersectional. Unlike Butler, Derrida does not focus on corporeal existence as a product of gender norms. For him, sex is originally impure and plural, and something that is not made or fashioned but consumed in the dynamic and fluid movement of *différance*. It is in that movement in which corporeal existence is inscribed that sex may signify, shine, and fade in non-sense.

Sexual difference is addressed in terms of the dispersion in the world of *Dasein* as a thrown being. The novelty of Derrida's account lies is its suggestion that the question of sex as an ontological question can be properly discussed only in an ontology that does not limit ontology to the entities of the kind present-at-hand. Heidegger is the philosopher who opened that field of ontological research. Jean-Luc Nancy too pursues the Heideggerian path, even though he does stay within the limits of an exegesis. Rather than focusing on the question of sexual difference, he concentrates on the "there is" of sexual relation as a site for the erotic experience understood as possibility of an infinite intimacy. He also rethinks the question of what it means to exist as sexed in a broader reflection on the philosophy's relation to Eros.

Jean-Luc Nancy's *Sexistence* is the most recent attempt to go back to a philosophical starting point at which existence is read as sexual, and sex opens itself to interpretation as a relation. Derrida and Nancy seek a third way to avoid the alternatives of naturalism and social constructivism. Their ontological approaches accommodate the innumerable differences that queer theory might need, without falling in the trap of the opposition between nature and culture. Jean-Luc Nancy's discourse on sex is a discourse on desire and language, on sense and signification. His account of erotic experience is not simply about how a subject relates to another in sexual desire; it concerns a fundamental way in which reality gives itself. For him, erotic signification cannot be separated from the question of the sense of the world.

In the sixth chapter, "Subjects of Rights: From Vulnerability to Autonomy," I discuss Ricoeur's political phenomenological theory of subject of rights in relation to feminist theories of oppression. My main themes are *"autonomy"* and *"vulnerability."* This chapter is interested in vulnerability as an effect of structural oppression, which deprives the subject of the possibility of exercising its capacities to become an autonomous subject. I argue that Ricoeur's account of autonomy is relational, and it implies relation to the other and the third. By *"subjectivity"* he means a process that involves becoming a speaking subject, a subject of action, a narrating subject, an ethical subject, and a subject of rights. Ricoeur does not take into account the question of sexual difference and erotic experience. By including Iris Marion Young, Marilyn Frye, and other feminist thinkers who wrote on sexual oppression, I argue that we cannot exclude sexual difference and erotic experience from the process of the formation of political subjectivity. And here by *"political subjectivity,"* I mean a subject prepared to resist systematic oppression.

Ontologies of Sex: Philosophy in Sexual Politics comes from my 400-level undergraduate course titled "Philosophical Perspectives on Gender" which I have been teaching at Koç University in Istanbul, Turkey, every two years. The course belongs to the curriculum of the gender certificate program of KoçKam, and students coming from the other disciplines take it with philosophy students. I designed the course so that students coming from different disciplines realize that multiple feminisms, queer theories, and philosophies of sex offer their own philosophical comprehensions of being sexed; that is, they have a specific understanding of the self, the others, and the world. In this course my main themes are "erotic experience" and "sexual difference." I start with French existentialism and phenomenology, which is informed by the French philosophical reception of Hegel's philosophy. The problem of freedom, the phenomenological concepts of intentionality, immanence, transcendence, alterity, relation to the other, master and slave dialectic, and relation to the Absolute are necessary components of my itinerary. They help to illuminate Beauvoir's ontology of sex. In my discussion of Bataille's erotic experience, the student discovers how structuralist anthropology provides for a comprehension of the patriarchal economy in which women appear as taboo and abject. In discussing the psychoanalytical tradition, I offer an analysis of Freud and Lacan's articulation of sexual difference and focus on Lacan's dialectic of desire, his early and late configurations of the real, the imaginary, and the symbolic, and his concept of jouissance. I explain Irigaray's engagement with Freud and Lacan, because without a good introduction we cannot make sense of her phenomenological and hermeneutical ontology of sex. I also discuss gender as conceived by Butler's queer theory and show how the concept of life is opposed to it, in naturalist evolutionary accounts of sexual difference. I consider the ontological approaches of Derrida and Jean Luc Nancy and what they contribute to the philosophy of sex. There we are introduced to the concepts of an ontology of sex such as "dissemination," "sexed body," "sexistence," "relation body," "making body with the other," etc., which serve to account for erotic experience in dissociation from the questions of power, such as abjection, exclusion, domination, sovereignty, and sexual oppression. I also explore the capability approach to subjectivation in Ricoeur's philosophy and show how it can be pertinent to feminism, queer theory, and transgender studies. This book is helpful for students and readers who may want to connect philosophies of gender and sexual difference with major philosophical currents in contemporary philosophy. It is hard to make sense of feminism and queer theory without understanding in what ways they are based on problems of philosophy.

In highlighting the indispensable concepts, strategies, and arguments that are worth keeping, my ultimate objective is to create a philosophical account of sexual difference and erotic experience. As it must be clear for the reader by now, I did not strongly impose a single understanding of sexual difference and erotic experience in my engagement with different philosophers. I tried to do my best to lay out and discuss their views, and, in the process, I revised my own theoretical tendencies. The novelty of my approach consists in its redesigning and enlarging of the ontological field: it fashions an ontology that takes into account feminism, queer theory, and philosophy of sex and love and its focus on the political implications of a new reflection on erotic experience and sexual difference. The reader can also see my own theoretical inclinations throughout the manuscript. I recapitulate them in the conclusion.

This book is written as part of a long engagement with teaching feminist philosophy. First, I would like to thank all my students at Koç University who took my "Philosophical Perspectives on Gender" class and shared my enthusiasm about thinking sexual difference in relation to erotic experience and the possibility of ethics of Eros throughout different philosophical figures. My student assistant Elif Çağatay, who is an undergraduate in the Department of Philosophy, has helped me at the stage of manuscript preparation, in styling my manuscript, and in checking and standardizing my references. Indeed, she has been my first attentive reader. Secondly, I thank Laverne Maggins, an editor at Penn State University, who proofread my first two chapters. Thirdly, I am grateful for the friendship and support of my former professors, Robert Bernasconi and Leonard Lawlor. I started doing feminist philosophy with Tina Chanter back in the 1990s in University of Memphis during my PhD years. I will always be grateful for her friendship and contribution to my philosophical formation. Fourthly, I am grateful to Jean-Luc Nancy, who has always been so supportive of me in the worst times of academic life in Turkey as a friend and made possible for me to work on his manuscripts. I also profited very much from Evert van der Zweerde's and Alison Assiter's valuable comments on the first draft of this manuscript. Finally, I thank my caring friend Bahire Boyra; my mother, Nuran Direk; and my children, Hasan Eflatun Akay and Baran Eflatun Küpüşoğlu, for understanding and supporting me in the process of writing this book.

Istanbul, September 2019

Chapter One

Simone de Beauvoir

An Ontology and Ethics of Freedom

Simone de Beauvoir's account of sexual difference is grounded in an ontology and ethics of freedom. Jean-Paul Sartre, in *Being and Nothingness*, starts with freedom as an ontological problem and then moves to a discussion of the possibility of free action. The debate over free action paves the way in Beauvoir's *The Ethics of Ambiguity* for a moral notion of freedom. In Maurice Merleau-Ponty and Sartre, the question of the possibility of free action culminated in a reflection on freedom in history, via a new dialectical account of historical reason. *The Second Sex* takes the step from moral freedom to an existentialist analysis of sexual oppression, which is rooted in history. Beauvoir explains the structure of oppression and demands the inclusion of women in history. Indeed, she believes that history will give rise to freedom and equality for all only if we personally commit ourselves to these values.

In this chapter, I situate Beauvoir within the existentialist philosophical debates over freedom and show how her ontological commitments have led to feminist ethical and political commitments. My discussion of Beauvoir's ontology and ethics of freedom explains her original contribution by situating it within her philosophical relations: I start with Sartre's early theory of free action, Merleau-Ponty's criticism of it, Beauvoir's response to Albert Camus's *The Myth of Sisyphus*, and Beauvoir's reinterpretation of Hegel's idea of the Absolute. This complex background helps to explain both Beauvoir's account of oppression and the nature of her ethical response to it, and sheds light on her discussion of sexual oppression in *The Second Sex*. For Beauvoir, sexual oppression plays a major role in the constitution of sexual difference. Her ethics of Eros, understood in terms of conversion and generosity, is premised upon the abolition of sexual oppression.

I first discuss Sartre's ontological notion of freedom in *Being and Nothingness* in relation to his theory of action, which accounts for the structure of free action. Second, I argue that Beauvoir in *The Ethics of Ambiguity* takes up the experience of freedom in the light of the problem of oppression, responding, although implicitly, to Merleau-Ponty's criticism of Sartre's notion of freedom in *Phenomenology of Perception*'s "Freedom" chapter. Third, I show that by developing a notion of moral freedom in *The Ethics of Ambiguity*, Beauvoir also responds to Camus's discussion of freedom, in *The Myth of Sisyphus*, as an encounter with the absurdity of the world. Last, I lay out how Beauvoir problematizes sexual difference in *The Second Sex*, by briefly exploring her response to Hegel and her approach to the biological facts.

SARTRE'S THEORY OF FREEDOM

Sartre in *Being and Nothingness* does not prove freedom. Just like Descartes and Kant did, he postulates it. For Descartes the faculty of the will is infinite, and for Kant freedom is a transcendental fact (moral law being the essence of freedom, human beings are free because, Kant claims, as rational beings they are capable of acting for the sake of moral law alone) (Kant 1997, 28). Sartre, in *Being and Nothingness*, refuses to discuss freedom on the basis of the faculty of the will; instead, he begins with the postulate that consciousness (being-for-itself) is free. This makes freedom the ground not only of decision-making, but also of all cognitive activity. Thus, Sartre develops a radical notion of freedom, which is expressed by the renowned statement "I am condemned to be free" (Sartre 2003, 462). The subject is free as thrown into the world; it is responsible for everything it does. If all human situations are created by freedom, we do not have the possibility of not being free; we cannot escape freedom. To believe that one has succeeded in escaping freedom is to live in bad faith (self-deception). Sartre is aware that his theory gives rise to several difficulties, the most serious of which is holding the oppressed responsible for their oppression.

Sartre's notion of freedom is ontological not simply because he asserts that human existence is free or that freedom belongs to human existence. What makes freedom ontological is the role it plays in the possibility of the experience of the world. In *Being and Nothingness*, experience of the world rests on the encounter of the being-for-itself with the being-in-itself. The being-for-itself nihilates the being-in-itself and brings nothingness and lack (that which does not yet exist) in the world. This is to say, being-in-itself does not include non-being; consciousness introduces the non-being into the world. Indeed, the first manifestation of freedom should be sought in that nihilating encounter of the being-for-itself with the being-in-itself, an encounter that, as Sartre argues, gives rise to "human reality." The world we experience stems from the entanglement of these two beings—postulates of the phenomenological analysis. Beauvoir recapitulates this entanglement very well when she writes in *The Ethics of Ambiguity*: "One can not deny being, this pure positivity; one does not escape this fullness: a destroyed house *is* a ruin; a broken chain *is* scrap iron: one attains only signification and, through it, the for-itself which is projected there; the for-itself carries nothingness in its heart and can be annihilated, whether in the very upsurge of its existence or through the world in which it exists" (Beauvoir 1976, 31).

In *Being and Nothingness*, Sartre takes freedom to be an ontological given, for he identifies freedom with the movement of consciousness, a movement that is intentional, with different layers of constitution, in accordance with the phenomenological tradition, in which intentionality is constitutive of even the underlying flux of temporality. The consciousness of time is constituted by the passive synthesis of the unreflective consciousness. The ontological notion of freedom is associated both with intentionality and negativity; Sartre takes them to be inseparable because he commits himself to the view that "every determination is a negation" (Sartre 2003, 38). That consciousness "is what it is not and is not what it is" implies that it cannot be fixed. The ultimate experience of the ontological freedom is the impossibility of arresting the movement of consciousness by giving it a fixed form.

Sartre gave the term "action" a specific weight. Given ontological freedom, the question still arises if we are really free in the world. To act means to modify the "shape of the world" by achieving particular aims, which one freely chooses (Sartre 2003, 455). But are we free to act, and what is free action? Sartre begins his chapter "Being and Doing: Freedom" by stating:

> To act is to modify the shape of the world, it is to arrange in view of an end, to produce an instrumental complex such that by a series of concatenations and connections the modifications effected on one side of the links causes modifications throughout the whole series and finally produce an anticipated result. (Sartre 2003, 455)

The citation makes manifest the main thesis of Sartre's philosophy of action, namely, that intention precedes and makes possible causes and motives. He frames his thesis as a response to the classical metaphysical debate over freedom and determinism. He insists that "what is" cannot determine "what is not" (Sartre 2003, 458). This claim, which is of ontological consequence, gives us, in a nutshell, the ground of Sartre's philosophy of action. Sartre rejects all kinds of determinism, but first of all natural determinism, which reduces action to movement in accordance with the laws of nature. For Sartre, action as voluntary intentional movement cannot be philosophically explained without appeal to freedom. In order to act, we need to have a relation to non-being. "What is not," in other words, non-being, appears because being-for-itself is free. What is not cannot be given to consciousness by what is; being-in-itself can only give what it has (Sartre 2003, 458).

Sartre rejects the account of freedom that is based on free will. He rejects the Cartesian tradition in which free will is opposed to the determination by the passions of the soul. He opposes the soft deterministic view that our acts can spontaneously introduce new causal chains in the causal phenomenal world. For Sartre, being-for-itself, in other words, consciousness, cannot be understood in any sense as predetermined. Freedom is a fundamental property of consciousness because consciousness chooses its determinations, and in doing so negates itself. As Sartre argues, if the consciousness *is what it is not and is not what it is*, consciousness implies a rejection of all determination that cannot be negated.

Indeed, in *Being and Nothingness*, Sartre also rejects psychological and historical determinism (Freudian psychology and Marxist historical materialism). He is critical of Marxism's understanding of what it means to be in a "historically determined situation of oppression" in his example of the worker (Sartre 2003, 457). The worker revolts not because his situation is determined by exploitation and oppression; he deems his situation to be unbearable only because he envisages the possibility that a different state of affairs can be created. If he does not revolt, even though his situation involves substantial exploitation, this is because he does not think there is a situation from which he must emancipate himself. The worker is not by natural observation aware that he or she is in a situation of oppression. Sartre argues that the worker may have different explanations of his situation and may not think it is oppressive unless he grasps the possibility of changing it by adhering to an emancipatory project. Clearly, a worker whose experience is theologically framed, which presumes a divine providence that assigns him to an unchangeable destiny, to a particular role and place in the world, would have an account of his situation different from that of a worker who shares the Marxist project of revolution and interprets his situation as oppressive and calling for revolutionary action. Workers may not even sufficiently reflect on their situation because of their low education (Sartre 2003, 457).

In "Being and Doing: Freedom," Sartre gives us a theory of action: determinism presupposes that there are causes and motives that precede action. Sartre opposes this thesis by claiming that causes and motives do not precede the intention to act; they manifest themselves in a situation, depending on the project the agent adopts. Projects enable the agents to portray ends and means. The accomplishment of a project may involve the achievement of several intermediate ends. For Sartre a project or an end entails the nihilation of both the being-in-itself and the being-for-itself. In other words, by way of nihilation we give both a new shape to the world and may invent for ourselves a style of existence. To set oneself an end makes the subject a being who lacks something in the world, and the world appears as that from which something is lacking. Now, it is the experience of the world through the threefold structure of the lack (the world as lacking, the subject who lacks something, and that which is lacking, i.e., the lack itself) that makes apprehensible the causes of and motives for the action. Thus, Sartre is not saying that the agent is not determined in a causal and motivational context of action; he stresses that the agent chooses to be determined in one way rather than another. Causes and motives do not determine the action; they serve to give an account for it. Sartre seems to think that reasons for actions, causes, and motives appear only after the manifestation of the intention to do something.

Then the question becomes whether intentions themselves are not determined by one's facticity, or in other words, by the conditions constituted by one's past. Sartre refuses to describe facticity as a web of causal relations. The past pre-delineates our possibilities in the world; however, the meaning and value of these possibilities for the subject depend on freedom's relation to the future, our projects, and ends. "There is freedom only in a situation, and there is a situation only through freedom" (Sartre 2003, 511), he claims. He does not deny the fact that our future possibilities become available to us within the horizon of the past. However, past facts do not determine present actions; what is delivered to me by my past cannot deprive me of my freedom. On the contrary, only because there is freedom can the past delineate future possibilities; there are no possibilities, understood in the existential sense, without freedom. Sartre argues that what is given has no effect on the individual's actions, and that what the individual is up to confers meaning and value to the psychological, sociocultural, economic, hereditary, or environmental givens. By contrast, in a deterministic scheme, consequences follow from certain precedent conditions, without there being any room for freedom. As Sartre says, to be is to choose, that is, not being part of the "unbroken continuity of existence" (Sartre 2003, 462–63).

Free agents create their "situation" insofar as they aim at determinate ends, to be transcended toward future possibilities. The agent may appeal to causes and motives as reasons for explaining his or her actions (Sartre 2003, 468). But this is just a retrospective way of speaking of the agent's action to justify the action in question; it does not show that there is causal determination. If one looks at the action in a prospective manner, one may see that the freedom of an agent rather conditions the givens of a situation so that they appear and make sense as motives and causes. The world of utilities and obstacles appears because our freedom opens a situation for itself in which it can fail or succeed, choose to act on this or that motive, or simply retreat in the face of difficulties. The implication is that we are not always already in a situation that benefits or limits us. Even my *facticity* is revealed to me thanks to my pursuit of ends. This is why it makes sense to speak of freedom as the apprehension of my facticity. My intention to act reveals to me the risks and dangers I will have to face. I discover the current state of affairs by nihilation, which carries my desire to replace them with some future state of affairs. Yet to pursue goals we need to have possibilities, which make it possible for us to reach our goals. Sartre expresses the symmetry between facticity and freedom as follows: "Without facticity freedom would not exist—as a power of nihilation and of choice—and without freedom facticity would not be discovered and would have no meaning" (Sartre 2003, 517).

Facticity is not a pre-given that predetermines freedom. Everything pre-given is subject to reevaluation by freedom. Facticity does not mean a constellation of some bare existents (Sartre 2003, 468). It is composed of givens such as family, its methods of child raising, the habits one has acquired, the class and the income of one's family, one's chronic health problems, the historical-cultural world into which one is born, the language one speaks, one's age, one's profession, the climate of the country in which one lives. These are objective facts that can be described without any reference to a free subject. They would remain as facts no matter what the agent chooses to do. However, for these mere facts to have meaning, freedom is needed. The meaning of facticity is determined by the agent's commitment to his/her ends and the perspectives from which he/she evaluates facticity. Situation is only a particular constellation of meaningful facts that belongs to the realm of facticity, but what makes them meaningful and turns them into an encompassing whole called "situation" is the free agent's meaningful relation with those facts. This also explains why Sartre in his *Critique of Dialectical Reason* speaks of situation as a function of totalization (Sartre 2004).

For Sartre an obstacle does not harm freedom; on the contrary, an obstacle comes into existence through freedom (Sartre 2003, 470). An obstacle has its quality as an obstacle if it makes it harder for the free subject to realize his/her projects. In the crag example, Sartre talks about how future projects determine the meaning of the facticity surrounding individuals (Sartre 2003, 504). The meaning of a crag will change depending on how one intentionally relates to the crag. If one intends to climb the crag, its steepness will appear, as offering resistance to the climber, but if one desires to take a photo, the climb is approached as an object of memory, for objective or subjective reasons. "Resistance" that the world presents to the agent does not deny freedom; on the contrary, it is an evidence of freedom (Sartre 2003, 505). Hence, for Sartre facticity is a neutral ground in which freedom manifests itself by giving rise to a meaningful situation. The situation does not constrain freedom but is a result of it because it appears only if one has freely chosen an end, with reference to which the facticity gains meaning and gives rise to a situation (Sartre 2003, 509). This illustrates the dialectical relationship between situation and freedom.

I showed how Sartre's ontological notion of freedom and existentialist account of action challenged the metaphysical tradition of free will and determinism. Sartre defends freedom against the tradition that frames the question of freedom in terms of free will and determinism. He proposes a theory of action that refuses to explain action by the assumption that past causal sequences inevitably produce present and future effects. For Sartre, to account for action in terms of the introduction of a new causality into the existing causal nexus of the world is equally unacceptable. Agency requires that the agent recognizes a desideratum, sets an end, makes a future projection, knows what he or she is doing, and acknowledges the consequences of his or her act.

To what extent does Beauvoir agree with Sartre's view that freedom has to do with our capacity to set ourselves ends or goals? She appropriates from Sartre's account the importance of the project, the adoption of a goal, the embracing of a value, which presuppose the representation of the given reality of the world as lacking, as a reality to be surpassed. She writes in *The Ethics of Ambiguity* that "to be free is not to have the power to do anything you like; it is to be able to surpass the given toward an open future" (Beauvoir 1976, 91). Although Beauvoir is using the terms that Sartre uses, I argue that her concept of freedom is different from Sartre's. However, Beauvoir is not making her criticism of Sartre explicit. To shed light on the differences of her account from Sartre's, I will make a detour through Merleau-Ponty's objections to Sartre's theory of freedom.

MERLEAU-PONTY'S CRITICISM OF SARTRE'S NOTION OF FREEDOM

Merleau-Ponty in his "Freedom" chapter is not critical of Sartre's rejection of determinism. He writes: "To repeat, it is clear that no causal relation can be conceived between the subject and his body, his world, or his society" (Merleau-Ponty 2012, 497). The agent may be certain that his or her actions were caused and motivated by such and such factors, that his or her character is as others regard it to be; nonetheless, these certainties will be lost if the I's presence to itself is phenomenologically investigated in the anonymous flow of consciousness.

Merleau-Ponty describes freedom as follows:

My freedom, that fundamental power I have of being the subject of all of my experiences, is not distinct from my insertion in the world. I am destined to be free, to be unable to reduce myself to any of my experiences, to maintain with regard to every factual situation a faculty of withdrawal, and this destiny was sealed the moment that my transcendental field was opened, the moment I was

born as vision and as knowledge, the moment I was thrown into the world
(Merleau-Ponty 2012, 377).

Merleau-Ponty agrees that there is an ontological fact of freedom, which
does not lend itself to causal explanations, even though he locates freedom in
the corporeal insertion into the world. Freedom accompanies the opening of
the transcendental field, the apparition of a meaningful world and all cognitive activity, the subject as vision and knowledge. It is felt as a faculty of
withdrawal from every factical situation. He also remarks that this freedom
and its universality cannot be obfuscated: "My freedom and my universality
cannot be eclipsed" (Merleau-Ponty 2012, 498). Although Merleau-Ponty,
too, has an ontological notion of freedom, his notion differs from Sartre's.
On the one hand, he agrees with Sartre's claim that causality and motivation
depend on freedom (Merleau-Ponty 2012, 498); on the other hand, his own
ontological and phenomenological account of freedom arises from a critique
of Sartre's conception of freedom. Indeed, Merleau-Ponty's concept of freedom leads him to different notions of *situation* and *facticity*.

Merleau-Ponty makes a distinction between *the particularity of consciousness* and *the generality of consciousness*. He argues that Sartre's notion of ontological freedom does not consider the generality of consciousness. He postulates that no particularity can be attached to the *insurmount-
able generality of consciousness*. The generality of consciousness that he
refers to is also described as *a vast power of evasion* (Merleau-Ponty 2012,
498). To grasp what he means by the generality of consciousness, it is worthwhile to appeal to the notion of corporeal operative intentionality, which
consists of centripedal and centrifugal intentionalities, which, as Merleau-
Ponty explains in the previous chapters of *Phenomenology of Perception*,
make possible the communication between the body and the world. The
generality of consciousness is distinguished from the particular consciousness such that only the latter accommodates *Sinngebung*, in other words, the
act of giving meaning, which played a central role in the Husserlian phenomenological conception of intentionality. The disability example that Merleau-Ponty gives sheds light on this difference. At the particular level of
consciousness, the disabled person is induced by society to believe that she is
incomplete, while at the level of generality of consciousness, in her corporeal
communication with the world, she does not acknowledge that she is incomplete and unable to do certain things. This person is conscious of her disability at the level of particular consciousness, but at the level of generality, she
does not experience any lack; hence she does not see herself as "disabled."
Therefore, the experience at the level of particular consciousness and the
experience at the level of the generality of consciousness may not overlap.
This justifies Merleau-Ponty's rejection of the view that associates freedom
with voluntary decision. We do not deliberate or weigh reasons and motives

to make a decision about a specific course of action. Most of the time, decision precedes motives.

> We often seek freedom in voluntary deliberation, which examines each motive one by one and appears to go along with the strongest or with the most convincing among them. In fact, the deliberation follows the decision, for my secret decision is what makes the motives appear and we could not even conceive of what the force of a motive might be without a decision that confirms it or counters it. (Merleau-Ponty 2012, 499)

The term "secret decision" implies that the subject may not be reflectively aware of the decision he or she has made. This expands freedom to the level of the generality of consciousness. Although we may continue to communicate with the others using the model of deliberative choice, we need to give a different account of free action. The disparity between my decision and motives becomes apparent when I do not wholeheartedly pursue a project and resort to a volitional act by going against my original secret decision. I even invoke motives to fight my own inertia, my lack of power. "When I have abandoned a project, suddenly the motives that I believed I had in favor of sticking with it fall away, drained of all force" (Merleau-Ponty 2012, 499).

The difference between Sartre's and Merleau-Ponty's accounts of freedom should not eclipse what they have in common: the problem of freedom is an ontological problem because it is as free beings that the world appears to us.

> Even those things described as obstacles to freedom are in fact deployed by freedom. An unclimbable rock face, a large or small, vertical or diagonal rock face—this only has sense for someone who intends to climb it, for a subject whose projects cut these determinations out of the uniform mass of the in-itself and make an oriented world and a sense of things suddenly appear. Thus, there is ultimately nothing that could limit freedom, except those limits freedom has itself determined as such through its own initiatives, and the subject has only the exterior world that he gives himself. Since the subject himself, by suddenly appearing, makes sense and value appear among things, and since nothing could reach him except through his giving them a sense and a value, then there is no action of the things upon the subject, but merely a signifying (in the active sense), and a centrifugal *Sinngebung*. (Merleau-Ponty 2012, 460)

Although this looks like a recapitulation of Sartre's theory of freedom, Merleau-Ponty promptly turns against it to question its limits. The distinction between the generality and the particularity of consciousness allows him to expand freedom to the generality of the corporeal consciousness. He therefore makes room for an experience of freedom even when in the reality of particular consciousness freedom is imperiled or entirely absent. This is how the ontological notion of freedom can take into account the situation of oppression in which the general consciousness of freedom contrasts with the particular consciousness of not being free.

> Yet this first reflection on freedom might result in rendering freedom impossible. If freedom is indeed equal in all of our actions and even in our passions, if it is incommensurate with our behavior, or if the slave displays as much freedom by living in fear as he does in breaking his chains, then it cannot be said that there is such a thing as *free action*. Freedom would then be prior to all actions, and in no case can it be said that "here is where freedom appears," since in order for free action to be detectable it would have to stand out against a background of life that is not free, or that is less free. Freedom is everywhere, so to speak, but also nowhere. (Merleau-Ponty 2012, 500)

Although Sartre, too, distinguishes the freedom of consciousness and free action, his distinction does not allow for the existence of actions that are not free. By contrast, Merleau-Ponty sees the generality of consciousness as both open to emancipatory possibilities that enable free action and as involving historically sedimented habits and ways of behaving that block free action. I believe that this duality, which stems from the ambiguity of the corporeal situation, helps Beauvoir to theorize sexual oppression.

To recapitulate, Merleau-Ponty postulates a natural self to which general intentions belong (Merleau-Ponty 2012, 503). Instead of interpreting these intentions as the psychological expressions of some causally determining processes, he comprehends them as organizing my body's relations with the environing world in ways that I do not determine. The model of operative intentionality allows for the communication between the body and the environing world, which is irreducible to internal or external causation. The operative intentionality forms a system in which my body, things, and others are enclosed. Merleau-Ponty does not think of such intentions as only mine. They also belong to other psychophysical beings with corporeal organizations similar to mine. Such general operative intentions underlie the system of I–the world–others. This system, rather than being a mechanistic system, bears in itself *Gestalt* forms, which are the primitive forms that function to make the world appear as making sense to a corporeal being. Indeed, this model contests the subject-centered experience of the particular consciousness, because the phenomenological reflection uncovers that "[e]verything happens as if, prior to our judgment and our freedom, someone were allocating such and such a sense to such and such a constellation" (Merleau-Ponty 2012, 504). Perceptual structures are called *Gestalt* forms because "these are the floating figures that propose in turn different significations" (Merleau-Ponty 2012, 504). We are ontologically free because such structures do not always impose themselves on us and make us hesitate between alternative ways of perceiving reality.

What kind of impact does that new theoretical contribution make on Sartre's theory about freedom of action? Merleau-Ponty agrees with Sartre's contestation of the classical model of deliberative action according to which free action is grounded in a voluntary decision taken through a deliberative process. According to the classical model, motivations precede the decision and reasons are weighed in the deliberative process so that their balance determines the outcome. Merleau-Ponty agrees with Sartre that deliberation follows the decision; however, they have different grounds for making the same claim. Sartre makes it because he defends an absolute notion of freedom, which opens a situation, and without which the elements of facticity will not have the sense and value of obstacles and utility. Merleau-Ponty argues for the same claim because of the distinction he makes between the particularity and generality of consciousness, which leads him toward a different conception of *situation*.

The situation does not only appear to me in virtue of the project I pursue. For Merleau-Ponty, the crag does not appear large to me because I want to climb it, but because my body experiences it as large. The sense does not accrue to the world and the things that surround me centrifugally, from me to the world (*Sinngebung*), but also centripetally, from the world to me. We shape our experience of the world as the world shapes us. When I give meaning to the world, I in fact give back to the world what I took from it. "The sensible gives back to me what I had lent to it, but I received it from the sensible in the first place" (Merleau-Ponty 2012, 222). Merleau-Ponty believes that Sartre's theory of freedom is idealistic because Sartre ignores the two-way, bidirectional relation between consciousness and objects. Although he contests the classical causal model of freedom, Sartre is still using a deterministic model in questioning freedom, which leads him to idealism.

Merleau-Ponty explores the experience of freedom in the complexity of the corporal existence. He holds that we have made some implicit or secret decisions at the level of generality, which might contrast with our explicit intentions at the level of particular consciousness. First, we may not be conscious of some of our implicit intentions. Take the example of a young woman who stops eating after she breaks up with her lover. She may not explicitly intend to starve herself, though her being unable to eat is a somatic response to her loss. Merleau-Ponty acknowledges that there are intentions that do not derive from the subject's interiority but originate in one's field of perception. The world may provoke me to feel and act in certain ways. A situation, in which I am corporeally anchored, can be ambiguous because of the complex interconnection of all these factors. The fact that it is more open to some possibilities rather than others does not make it deterministic. For Merleau-Ponty, the situation is open and ambiguous because it lends itself to being understood in respect of floating *Gestalt* forms; it can make sense differently given the implicit and explicit decisions, and particular and general consciousness. This is not to say that for Merleau-Ponty all situations are ambiguous or open. He admits that there can be closed situations, indicating a complete absence of freedom.

Merleau-Ponty's discussion of the class-consciousness alludes to Sartre's example of the worker and illustrates the essence of Merleau-Ponty's notions of situation and facticity. It is not up to the worker to choose to experience his or her situation in this or that way. First, a worker's recognition of the other workers as other workers depends on his or her awareness that they have similar experiences. As Merleau Ponty argues, "the structures of the For-Others must already be the dimensions of the For-Self" (Merleau-Ponty 2012, 474). This is to say that there is an intersubjective dimension in subjectivity. One makes sense of one's experience also by learning from the others' experiences, by acknowledging their gains and losses in an effort to improve their conditions as workers. If class-consciousness is born, "this is not because the day laborer has decided to become a revolutionary and, consequently, to confer a value upon his actual condition, but rather because he perceived concretely the synchronicity between his life and the lives of the workers, and the community of their lot in life" (Merleau-Ponty 2012, 508). This is how "the social space begins to become polarized, and a region of 'the exploited' appears. Upon every upsurge, coming from any point on the social horizon whatsoever, the regrouping takes shape beyond different ideologies and trades. Class is coming into being, and we call a situation 'revolutionary' when the objectively existing connection between the segments of the proletariat (that is, those connections that an absolute observer would ultimately recognize between them) is finally experienced [*vécu*] in the perception of a common obstacle to each one's existence" (Merleau-Ponty 2012, 509).

Merleau-Ponty's interpretation of the origin of class-consciousness is different from Sartre's, because he understands being-for-others differently. "The other is neither necessarily, nor even ever fully, an object for me" (Merleau-Ponty 2012, 474). Experiences of sympathy reveal that I can perceive others as bare existence or as freedom as much or as little as I perceive myself. "The-Other-as-an-object is only an insincere modality of the other, just as absolute subjectivity is only an abstract notion of myself" (Merleau-Ponty 2012, 474). The absolute notion of freedom is abstract because it forgets my absolute individuality is surrounded by a halo of generality, or an atmosphere of "sociality" (Merleau-Ponty 2012, 512).

Merleau-Ponty's facticity puts the worker in a situation in which he learns from the experiences of the other workers. According to Merleau-Ponty, lived experience is sedimented. The habits acquired in the past play a role in the constitution of the sense of lived experience. This adds to Merleau-Ponty's notion of situation as thickness, which Sartre neglected in his own account of situation. The analyses of fatigue and laziness are particularly relevant at this point. They contribute to our understanding of what Merleau-Ponty means by not being free. And freedom appears behind this background of not being free as a new way of being-for-others.

To conclude, like Sartre, Merleau-Ponty denies the terms of the determinism and free will debate; however, he lays down a theory of freedom that differs from Sartre's. As William Wilkerson argues: "Merleau-Ponty's solution to this problem is difficult to pin down: We may be both entirely passive and entirely active (1945, 491; 2012, 452) or neither determined nor free (1945, 518; 2012, 480). Despite these doubly contradictory formulations, his point is simply that we can never separate the contributions of socialization, environment, and the whole of the past, which is felt as "personal time" (Wilkerson 2017, 228). I put the stress on Merleau-Ponty's argument that freedom depends on the interpretation of a situation as an open situation. However, there are layers of generality, sedimentation, and sociality of facticity which are already at work in how the situation makes sense to us. We do not voluntarily confer meaning on a situation; meaning is already in the process of formation at the thickness of our experience.

I think Beauvoir's *The Ethics of Ambiguity* is inspired by Merleau-Ponty's critique of Sartre's notion of freedom. She draws the ethical implications of this ontological phenomenological notion of freedom. I think that a revision, in the Merleau-Pontian style, of the notions of *situation* and *facticity* stands at the background and inspires Beauvoir's feminist analysis of oppression. The intersubjective and interpersonal nature of moral freedom implies that we are also responsible for the emancipation of other women from sexual oppression. Beauvoir learns from Merleau-Ponty that one is not just a for-itself but an embodied consciousness, a socially situated and conditioned freedom. Her concept of freedom, which is rooted in ambiguity and intersubjectivity, is closer to Merleau-Ponty's concept of freedom than to Sartre's. It is also possible that her thinking of the notion of situation in terms of oppression inspired Sartre's later reflections on oppression. Sonia Kruks, in "Teaching Sartre about Freedom," argues that Sartre in the late 1950s came to grips with the necessity of addressing individual freedom by taking into account the weight of institutions and social structures. The role that history and the concept of practico-inert play in the *Critique* shows that Sartre revises his early understanding of freedom. Kruks says that a comparison between *Notebooks for an Ethics* and *The Second Sex*, written more or less at the same, would show that "he is still clinging to his early philosophy, finds himself in difficulties that do not arise for Beauvoir" (Kruks 1995, 91). She remarks that, in the *Critique of Dialectical Reason*, Sartre abandons his absolute subject and begins to speak, like Beauvoir, of a destiny that is not natural, but is the result of oppression. Thus, Sartre learns both from Merleau-Ponty and Beauvoir (Kruks 1995, 92).

CAMUS'S ACCOUNT OF FREEDOM
IN *THE MYTH OF SISYPHUS*

The Ethics of Ambiguity does not make full sense when we set aside Beauvoir's reaction to Camus's discussion of freedom in *The Myth of Sisyphus*.
The notions of the authenticity and the inauthenticity of freedom and moral
freedom are developed as a response to Camus's experience of the absurdity
of the world. According to Camus, the most important philosophical question
is whether a meaningless life is worth living. This is indeed a peculiar philosophical question, blatantly different from the perennial questions of philosophy, which have no unique solution. The perennial questions of philosophy
point to the limits of the knowable, although, notwithstanding the existential
questions, no one is prepared to die for them. As Camus points out, one's
very life is at stake in the existential questions. Should one commit suicide or
invent a new style of existence to continue living? The feeling of the absurd
that Camus spoke about is not to be eliminated; such an experience of the
endurance of the absurd implies the rejection of endorsing ungrounded
hopes, which lead to self-deception. Of course, Camus does not recommend
suicide at the face of a meaningless world; he suggests that the subject can
still create a meaningful life by his efforts and engagements.

   Suicide is an option for the individual who confesses that life is unbearable, overwhelming, and devoid of meaning. Such a person feels alienated in
a world, which no longer appears to her as "familiar." Hence, the act of
suicide takes place in the feeling of absurdity. But why does the individual
feel that way? What is the cause of absurdity? Camus argues that the feeling
of absurdity is created in us by diverse and fragmented reality, which is hard
to understand in a rational way without an irrational remainder. Although it is
possible to flee from the absurd by making religious or ideological commitments, Camus warns us against the metaphysical human tendency or the
nostalgia of finding an absolute and clear unity in the world. However, the
meaninglessness of life does not necessarily make it "not worth living" (Camus 1955, 8). The stranger, he says, does not attempt to make the world a
familiar place by trying to rationally account for it, but continues to live
(Camus 1955, 18). The feeling of absurd is there in the encounter of the
individual in search of a meaningful reason for his or her life within an
irrational world devoid of meaning. There is a discrepancy between people's
disproportionate expectations from the world, and what the world offers
(Camus 1955, 29). How to solve this problem? In dealing with this problem,
Chestov, Jaspers, and Kierkegaard committed "philosophical suicide" because as soon as they realized reason's insufficiency, they made an appeal to
something beyond reason (Camus 1955, 41–42). Camus's proposal is that we
learn to live with the feeling of absurdity, by recognizing that reason is
limited, and give up the effort to transcend its limits. He stresses that we need

rationality even though it cannot account for everything; rationality does not emancipate us from absurdity. We can be free only if we give up the hope of finding meaning in life as a whole.

Given that there is no possibility of making recourse to a higher court of appeal because no greater point of reference exists that can render a life useful or useless, and if absurdity is indeed inevitable without hope of escape, consciousness should adopt a *revolting attitude* (Camus 1955, 59). Revolt makes life valuable, and both real suicide and philosophical suicide are wrong because they dissolve the absurd and bring revolt to an end. Individual freedom is possible only on the condition that one accepts the absurd and refuses to flee from it to some transcendence in faith or philosophy. If the absurd is the source of passionate revolt, and does not rob life of its worth of being lived, how should one live?

The last question concerns the possibility of an ethics of revolt. For Camus, revolt does not have an ethical program. It does not provide an ethics based on principles or a set of universal ethical values that orient action. He argues that "adventurers" can create their "own" ethics, and in it what matters is the quantity of the experiences accompanied by the revolting attitude (Camus 1955, 62). Sisyphus can be happy even though he gave up the hope for accomplishment. He can be the symbol of those absurd men who are aware of the meaninglessness of their life but continue to live in a passionate revolting attitude (Camus 1955, 64).

BEAUVOIR'S *THE ETHICS OF AMBIGUITY*

In contrast to Camus's absurdity of existence, Beauvoir focuses on the ambiguity of existence in *The Ethics of Ambiguity*. *Pyrrhus et Cinéas* (Beauvoir 1944) had already made clear that I can be free only in relation to the other and, thus, asserted the possibility of reciprocity. Debra Bergoffen argues that, taking a developmental perspective on Beauvoir's work, "we might say that as *The Ethics of Ambiguity* abandons the *Pyrrhus et Cinéas* position of absolute freedom, for the concept of situated freedom, *The Second Sex* concretely develops *The Ethics of Ambiguity*'s thesis that one's freedom is historically conditioned rather than ontologically guaranteed" (Bergoffen 1997, 142). I think freedom is an ontological possibility, but it must be actualized by the assumption of subjectivity. *The Ethics of Ambiguity* remarks that we first assume subjectivity in childhood and adolescence. Moreover, a person's historical situation can bring about a deficient fulfillment of the ontological possibility of freedom. In *The Ethics of Ambiguity*, Beauvoir is concerned with deciphering mechanisms of oppression and shows the interrelatedness of types of oppressions such as anti-Semitism, sexism, and racism. As Ursula

Tidd claims, these analyses will be made pertinent to the analysis of gendered subject in *The Second Sex* (Tidd 2004, 30).

In "Gendering the Perceiving Subject," Bergoffen points that even though in the early *Pyrrhus et Cinéas* or the later "Must We Burn Sade?" the themes of ambiguity, generosity, and the gift are present, in the more abstract *Pyrrhus et Cinéas* and *The Ethics of Ambiguity* the ambiguity and the generosity of the subject is bodied but not sexed. In *The Second Sex*, "Must We Burn Sade?" which dates from 1951–1952 (Beauvoir 1966), and in *The Coming of Age*, which was published in French in 1970 (Beauvoir 1972), "Beauvoir ties the issues of subjectivity and embodiment to the concepts of sex and gender" (Bergoffen 2000, 62). This is a good general outline for the development of Beauvoir's thought from *The Ethics of Ambiguity* to *The Second Sex* as a transition from the ambiguity embedded in the existence of the corporeal subject to the situation of subjectivity in its sexual difference.

In my interperation, *The Ethics of Ambiguity* reevaluates the debate over freedom between Sartre and Merleau-Ponty and includes Camus in the discussion. Beauvoir's agreements and disagreements with Sartre, Merleau-Ponty, and Camus shed light on the philosophical itinerary that culminated in *The Second Sex*. Beauvoir defends the existentialist thesis that human existence is the source of values. However, she agrees with Merleau-Ponty in criticizing Sartre's absolute and abstract notion of ontological freedom. She rethinks ontological freedom by affirming with Merleau-Ponty the ambiguity of the situation, which she generalizes as *the inevitable ambiguity of life*. Finally, she sides with Camus in warning against fleeing from one's freedom by making some value, desire, or passion absolute.

The Ethics of Ambiguity also rejects, along with Merleau-Ponty, the Sartrean view that the struggle for freedom must necessarily be a struggle for domination. While Merleau-Ponty proceeds toward a dialectical notion of freedom, Beauvoir explores the connection between this new ontological notion of freedom and a moral notion of freedom. Her moral notion of freedom helps her to respond to Camus's concerns. For her, the revolting attitude as described in Camus's text belongs to an adventurer and will culminate in a betrayal of freedom, if it does not involve care and support for others' freedom.

It must be stressed that beginning from the late 1940s, Sartre's views about freedom start to change. Beauvoir witnesses the transformation of Sartre's views on freedom. She grants that Merleau-Ponty's notion of general intentions and "body" have influenced her, but she also remarks that Merleau-Ponty's reading of Sartre is partial and reductive because Merleau-Ponty did not address Sartre's subsequent discussion of freedom in *Critique of Dialectical Reason*. Indeed, there are similarities between Merleau-Ponty's *Adventures of Dialectic* and *Humanism and Terror* and Sartre's *Critique of Dialectical Reason* because both philosophers are critical of the classical

Marxist account of dialectic and seek a new, more phenomenological account of freedom as a dialectical experience.

Let us turn to the moral of freedom, which is Beauvoir's specific contribution to the debate over freedom. *The Ethics of Ambiguity* does not offer a normative ethics or an axiology, which would give us a stable and unchanging ranking of values, applicable to all situations. Such a fixed hierarchy of values would have contradicted the spirit of Beauvoir's existentialism. There is no unchanging value of values. She holds that when deciding in a moral situation one should try to remain at a "distance" from oneself and conduct an unending reflection on one's aims and values. Such a reflection resembles an existential conversion that results in the apprehension of human existence as the source of values. These values serve to evaluate our actions, which shape the world; and if actions rest on evaluations, our evaluations make us responsible for our acts. Why are we responsible for our evaluations? Beauvoir interprets the unjustifiability of life as meaning that there is no value independent of life that can justify life. Hence, there can be no given universal values by which we can evaluate ways of life. On the contrary, the source of values is "concrete, particular men" with differing aims, whose subjectivities are inevitable and an objective fact (Beauvoir 1976, 6).

Beauvoir does not give us an ethics of principles; she is aware that depending on the situation we make sacrifices of our principles and values for the sake of other principles and values. Because she rejects upholding a unique universal moral principle, she can be described as a particularist in ethics. She acknowledges that in extreme situations, freedom, too, can be sacrificed to preserve some other value, such as one's own life or other people's lives. That does not stop her from ranking freedom as the highest value, as an absolute ideal.

It is true that Beauvoir's concept of freedom shares some Sartrean assumptions about freedom. She postulates with Sartre that we are ontologically free. First, she agrees with Sartre's claims that people "want themselves free" and try to disclose their being, and to do so they negate the world to make it appear as lacking, which is a manifestation of their freedom. Second, freedom being the only source of all meaning and value, life can be meaningful only through people's actions and due to the goals they pursue. Third, the "human reality" is interwoven by "significations" and is partly constituted by persons' creation of values stemming from the experience of their own existence, and this is the reason why freedom has an ontological sense. Even if Beauvoir agrees with Sartre that actions can make life meaningful, she thinks Merleau-Ponty is right in arguing that ontological freedom is too abstract, and she affirms Camus's view that life cannot be justifiable with reference to universal values. Merleau-Ponty's criticism of abstract understanding of freedom leads Beauvoir first to a moral notion of freedom in *The Ethics of*

Ambiguity and immediately afterward, to a political philosophical analysis of oppression in *The Second Sex*.

In *The Ethics of Ambiguity*, ambiguity implies that there are diverse ways of making sense of the world. The manifestation of the sense of the world is often constituted with the inclusion of others' interpretations. However, I think that if the subject draws from a set of spatio-temporally coherent past experiences there can be situations that are definitive and stunningly univocal for a subject, situations that signify without needing confirmation from others' perspectives. This possibility does not refute the generality that experiences of situation are in principle inadequate, that is, open to negation in the future.

How different is the experience of ambiguity from the experience of the absurd? Absurd suggests that no meaning can be given to life, whereas ambiguity concerns the plurality of possible interpretations. In Merleau-Ponty, the situation is ambiguous because it is indeterminate and open to possibilities. Beauvoir writes in her review of *Phenomenology of Perception*:

> It is impossible to define an object in cutting it off from the subject through which and for which it is an object; and the subject reveals itself only through the objects with which it is engaged. Such an affirmation only makes the content of naive experience explicit, but it is rich in consequences. Only in taking it as a basis will one succeed in building an ethics to which man can totally and sincerely adhere. It is therefore of extreme importance to establish it solidly and to give back to man this childish audacity that years of verbal submission have taken away: the audacity to say: "I am here." This is why *Phenomenology of Perception* by Maurice Merleau-Ponty is not only a remarkable specialist work but also a book that is of interest to the whole of man and to every man; the human condition is at stake in this book. (Beauvoir, 1945)

One might wonder why Beauvoir, in reviewing a book that sets itself the task of going beneath the object/subject divide and exploring the ambiguity in the corporeal communication with the world, chooses to account for ambiguity in terms of the subject/object divide? Monica Langer, in her essay "Beauvoir and Merleau Ponty on Ambiguity," argues that Beauvoir's ambiguity in *The Ethics of Ambiguity* differs from Sartre's paradoxical ambiguity and resembles Merleau-Ponty's ambiguity, despite the fact that Beauvoir invokes Sartre and strategically omits Merleau-Ponty's name from her text (Langer 2003, 88–90). We can only speculate about the possible reasons for that. It could be her commitment to Sartre or her desire to say something different from Merleau-Ponty despite their affinities. I agree with Langer that her ambiguity is closer to Merleau-Ponty's, but I also think that Beauvoir goes beyond Merleau-Ponty in carrying ontological ambiguity into the ethical realm. And why would Beauvoir refer to Sartre's ambiguity affirmatively, if that were to make her contradict her own theory?

I believe an answer can be given to the puzzle raised above by acknowledging that for Beauvoir ambiguity is spread at all the levels of constitution. The epistemic subject/object relation manifests it as well. Ambiguity in the ethical realm is found in the condition that our natural freedom must make the transition to the moral realm in order to become genuine freedom. Our natural freedom "merges with the very movement of this ambiguous reality, which is called existence" (Beauvoir 1976, 25). In existence, acts that originate from our natural and ontological freedom can be objectified (experienced) from different perspectives; they may be judged or evaluated differently from different normative perspectives. This is why ethics is in general irreducibly ambiguous and the elaboration of its issues must include a plurality of perspectives and interpretations. Although this ambiguity may lead to ethical relativism, Beauvoir has grounds to escape it.

In *The Ethics of Ambiguity*, natural freedom becomes genuine freedom if one wills oneself to be free. This is the original upsurge of our existence, the disclosure of the world, escape from the absurdity of the pure moment, the beginning of the movement of transcendence. Desire for freedom must be absolute if existence is to be justified. Existence is justifiable in the ethical realm not by getting rid of ambiguity, but by embracing freedom. The ambiguity of existence implies that there are no objective values that precede choice; however, Beauvoir acknowledges that the moral sense of the situation is not solely a function of the subject. The reality of the moral situation depends on how the subject intends it, but it is also independent of individual attitudes and beliefs. Indeed, her emphasis on the ambiguity of the situation enables Beauvoir to escape from the charges of voluntarism and ethical individual relativism.

That she is beyond individual ethical relativism also becomes clear from Beauvoir's exploration of the Merleau-Pontian intuition that others figure in my experience of ambiguity. This means that the experience of ambiguity opens the door for intersubjectivity and reveals that genuine freedom is already an interpersonal and intersubjective matter. It is worth stressing that not Merleau-Ponty but Beauvoir explores the ethical implications of this phenomenological ontological analysis of freedom. Because the sense of the moral situation is always already intersubjective and constituted by how I make sense of other people's similar experiences, to deliberately will myself to be free cannot be separated from willing others' moral freedom.

Intersubjectivity, which has already been part of Merleau-Ponty's analyses of freedom in *Phenomenology of Perception*, is at the core of Beauvoir's concept of moral freedom. But Beauvoir is very clear about the risks of identifying one's self in interpersonal relations by one's social roles, and she sees that as a way of fleeing from one's freedom. She is very far from being a normative ethical cultural relativist because in *The Second Sex* she wants to be a reformer. If sexual inequality is injustice and not be tolerated, this is freedom committing itself to objective values that are universally valid. The question of intersubjectivity of freedom is, in *The Ethics of Ambiguity*, tied with the problem of authentic and inauthentic experiences of freedom. The authenticity of an act is a necessary though not a sufficient condition of its morality. The subject is inauthentic if she identifies herself with an occupation in the world. This is a Heideggerian and Sartrean element in Beauvoir's thinking. The serious man flees from his freedom because he understands himself by what he does in the world. A dictator who attains absolute power over everybody else is not free because he is a special kind of adventurer who not only fails to promote others' freedom but destroys the possibility of freedom for others. What makes freedom a moral goal is that one wants it for others as well. We cannot be free if others are not free, and therefore freedom must be fostered in interpersonal relations. Indeed, there is no freedom in the moral sense without the recognition of others' freedom at the interpersonal and institutional levels. If a person dominates others and reduces them to objects, he does not merely harm others; he also hurts his own freedom because he deprives it of the possibility of being accomplished in moral freedom.

Insofar as Beauvoir's notion of genuine freedom embraces ambiguity, it opens the door for moral uncertainty, not so much because of disagreement over the facts, but because different principles may apply to different situations. I believe Beauvoir is a moral pluralist because she knows moral rigidity can be avoided only if one remains open to criticism. Authentic freedom implies a constant effort to reevaluate values and to test them in existence. Beauvoir is very close to Camus when she emphasizes that the possibility of failure should not affect freedom adversely. One should not retreat in the face of obstacles. Freedom is realized by acting despite the possibility or inevitability of failure (Beauvoir 1976, 11). She probably has Camus's figure of Sisyphus in mind when she refuses to evaluate a situation of failure as tragic. According to her, an action is not valuable because of what it accomplishes, but as an exercise of freedom that manifests a value.

Camus in *The Myth of Sisyphus* was not interested in evaluating all suicide. He addressed only suicide that is committed as a response to the feeling of the absurd and that results in the elimination of the possibility of revolt and freedom. Beauvoir agrees with Camus in endorsing freedom as the highest value and the absolute end of human existence even though she thinks that "revolt" does not have any positivity unless it gains content through action and turns into "struggle and revolution." In situations where this is impossible, suicide becomes a "death freely chosen," and a way to reject the "imposed situation" (Beauvoir 1976, 12). If one needs to fight the absolute forces one cannot beat, suicide becomes a manifestation of freedom. Hence,

Beauvoir is far from being a Stoic philosopher who, under conditions of oppression, would recommend withdrawing into interiority and define freedom as a balance in the soul.

What is the relation between ethics and politics in Beauvoir's philosophy of the late 1940s? *The Ethics of Ambiguity* claims that freedom must accomplish itself in a moral life. This moral freedom paves the way for an ethics, which accounts for the right and wrong ways of living a life of freedom, without reference to a transcendental ground. There are authentic and inauthentic types of living freedom (Beauvoir 1976, 13–14). She concentrates on experiences of freedom such as those of the adventurer, the serious person, the passionate man, and the genuinely free man. The adventurer has a vital energy and reflects on his own experiences of the world though he does not take politics seriously. He runs the risk of absolutizing his love of adventure. If he does so, he will resemble the serious person who treats others as objects and fails to care for their freedom. The serious person is an inauthentic figure of freedom because he takes human beings to be mere means of the "unconditioned universal" values they serve (Beauvoir 1976, 20–25). What distinguishes the free man from the adventurer is that the former cares for others' freedom, whereas the adventurer treats others as objects of his actions and therefore can turn into a "tyrant" (Beauvoir 1976, 25). Although the adventurer exercises his freedom of action and is closer to being free than the serious person, as long as he neglects to care for the freedom of the others, he ends up being a slave of his own aims. Both the adventurer and the serious person are concerned with their wealth and power and do not support others' freedom. Neither will act to subvert oppression and directly or indirectly help the existing oppressive regimes to remain in power. At the end, they become the slaves of the things that they try to protect (Beauvoir 1976, 26–27). Hence Beauvoir's adventurer, as a figure of inauthenticity, invokes and criticizes Camus's individualistic account of freedom and revolt. Camus was critical of the serious man's life and repudiated the absolute ideological and religious commitments the serious man makes to flee his freedom. Remarkably, he did not associate caring for others' freedom with the revolting attitude. He did not share Beauvoir's commitment to intersubjective freedom. Her emphasis on intersubjectivity as a condition of being free can be interpreted as a Hegelian and Marxist element in Beauvoir's thought. One cannot be free all alone, as a single person; solitary freedom is insufficiently free.

Beauvoir thinks that a meaningful manifestation of freedom takes place in intersubjective relations in the social realm, which involves the presence of other individuals whose freedom is respected and fostered. Although Camus did not declare that others' freedom is not worth caring for, he seemed to believe that one can be free among others without fostering their freedom. Clearly, he did not choose to develop this theme of moral freedom that Beauvoir picked up. According to Beauvoir, caring for the freedom of others can protect us from sinking into absurdity. There are two reasons for that: First, although life does not get its meaning from a transcendent or transcendental ground, we can cope with the absurdity that stems from our encounter with the world by the reasons or justifications that we derive from our own existence. We present our reasons and justifications to others, because reasons cannot count as objectively valid reasons without being evaluated by others. I need others, who can make moral evaluations freely and autonomously, to justify my existence to myself. The moral realm is for Beauvoir a realm of losses and gains and involves, as a matter of course, considerations of others' happiness; but most important, the moral realm presupposes others' freedom. Second, only if we care for others' freedom and make their freedom our end, can we form a collectivity of persons with different aims. The world can become a meaningful place if this collectivity shares some common values and principles that foster equality and justice. I think this is also where Beauvoir's notion of moral freedom becomes political, for it is not simply to justify my own existence that I care for others' freedom, but to create a free society that appropriates and expropriates values in reflective and critical processes. Ambiguity here would safeguard existentialist ethics from falling into formalism, dogmatism, and solipsism.

In my view, Beauvoir imagines a just society based on the recognition of the others by the subject as free beings. But this proves that ontological freedom, capacity for transcendence, can be fulfilled only by moral freedom. People do not support others' freedom, because they benefit from the social and economic system in which relations of oppression are consolidated. For Beauvoir, oppressors are not free in the authentic sense because they lack the *Mitsein* in which they can justify their existence. Dictators are not free, even though they may exercise violence with mob support. The mob consists of passionate people who seek to avoid facing the ambiguity of the situation, in self-deception.

In contrast to Beauvoir, Camus does not see political freedom as the ultimate moral end. And he takes the aspiration for it as incompatible with the revolting attitude. For the stranger who refrains from striving to know the things that are uncertain, others' freedom is irrelevant. Camus promotes the adventurer who is invested in his own freedom. For Beauvoir, at the face of absurdity, an ethics of ambiguity is a better alternative than a revolting attitude. Both Camus and Beauvoir agree that freedom is possible only if one lives a life "without appeal," without God-given or universal natural or transcendental values. However, Beauvoir thinks that "willing oneself free" amounts to "willing oneself moral," because freedom as the source of value and meaning can be maintained only in the moral attitude; all other attitudes result in the loss of genuine freedom. The moral attitude Beauvoir has in mind culminates in the creation of a shared set of values. Camus does not see morality as the precondition of freedom, and the creation of a common set of values is not really a problem for him. Even though Beauvoir and Camus agree that no values exist independently of human existence, for Beauvoir we can create and share values, whereas Camus does not consider that an integral part of freedom. For Beauvoir ontological freedom fulfills itself in moral freedom whereas for Camus freedom can be experienced properly in the revolting attitude without making any commitments to others' freedom.

Beauvoir stresses "ambiguity" as a feature of human life and argues that moral freedom, working to promote others' freedom, can be a way to overcome an "empty subjectivity" (Beauvoir 1976, 2–3). She repudiates existentialism, which takes the form of a solipsistic philosophy without moral concerns. In her view, existentialist ethics is not formalistic; it is not based on some general principles without appeal to life. Values and principles that our actions exemplify cannot be justified independently of our active affirmation of them. Even though people can inherit historical values, values are sedimentations that do not really exist as values unless agents bring them into actual existence by acting on them. Acting in accordance with values is the real source of the social existence of values. Both Beauvoir and Camus share the view that there is no higher court of appeal than the individual's existence when it comes to such questions concerning meaning of life, freedom, and action, even though for Beauvoir intersubjectivity gains a central role in ontological freedom's accomplishment as moral freedom.

THE SECOND SEX

How is this new existentialist ontology of freedom transformed into an ontology of sex? I do not think that the notion of freedom in *The Second Sex* can be explained with reference to Merleau-Ponty's influence on Beauvoir without taking into account Beauvoir's concern to respond to Hegel's conception of freedom as the Absolute.

I agree with Sonia Kruks's view that Beauvoir's concept of "situation" makes better sense when it is interpreted in the light of Merleau-Ponty's phenomenology in *Phenomenology of Perception* rather than Sartre's in *Being and Nothingness*. Kruks argues that Beauvoir understands "situation," like Merleau-Ponty, in corporeal terms (Kruks 1990). The duality between the body as a thing or object in the world and the perceiving and lived body organizes *Phenomenology of Perception*. The body as our "hold on the world" or "grasp of the world" opens the way for the notion of "body as situation." Although they are the same entity, the body as being-in-the-world is irreducible to the body as an object of biology. The lived experiences and the relation to the world that belong to the body as being-in-the-world make sense within certain cultural and historical horizons. The lived experiences that belong to woman's corporeal being-in-the-world are lived, as they are, as experiences of sexism and patriarchal oppression because of the way her body is sexed female. Patriarchal oppression presupposes a hierarchy of sexes in which males have supremacy and this hierarchy is perpetuated by the institutional structures of the society. Such a hierarchy exists to control the reproductive labor of women. Beauvoir explains the stages of the patriarchal history and lays it out as a background in which lived experiences of women make sense. This is not to say that all lived experiences can be analyzed into its components of historical sense. Beauvoir is interested in exploring both the general and impersonal layers of sense of the bodily experience, and the particular forms of consciousness that a certain situation may give rise to. *The Second Sex* takes up the way consciousness is embedded in a body and phenomenologically explains how this situation, because it is one of sexual oppression, gives rise to an inauthentic consciousness. However, the ambiguity of the situation holds in reserve the possibility of new ways of experiencing it. *The Second Sex* casts the problem of the authenticity and inauthenticity of consciousness in terms of a proto-feminist theoretical analysis of sexual oppression. Notably, Merleau-Ponty's discussion of the emergence of class-consciousness is analogous to Beauvoir's discussion of the emergence of what we call today "gender consciousness."

In *The Philosophy of Simone de Beauvoir: Gendered Phenomenologies, Erotic Generosities*, Debra B. Bergoffen argues that "Beauvoir was sensitive," even in her abstract works such as *Pyrrhus et Cinéas* and *The Ethics of Ambiguity*, "to the ways in which women were assigned inferior roles and relegated to passive positions!" And this becomes a central issue in "Must We Burn Sade?" (Bergoffen 1997, 142). Beauvoir explains her attainment of the awareness of woman's situation: "Wanting to talk about myself, I became aware that to do so I should first have to describe the condition of woman in general" (Beauvoir 1975, 195). This led to a reflection on what constitutes the specificity of a woman's situation. She thus sets herself the task of explaining what constitutes the specificity of woman's situation and the conditions of the formation of a genuinely free consciousness that the situation may bring about. Values should be considered as belonging to this existence; and as a matter of general philosophical principle, existence does not possess value properties simply because of individual projects. Beauvoir writes:

> But what singularly defines the situation of woman is that being, like all humans, an autonomous freedom, she discovers and chooses herself in a World where men force her to assume herself as Other: an attempt is made to freeze her as an object and doom her to immanence, since her transcendence will be forever transcended by another essential and sovereign consciousness. (Beauvoir 2010, 17)

Given that both women and men are human beings, from an ontological point of view, their being must be in principle the same. Hence, we can use the same kind of ontological explanation to account for both. How, then, to conceive the being of human being, *human reality*? According to Beauvoir, the being of human being is "transcendence," which can give rise to autonomy. She also acknowledges that historical and social conditions can impede transcendence. For example, a woman who needs the permission of her father or husband to leave the house, work, write, or see her friends, cannot live her transcendence. "Transcendence" is the human capacity to overcome one's situation. It is to leave the house; to exit from one's self to go out to the world in order, eventually, to return home, to the self.

The implication is that after all that we have achieved out there in the world, we need to return home, to our own center, to what may be properly "immanence." Whether or not the fundamental terms of her ontology, such as "transcendence" and "immanence," derive from her reading of Hegel has been the subject of various studies in Beauvoir scholarship. Here I will not go into this literature (see Direk 2011). Immanence does not just refer to the domestic sphere; it also refers to the body. Even though we are ecstatic beings, because in the movement of existence we tend to be outside of ourselves in the world, we also need to return to ourselves and remain in our bodies. Transcendence is the movement of our being that cannot be objectified and frozen; it refers to the human capacity to transform, create, and form a world. Freedom is a manifestation of transcendence and synonymous with it. Nonetheless, the being of human being is not just transcendence; it also inheres the dimension of immanence. In Beauvoir, immanence describes the sphere in which the physical and psychological needs of life are satisfied. Transcendence is of the desire that struggles and obtains the means of survival and the desire that expresses itself in the world. Home is, in principle, the place of rest, a realm of intimacy. This is where a human being self-relates, gathers its pieces from dispersion in the world, and comes back to its own center as a subject. Necessities of survival, daily habits of life, and desires for comfort and luxury repeat themselves and reveal circular temporality. Immanence is also the realm of shared intimacy with the intimate partner and a sharing of self with the others for whom one cares.

In principle, the sphere of immanence is a sphere of ethical relations. However, in patriarchy, immanence can become a site of violence. Intimate relations of care and love can become oppressive. Beauvoir argues that in the history of patriarchy women are forced to spend their lives exclusively in this realm, which makes them subject to an ontological violence that impedes the actualization of their ontological possibility of transcendence. Woman who does not have the conditions of self-realization as human being is reduced to an object surpassed by someone else's, man's, freedom.

Patriarchal order is an ontological obstruction for woman because it forces her to devote herself to the family—to her husband, children, and other family members for whom she is expected to provide care. Why speak of "coercion" and "force" here? The lived experiences of her sexed body—as girl, teenager, young woman, old woman—signify as they do, in virtue of the historical effectiveness of the cultural and social practices. Patriarchy begins to confer on her body the meaning of her corporeality as soon as she comes in the world. Biologically she is female when she is born, but what does being female mean? How does the given signify at all? This is not apparent at all phenomenologically speaking, if we do not have the horizon of the patri- archal history in which this body is inserted in the world. In this horizon, her being as a psychophysical unity is organized to perpetuate the system that produced it, even though she may not embrace what is expected of her, that is, the cultural injunction to dwell in immanence and reaffirm her own coer- cion. She is forced to accept her devotion to the others in the family as an injunction of her nature or as a moral virtue. The oppressed people may perceive the conditions of oppression as natural; they may not problematize inequality and lack the consciousness of coercion. But this does not prove the nonexistence of oppression; it only makes manifest that it is lived as natural or as destiny, and rendered invisible by some kind of legitimation. A woman can assume the devotion to family that is expected of her as a value, may want to practice it and defend it, and may demand it from her sex and even impose it on other women as a norm. There are women who actively contrib- ute to women's oppression. But there are also women who strive to oppose the imposition of this way of being as a norm for women in general, even though they could not save themselves from subordination and intimate vio- lence in the sphere of immanence. It is perhaps more important to see if an individual gives support to the historical perpetuation of a situation of op- pression than to judge her by considering whether she can actually exit it. Even though a person may not under certain circumstances incorporate an ideal of freedom in the existential sense, she may find the value of freedom worth supporting. It is worthy to make others recognize that the inhabited situation is actually unequal.

Beauvoir describes woman's situation as one in which woman's freedom is not considered as essential as man's and is surpassed by it. How come her freedom is surpassed by his freedom? And if patriarchy made it possible, how is the latter constituted? That man is physically stronger than woman is not explanatory at all, because physical force can always be exceeded; force can guarantee domination only if it justifies itself. A strong person's strength can always be surpassed by a group of people, which consists of individuals of lesser strength. In order to justify male domination, man must socially construct woman. Beauvoir argues that man justifies his sovereignty by de- fining woman as "the Other" and the effect of that resembles freezing her in being, making her an object. Woman is condemned to immanence and de- prived of her transcendence by being represented as "the Other." Here we have a case in which the symbolic brings a historical concrete human reality into being; at stake is the creation of a body in situation. In my understanding, Beauvoir does not deny the biological reality of the female body, but the historical reality of the body as situation is about the constitution of the material existence as meaningful. Beauvoir is talking about history of sense, of the dialectical genesis of the patriarchal symbolic, which she grounds in the changing historical balance between the forces of production and those of reproduction.

Although woman's situation affects the way she relates to the possibility of freedom that ontologically belongs to her very being, she is not bound by destiny to immanence. It should be stressed that, according to Beauvoir, woman's situation is not merely ambiguous but essentially conflicting. Man profits from it; his interest lies in perpetuating it, whereas woman might seek ways to contest it in order to realize her own being. What paths are open for woman to realize her being? "Which ones lead to dead ends? How can she find independence within dependence? What circumstances limit women's freedom and can she overcome them?" (Beauvoir 2010, 17). *The Second Sex*'s feminist agenda contests the historical ruse that defines woman in relation to man and calls for self-definition. The definition of her being as wife and mother is not made by an independent access to the *definiendum*. This is a phenomenological problem: when we do not take our departure from the very being we aim at describing, we appeal to constructions that might be arbitrary and distort the being of the entity we describe. We operate with a negative definition of freedom when we understand freedom as liberation from male domination. Of course we need to fight oppression and domination, but the real aim is to reach freedom in the positive sense, which is the expression and manifestation of human freedom in its world-building creative capacity.

The social roles of wifehood and motherhood can be obstacles on the way for women's liberation in the sense of self-realization. Stella Sandford argues that although Beauvoir writes that "the female organism is wholly adapted for and subservient to maternity such that her individual life is subordinated to the function of the reproduction of the species through her, 'absorbing' her individual life. . . . Beauvoir's pessimism is partly rhetorical. The burden of the human female is accentuated in order that the rather different plight of the woman might emerge more clearly" (Sandford 2006, 74). Although her rhetoric is equivocal and invites misinterpretation, and this is so well-documented in the literature on Beauvoir, I agree with Julie Ward's argument that Beauvoir is not against motherhood as such when she objects to the traditional roles that perpetuate male domination (Ward 1995, 234–40). Being a mother might not be a handicap in a world in which there is gender equality.

The introduction to *The Second Sex* promises to explain how woman's situation is constituted and what enables it to perpetuate itself. The section titled "Destiny" takes up the question in the light of biology, psychoanalysis, and history. Indeed, the multidisciplinary perspective is required by the complexity of the situation, which no single discipline can fairly explain. We should begin with the question of what, if anything, biology has to contribute to it? Surely it is important to highlight the contribution of biological elements to the woman's situation, though we need to reverse the order and make a detour through historical materialism to make that assessment. Simply put, even though biology tells us that the human female can give birth and the human male can fertilize her, their roles in reproduction do not help us understand why man is the subject whereas woman is the Other. It follows that the issue would be better addressed in terms of psychoanalysis and historical materialism. Nonetheless, psychoanalysis is under the domination of the phallus; it is phallocentric. Even though it gives us a clue about how patriarchal cultures situate woman, it does not make room for an ethical problematization that opens the way for sexual emancipation. The inadequacy of the psychoanalytical perspective brings us to the historical materialist perspective. In *The Second Sex*, Beauvoir is concerned with the question of history because she would like to give an account of sexual oppression. Rather than focusing on the history of facts, she is interested in the dialectical evolution of historical structures. She works on the genesis and the structure of sexual oppression by using a philosophical method that combines phenomenology and existentialism. In so doing, she draws from Hegel's phenomenology as well, even though she knows that he fails to address the problem of sexual oppression.

Beauvoir refers to Hegel's master and slave dialectic when she speaks of the difficulties of women's emancipation. The situation of woman as wife is different from that of the slave. "The tie that binds her to her oppressors, is unlike any other" (Beauvoir 2010, 9). Evidently, there are female slaves whose situation may involve sexual exploitation and which complicates the distinction that Beauvoir would like to make between the relative other and the Absolute Other. Woman is characterized as "Absolute Other" in contrast to the slave who, because he is man, is a "relative other" other than the male master. This distinction serves to discuss the specificity of sexual difference in its irreducibility to other forms of oppression. At the end of the master and slave dialectic, the slave obtains a new relation to himself in the activity of transforming nature to build a world. A positive image of himself is reflected to him from the world he built, a reflection that paves the way for the formation of self-confident identity, which is necessary to reclaim independence. A situation is thus dialectically created, which demands the master's recognition of the slave. The same logic does not apply to woman insofar as she is condemned to immanence. Different from the slave, the tie that ties her to her oppressors does not undergo significant modification beyond the limits of immanence. Given that she cannot leave the domestic sphere, she does not attain the possibility of having a new self-relation in world-building activity and, as a consequence, the possibility of independence remains closed to her.

Although man can become the subject, woman is constituted as the Other and excluded from dialectical movement. This contrast lies at the heart of Beauvoir's tackling of Hegel's discussion of freedom. Hegel's account of the development of freedom in history is an account of how the male subjectivity becomes the Spirit. Beauvoir claims that this is made possible by the positing of woman as Absolute Other, which is a contingent though persisting structure of history. Her thesis is grounded in the dialectic unfolding of a historical materialist argument. Man subjectivated himself in a struggle for recognition between men, and reached the Absolute in which the Spirit attained self-consciousness and universal freedom. Woman could be excluded from this dialectical movement of freedom because she was constituted as the radical Other.

In Beauvoir's critical reading of Hegel, the idea of freedom implies the freedom of all human beings and not just of all men. To include woman in the course of history, she must be stripped of the characteristic of Otherness that patriarchy attributed to her. Beauvoir learned that woman is the "Absolute Other" from structural anthropology, and Hegel taught her that the Absolute Other cannot enter into dialectical movement. In *The Elementary Relations of Kinship*, Claude Lévi-Strauss described woman's status within kinship relations by following Marcel Mauss's insight. Accordingly, woman has the economic status of a luxurious present exchanged between groups of men. A subject, because it is by definition *self-posssessed*, can never be given as a present to another subject. Woman must be alienated from subjectivity by first being represented as Absolute Other so that she can be treated as a commodity, a luxurious present. She is different from a slave who is bought for work for she is consciousness possessed in flesh, a luxurious object of sexual enjoyment in whose sensuousness the proximity of immanence is sought. That female bodies are consumer goods for sexual gratification and service is the misogyny embedded in patriarchy.

Years later, when she wrote *The Coming of Age*, Simone de Beauvoir criticized herself for not having been able to give a stronger historical materialist account of woman's constitution as Other (Beauvoir 1972). Retrospectively, *The Second Sex* seemed to her to risk falling in the idealistic philosophy of consciousness that privileges representation over the material forces of production. Her hermeneutical tracking of alterity in various discourses and myths gave the reader the impression that the revealing of vacuous alterity may suffice to change beliefs and attitudes, and eventually result in the abolition of oppression. In my own reading, this self-criticism is not fair because *The Second Sex* gives an argument about how representations of alterity change in function of the relation of the productive forces to nature.

In the last analysis, what makes woman Absolutely Other is the fear that man feels at the face of her fecundity. Freud had associated the taboo of virginity with man's perception of the blood flowing from woman's body as a threat to his being, with his fear of death. Insofar as woman's body is associated with life's unknown, uncontrollable creativity, man's horror at the face of nature is projected on his relation to woman. Beauvoir sees a dialectical movement here and explains it by using Hegel's terms. We can unfold this dialectic as a conceptualization of a sequence of relations between the same (subject) and the Other. Initially, man posits woman as Other and essential as the wild and unintelligible nature to the capricious forces of which he is subordinate as the inessential. A term is essential if it determines the relation to the other term. In the first moment of this dialectic, man thinks that his relation to nature is determined by nature. In the second moment, society changes the mode of production and becomes an agricultural society and technological innovations are made that enable man to transform and control nature. As a consequence, he does not feel as weak and horrified as he did in the past. In the third moment, man realizes that he is the one who is essential, and he relegates woman along with nature to the position of the inessential. Woman becomes subordinate to man. It was man who had postulated woman as essential; now he makes her descend from this higher position and gives her the inferior status of servitude. At the end of this dialectic in which woman is subordinated, she is not released from being conceived as the Other. The Otherness that makes her radically different than men now serves to justify her subordination. In one and the same movement it serves to present her as incommensurable to man and defines her being not "in relation to herself" and "for herself" but "in relation to man" and "for man." This paves the way for the traditional ideas that woman's nature is biologically very different than man's because this is how God created her, and that she fulfills her essence in her function as wife and mother. This is a discursive regime that constitutes a contingent difference as Absolute alterity in order to subordinate the other to the same (subject).

As Absolutely Other, woman is both exalted and despised in her servitude to man. Besides, the oppositions and contradictions that the myth of the eternal feminine inheres mark her. Even though Beauvoir probes the patriarchal discourses in the structuralist style, she does not merely content herself with a static analysis; she addresses woman's situation historically in different cultures, tribes, various configurations of family and state relations. This is an indication of her awareness that despite the similarities of the structures, there is not a uniform patriarchy that operates homogeneously or monolithically.

So, woman must be evacuated from that site of problematic alterity and recognized as a free moral subject. This is a symbolic struggle as much as a struggle for independence. Even when woman is granted a place on earth as man's "respectable spouse," she is only enchained to her place if she is deprived of economic independence and social and political rights. Yet, in a world in which man continues to be the master, woman's freedom will be empty even if she has economic independence, for she will not be able to shape the world in accordance with her values. Using a term that Beauvoir herself did not know, but which is a conceptual innovation that occurred within the horizon of her philosophical achievement, we can say that unless there is *gender equality* this freedom would be "for nothing." Hence the goal is neither to possess rights in the abstract sense nor merely to gain economic independence; it is to make freedom actual, active in its world-making capacity. Freedom is the constitution and expression of one's own essence (character) in the movement of existence. Freedom is neither reached by emancipation from the obstacles on its way nor is it an inner feeling. It is forming the world, building the self in ethical relations to the others. The improvement of one's character in generous relationships with others, the relentless effort to organize a world in accordance with values. In other words, freedom manifests itself in the world if a person's relations to others, natural environment, and political institutions reflect the values the subject chose to embrace.

It is hardly possible to understand Beauvoir's ontology of sex without speaking of her relation to Hegel. Indeed, her interest in Hegel's philosophy goes back to the late 1920s, the period in which she was a philosophy student. In the late 1940s, she was reading Hegel's *Phenomenology of Spirit* while she was writing *The Second Sex*. The philosophical terminology in *The Second Sex* testifies to the influence of his thought on her. This is not surprising as French existentialism of the Second World War period engages with Hegel's philosophy. Sartre's phenomenological ontology in *Being and Nothingness* owes a great deal to Hegel's notion of negativity. In the literature on Beauvoir, the major differences between her relation to Hegel and her relation to Sartre are much debated (Lundren-Gothlin 1998). Sartre starts with the dualism of Being-in-itself and Being-for-itself and argues that nothingness enters the world thanks to intentionality and the nihilation of the Being-for-itself. In other words, nothingness appears as lack or absence at the interstices of Being, due to the negativity of the consciousness. By starting from the dualism of *Being and Nothingness*, Sartre gives a phenomenological account of nothingness and absence in its interrelation with presence. This is a refusal of a developmental phenomenological project that culminates in absolute knowing, conceived in terms of the self-reflection of the Spirit. Hegel also plays an important role in Sartre's text when being-for-others is addressed. There, too, Sartre does not subscribe to Hegel's concept of reconciliation and recognition between the two desiring self-consciousness; he contests Hegel by making asymmetry fundamental even though always possible to reverse. Beauvoir's relation to Hegel's philosophy is quite different. Notwithstanding Sartre's argument that depicts being-for-the-other as end-

less negativity and struggle for domination between the other and me, Beauvoir argues that the others' freedom is part of my situation. The other's
freedom does not have to be the negation of my freedom; the Hegelian idea
of reciprocal recognition between the other and me becomes the condition of
a political organization in which all human beings can be free. I think that in
her philosophy of history, Beauvoir is Hegelian in that she believes that
history holds in itself the promise of equality for all human beings. Absolute
freedom must include women's political freedom and equality. Hegel's philosophy of freedom did not include freedom for women because it was governed by patriarchy. If freedom is the Absolute ideal of historical being, it
must expand to all humanity. It is the future goal of overcoming all historically contingent relations of subordination, including sexual oppression.

However, oppression will not come to an end due to the impersonal forces
of history without there being need for human action. Political oppression
will cease to be if the oppressed chose to organize to resist oppression.
Beauvoir argues, "a freedom which is interested only in denying freedom
must be denied" (Beauvoir 1976, 91). Both Sartre and Beauvoir advocate
freedom and take determinism as the metaphysical manifestation of a freedom that must be fought. Sartre rejects that the motivation to surpass the
world toward a new state of affairs that is not yet present derives from facts:
"No factual state whatever it may be (the political and economic structure of
society, the psychological 'state,' etc.) is capable by itself of motivating any
act whatsoever. For an act is a projection of the for-itself toward what is not,
and what is can in no way determine by itself what is not" (Sartre 2003, 457).
For Beauvoir the possibility of transcendence is preserved in the ambiguity
of life.

So far, I have few presented reasons to think that Beauvoir's understanding of the freedom of action as transcendence differs from Sartre's. Let me
add here the following remark: in phenomenology the problem of transcendence is closely connected with temporality. Sartre argues in *Being and
Nothingness* that our present reality and what the past signifies for us become
manifest to our consciousness in the light of a future projection. This seems
to contradict with the Hegelian idea in *The Science of Logic* that "essence is
past—but timelessly past—being" [*Wesen ist was gewesen ist*] (Hegel 2010,
337). For Hegel freedom is nothing but the unfolding of an essence, while for
Sartre it is the embracing of a possibility. Beauvoir holds that there is a
historical destiny that engulfs woman's situation because woman is constituted as the Absolute Other, though that does not abolish the ambiguity
thanks to which the possibility of transcendence remains open.

In *The Ethics of Ambiguity*, she makes future possibilities play a fundamental role in evaluating the present. In *The Second Sex*, on the other hand,
Beauvoir proceeds to explain oppression by making a genetic phenomenological analysis of the constitutive historical structures of patriarchy. This is

not a genealogy of oppression that deciphers the power structures that subordinate the female sex to the male sex, but it gives us a multifaceted description of the pervasiveness and continuity of oppression.

Her existentialist theory of action commits Beauvoir to a neat distinction between action and movement in the physical sense. Animals move in their environments and are immanent to their environing nature. In contrast, human beings have the capacity to act, to transcend the given state of affairs and shape the world in the social and political sense. *The Second Sex* calls for women to surpass the world in which they are enclosed in the realm of immanence, the domestic realm, which is socially constructed by the patriarchal tradition as a natural realm of difference and sexual subordination, and move toward a world of ethical and political equality of the sexes. This message may sound outdated, at least in some parts of the Western world, and Beauvoir's reference to the biological sexes in the binary form of female and male can be seen as a sexist view to overcome. However, the binary is important to recognize for defining what sexism is at its core and how it prevails in the rest of the world, especially in those places in which feminist movements fight against the traditional forms of patriarchy, which anti-democratic and authoritarian regimes reaffirm. The old definition of sexism is still relevant to make sense of the structures of oppression women's lived experiences reveal.

Beauvoir claims that those who suffer from sexual oppression may evade their freedom and instead participate in their own oppression. Even though the oppressed is in her situation half victim and half complicit, genuine moral freedom must have the *telos* of freedom and equality for all human beings. The ideal of absolute freedom does not imply the surmounting of all ambiguity, for ambiguity makes possible the upsurge of existence and temporalization. To uphold the ideal of absolute freedom is to embrace the goal of bringing all oppression to an end. Although, it is true that there is no such thing as absolute freedom in the world, and that freedom is fragile and contingent, something to conquer and reconquer.

Existentialism leads Beauvoir to philosophize about the concrete problems of existence. She refuses to begin with an abstract universal conception of human essence and looks for essences in existence. That strategy enables her to raise the question of the specificity of woman's situation. We may fail to realize the possibilities of our being under the conditions of oppression because oppression obstructs human action and prevents people from flourishing. Given the ontology of freedom to which she commits herself, and the existentialist axiom that existence precedes essence, Beauvoir argues that woman's essence is not pre-given but has to be found in historically shaped situation. The famous statement "One is not born a woman, one becomes one" (Beauvoir 2010, 283) can be interpreted in the light of the basic tenet of existentialism: *existence precedes essence*. By *existence* is meant human reality, which is contingent and superfluous. Human existence is not determined by a necessity, which will make it become what it is. Human essence is not a *telos* that is inscribed at the origin, which determines human existence as it unfolds. That sexual difference is the manifestation of a teleological essence is not just false but a justification of sexual oppression.

THE DEBATE OVER THE BIOLOGICAL

The most controversial issue in Beauvoir studies concerns the status of the biological in *The Second Sex*. Beauvoir does not deny that there are natural differences. As Aristotle remarked, nature is a realm of differences, but equality is our creation, a political achievement. She also sees, in the way a phenomenological ontologist would, that some differences may become more significant than others. Why do some differences matter and others do not? What makes some differences indicators of the specific ways in which reality is organized? Although there are natural biological differences, there is no such thing as being born a woman, if there is no essence that predetermines the differences that show themselves in existence. Differences may appear as signifying this or that depending on how one relates to and experiences them, in historically sedimented contexts.

The famous statement "One is not born a woman, but rather becomes a woman" is often interpreted as giving us a proto concept of gender. But what did Beauvoir exactly mean when she rejected that sex is biological? "The division of the sexes is a biological given, not a moment in human history" (Beauvoir 2010, 9). In the first chapter of *Destiny*, which she titled "Biological Data," she works within the Darwinist paradigm according to which sexual difference is a contingent product that belongs to the later stages of the process of evolution. It was not always already there in nature since the beginning and it is not universal. Moreover, "the very meaning of *division* of the species into the two sexes is not clear" (Beauvoir 2010, 21). "It does not occur universally in nature. In one-celled animals, infusorians, amoebas, bacilli, and so on, multiplication is fundamentally distinct from sexuality, with cells dividing and subdividing individually. For some metazoans, reproduction occurs by schizogenesis, that is dividing the individual whose origin is also asexual, or by blastogenesis, that is dividing the individual itself produced by a sexual phenomenon" (Beauvoir 2010, 21–22). Sex appears in complex life forms; however, in nature, sexual reproduction coexists with reproduction without sex. Indeed, the future is undetermined. A "society can be imagined that reproduces itself by parthenogenesis or is composed of hermaphrodites" (Beauvoir 2010, 24). In the future people may not need sex in order to reproduce. Clearly, this section summarizes the biological data that the Darwinist feminists work with. Sexual difference is a product of nature; sexual difference does not have to be limited by two in nature because the sexual differentiation continues. What is the mechanism that divides people as "woman" and "man" in accordance with the anatomical features of their genital organs, biological properties, and function in reproduction, in order to assign them to a group that is hierarchically positioned in relation to other groups? Are not our lived bodies, which offer us a perspective on the world and open the possibility of making sense of the world, rather affected by this classification or assignment than simply naturally determined? Beauvoir does not claim that bodies are produced or brought into being by discursive social construction. Bodies are born; as such they are natural and real. But this real body that is brought about into the human world by nature can neither be the ground of accounting for the lived experience of sexuation nor of the world as lived from the standpoint of the sexed body.

Although sexual division as male and female should be seen as a given of evolution, in order to find out what that signifies we need to turn to human beings' being-in-the-world, to the historical structures of *mitsein*, to the social organization of the world. The sexual division which nature brought into being is made to signify in a historical dialectic in which woman is constructed as the Other. One may ask the question whether sex as a natural given may not be the cause of the historical dialectic at issue. Can the situation which is created by a historical dialectic be an expression of natural being? This way of conceiving sexual difference risks legitimating male domination because, if historical domination is a reflection of natural difference, then there is no ground to complain about sexual oppression. Naturalist feminism contests the reading of nature in terms of determinism by neglecting the virtualities. Beauvoir rejects the naturalist thesis that comprehends the situation of being the second sex as a natural consequence. The apparition of sexual difference in nature being contingent, we have no ground to argue that, given sexual division, sexual oppression is necessary and inevitable. Why in the human world are women in the situation of being the second sex, whereas in animal species that sexually reproduce, females are not secondary to males? In distinction to animals, in human societies the balance between the forces of production and forces of reproduction changes; it takes on different configurations in different economic moments of history. In the early economy of hunting and reaping the fruits of nature, woman needs man's labor to keep her children alive. However, as soon as the forces of production and reproduction are reorganized, human relations, including the relation between man and woman, between parent and child, and between children, will change. Hence, to understand human reality we need to go beyond biology. Insofar as we remain within the biological paradigm, there is no way of taking into account the historically changing balance between the forces of production and reproduction.

Beauvoir seeks to give a phenomenological answer to the question of sexual oppression without neglecting the historical perspective. She focuses on how corporeal experiences are lived and represented. She explores how women's corporeality, the differences in their bodily processes are appealed to justify their being thrust into a situation of social inequality. But that phenomenology is loyal to the principle that existence precedes essence and committed to the view that human beings create the sense and value of the functions that they fulfill. I think Beauvoir is not so far from Foucault, even though it is well known that Foucault distances himself from phenomenology and existentialism, in her claim that the sexual institutions and practices determine the sense and value of sexual difference in its social dimension. Nature does not limit sex in a heteronormative way and subordinate women to men; sexual oppression is made possible by the historical institutions that are built on historical practices. There is no such thing as a given universal male or female human nature from which one can infer sexual activities that would be natural and necessary for individual men and women.

Existentialism commits to an ontology of freedom that denies that existence can be determined from the outside by facts and values. Existence is the movement of making the facts signify in accordance with a fundamental project and by one's assumption of values. Even though this is generally right, it is hard to explain sexuation without referring to historical conditions. Beauvoir agrees with Merleau-Ponty that the body is both a thing in the world and a perspective on the world. The analysis of sexuation must take this perspective seriously. A perception from a standpoint is not an outcome of the particular structure of the body; its difference must be sought in the specific historical situation and the conditions that constitute it. Beauvoir accepts that woman's biology makes her vulnerable to enslavement by the species' natural urge to perpetuate itself. Man's biology, on the other hand, gives him the possibility of maximizing the number of sexual encounters without assuming future responsibilities for the children that may be born thereof. But both man and woman have the possibility of not complying with what their species' being holds in reserve for them. Culture enables them to surpass their biological being. Beauvoir thinks that biological factors must be taken seriously because "they play a primary role in woman's history." Hence biological data constitute an element that belongs to the essence of the situation. The reason for that is not biological determinism. The role that biology plays in woman's history and its contribution to woman's situation is not grounded in causal natural processes. Beauvoir has a phenomenological reason to attribute importance to the biological data: "Because the body is the instrument of our hold [*prise*] on the world, the world appears different to us depending on how it is grasped, which explains why we have studied these data so deeply; they are one of the keys that enable us to understand woman" (Beauvoir 2010, 44). It is thanks to the body that we perceive the world; we

are in the world; we are anchored in the world. How we perceive and understand our own bodies is a key to how we perceive and understand the world.
This has nothing to do with biological determination. How we understand
and interpret biological data belongs to the constitution of the lived experience of the world. If determinism were true, Beauvoir should have said that
woman lived her natural destiny in history. She does not accept that. "But we
refuse the idea that they form a fixed destiny for her. They do not suffice to
constitute the basis for sexual hierarchy; they do not explain why woman is
the Other; they do not condemn her forever to this subjugated role" (Beauvoir 2010, 44). Then, the way biological facts are lived and what they signify
for us are more important to understand before we can say anything about the
modality of their effects on us. This strategy gives a basis for the invention of
our contemporary notion of "gender." Gender explores how the lived experience of "biological facts" is mediated by the historical and cultural practices.
The difficulties in making sense of the biology chapter gives rise to radically
different readings of Beauvoir. Judith Butler, for example, as Toril Moi says,
offered a reading of Beauvoir's 1949 essay through the lens of the 1960s sex/
gender distinction (Moi 1999, 3). Difficulties in the assessment of Beauvoir's
rhetoric style have led to major misunderstandings that depict her as if she is
saying that woman's biological being is a destiny that she cannot escape. As
a consequence, Beauvoir's historical, non-essentialist, feminist ontology of
sex, which stems from a debate over freedom in existentialism, has been lost
from sight.

For Beauvoir, it is a *misfortune* that woman's biological destiny forces
her to create life and provide the care necessary for the perpetuation of the
human species. But this statement is based on the philosophical view that
existence keeps always open the possibility that this destiny can be
transcended. If we forget this accompanying ontological commitment, Beauvoir may sound like defending male superiority and as practicing misogyny.

The repetition of life refers to the cyclical management or ritualistic
maintenance of the necessary means of human survival. This is concretized
in domestic organization of life, occupation with the house chores, such as
cooking and cleaning, providing comfort for man, caring for children and
elderly, feeding the animals and cultivating the environment. The sexual
division of labor makes her spend her physical and mental energy for the
maintenance of life, and it deprives her from the possibility of leaving permanent traces in the world. The products of her labor are often immediately
consumed: a room that she cleaned will be dirty again in a short time and the
meal she cooked will be eaten and gone. The labor is not visible, recognized,
appreciated, and paid for. A person caught up in the domestic sphere dies as
if she has never existed and will only be remembered by the people she cared
for in her closed circle. In contrast, a person who does more than reproducing
life builds a world, and can make lasting traces in the world. Important

achievements such as political deeds and artistic products will be part of the world and shall make their authors be remembered by the future generations. In Hegel's view, they become part of the different temporality of the spiritual world. Woman, as long as she remains in the domain of immanence, facilitates man's access to the spiritual world and assures him posterity at the expense of her own exclusion from the life of the spirit, which is superior and transcends the biological. If this is the case, is there any good reason for woman to devote herself to the realm of life's necessities rather than to try to realize her own freedom in the world? Why should a woman do something that obstructs her from achieving her personal goals, instead of working toward self-realization? More specifically, why should she have children and submerge in non-being in the whirlpool of circular time? Beauvoir highlights the contrast between man and woman: although man's personal goals do not conflict with the ends of the species, the conflict ensues in woman's case. Given that this difference is unfair, it is morally and politically just to eliminate it. The problem of inequality can be solved by making fair the distribution of responsibility in the domestic sphere, by the creation of institutions that reduce the burden on women, and by giving women the equal opportunity to play their role in building and organizing the world.

According to Beauvoir, women's bodies have specific physiological and psychological experiences because of their biological sex; they go through menstruation cramps, hormonal changes, pregnancy nausea and fatigue, birth, the transformations of menopause. Beauvoir recognizes these non-voluntary lived experiences and focuses on their negative impacts on women's life in patriarchal culture. In contrast, the second wave feminists celebrated these corporeal experiences as an affirmation of women's being. Even though it is forbidden to speak of these bodily experiences that are specific to women in the patriarchal culture, Beauvoir held that the strategy to reaffirm and revalue them is to make concessions to it. Why is that so? The affirmation of the feminine body, if it leads to the affirmation of a life of immanence, will result in alienation. For a woman to choose a life of immanence is to surrender to a life of repetition by renouncing to her economic independence and, more significantly, by giving up her productive activity in the world.

Ultimately, Beauvoir believes that to occupy oneself simply with the perpetuation of life is *alienation*. What are these alien forces that capture control over the being of the person? Women who are forced to leave their work because they have to take care for the family, and cannot go back to it because they have no social and institutional support, do not return to their original, authentic womanhood; they become alienated from their own being. Although this has to do with how labor is organized, it is also the case that the female body in its reproductive capacities sets the stage for alienation.

Nancy Bauer argues that the discussion of women's alienation should begin with her body. "To my ear, Beauvoir here points a scene of woman's body as the site of a life-and-death drama (something she at one point calls 'the theater of a play that unfolds within her' (Beauvoir 2010)" (Bauer 2001, 206). Focus on alienation may help us understand why Beauvoir is using a negative tone in speaking of women's corporeality. From menstruation to menopause, woman's body is the scene for the play of forces in a life and death struggle. Indeed, no body consists only of the life forces; all living bodies accommodate the forces of death. As such, death is not at all exterior to life; it pervades life. The real problem arises because this struggle in woman's body is framed or captured by patriarchal social conditions that alienate it. Here abjection and objectification are intertwined. On the one hand, this is a body that cannot be allowed to signify itself as a living being; it is chased away from the public sphere. It appears there in effacement, covered up and hidden. On the other hand, it is an object of the male gaze and woman herself assumes and performs her objectification. Her body is alienated when woman objectifies her corporeal existence under the male gaze. The objectification of the body opens the way for its colonization and exploitation. The concession made to objectification by the male gaze is part of woman's flight from freedom. Independence comes with anxiety: the fear of being alone and without social support in the world, the despair that one has lost love in seeking freedom; and the worries of the consequences of not complying with gender norms. Of course, these are the feelings with which we can cope if we realize that this is how gender internally operates to repress emancipation. If this is right, Beauvoir's existentialism recognizes sex and invites for the critical engagement with gender norms that alienate women from their own bodies and subjectivities. Subjectivity here is a search for authenticity that does not reduce to egoism or individualism; it accommodates the ethical and political care for the freedom of others and the readiness and willingness to assume responsibility for the world.

The Second Sex conceives woman's situation as a way of being-in-the-world; hence situation is not a spatiotemporal position in the objective space. It depends on the way the world is disclosed in the light of a projective understanding of being; this is the condition in which one acquires a place in the world. As Hannah Arendt said in *The Origins of Totalitarianism* (Arendt 1958), words and deeds have worth depending on how one is placed in the world. What is at stake in woman's situation is her social and symbolic status, a status that cannot be easily changed by the individual's projects as long as it retains its ambiguity. Although existence is disclosed by projects, it is at the same time historically sedimented. In women's case, this is sedimentation by the patriarchal structures in which she is constructed as the Other.

In *The Second Sex*, Beauvoir thinks through the historical dialectic that gives rise to patriarchy, and articulates the strange logic underlying sexual difference. The upshot is that woman's situation, her being-in-the-world as sexed or sexually differentiated, is grounded on sexual oppression. This is not to deny the reality of the biological sex, even though it is a denial of biological determinism. If the political and social inequality between the sexes is not a consequence of a natural necessity, but a product of contingent historical necessity, women can liberate themselves from the conditions of oppression by refusing to participate in their own oppression. Indeed, ambiguity leaves the door open for historical transformation, which is also named "conversion."

Beauvoir learns from the philosophical tradition, especially from Hegel, that alterity is a relative concept. Everybody is other than other people. There are myriad differences that could characterize us, but they can do so because we are always already placed in relation to other people whom we fundamentally resemble. Diversity implies relatedness, because it assumes the comparability of the beings that are given. To claim that woman is other than man and man is other than woman is to postulate the diversity of woman and man, who are similar in other essential aspects. Hence, man cannot take himself as the essential and woman as the inessential. One could object that to address feminine alterity in terms of relative alterity amounts to an understanding of woman in terms of man, which implies taking the male sex as an ontological model for an understanding of the being of human being. I disagree with the objection. I see no reason why Beauvoir's ontology of sex should be characterized as male. She strongly opposes a framework in which sexual difference becomes an essential difference in the being of human beings. She rejects all naturalist and essentialist accounts of sexual difference (keeping in mind that naturalism can have essentialist and anti-essentialist versions).

We cannot know what may become of sexual difference if oppression is abolished. Erotic experience shall no longer be framed in terms of a man's comfort and rest in immanence when he returns there from his unceasing struggle in the world with other men. "Thanks to her, there is a way to escape the inexorable dialectic of the master and the slave that springs from the reciprocity of freedoms" (Beauvoir 2010, 176). Erotic experience in the realm of immanence in the patriarchal context can never be authentically moral because it involves possession (Beauvoir 2010, 176). The possibility of erotic experience based on ethical freedom opens with the transformation of women's historical status of oppression grounded in a patriarchal understanding of sexual difference.

To conclude, woman's situation is characterized by sexual difference, which is constituted by oppression. How is this difference formed as characterizing a situation? There are plenty of differences in existence, but only some of them come to acquire the senses that determine one's social status. The constitution of a difference as making sense in this way is an effect of the past human practices on our lives. Beauvoir studies these practices by considering anthropological findings and articulates the laws that govern them in myths. She distances herself from a naturalist analysis of sexual difference by explaining women's oppression in an open-ended dialectic of history. For her, the intentions that operate in man's attitudes toward nature matter in the constitution of sexual difference. Man's attitude toward life and death mediates both his relation to nature and his relation to the female sex, which he associates with nature. Man is horrified at the face of women's reproductive powers, as he was horrified at the face of nature's forces. Nancy Bauer writes: "Man's fear of woman, Beauvoir says, thus came to manifest itself not in the form of veneration or awe—of the acknowledgment of other-ness and difference—but in the guise of resentment and hatred, or what we nowadays call misogyny" (Bauer 2001, 198). The logic of abjection is the logic of absolute alterity, which does not return to the same. It enables man's relation to himself in the realm of immanence through the Other. His relation to the feminine other is mediated by his relation with the Other. According to Beauvoir, the Other can have many faces, but it often has the woman's face. In patriarchy the Sameness of the absolute subject, which is male, is consti-tuted by the relation to the Other. This is the logical structure of her account of the male and female genders. For woman, gender is oppression because, as a figure of the Other, woman is both cut off from her transcendence and deprived of the possibility of self-relation, of return to herself through rela-tion with the other in an ethical erotic relation in the sphere of immanence. Women in the patriarchal tradition have been confined to the realm of imma-nence because they are constituted as absolute alterity, which legitimized and made invisible their oppression. It is because women were symbolically des-ignated as absolute others that they could be deprived of possibilities for the actualization of their capacity for transcendence and of self-relation through the other in the realm of immanence. My next chapter is devoted to Bataille's ontology of sex, in which I discuss how Bataille rethinks erotic experience with woman symbolized as absolute alterity, as a function of the anthropo-logical break with natural existence, and with reference to the general econo-my of the sacred realm. Bataille starts with an ontological economy of nature and speaks of the transition to the profane world. For an ontological analysis of erotic experience, an understanding of the history and symbolism of the sacred realm is indispensable.

Beauvoir's problem of freedom and determinism takes the form of the tension between freedom and historical constitution. Historical constitution does not annihilate the existential possibility of being free, but it creates conditions that hurt its realization in the form of actual freedom. Women for millennia have not found the conditions in which they could actualize their potential for freedom. Because freedom of action and ethical freedom belong to the accomplishment of human freedom, being free means being fully human. Full-fledged humanity is not a biological concept; it implies moral and political equality, but also fecundity in the sense of creative activity. If woman is something we become, the same can be said for human in general. Human implies both immanence and transcendence, and if immanence is about an impersonal immersion in the elemental to satisfy one's needs and if it gives the possibility to return to oneself in erotic desire and enjoyment, transcendence enables individuation as a person in the spiritual realm. One becomes truly human if it is possible to realize one's self in both dimensions of one's being.

REFERENCES

Arendt, Hannah. 1958. *The Origins of Totalitarianism*. New York: Meridian Books.
Bauer, Nancy. 2001. *Simone de Beauvoir, Philosophy and Feminism*. New York: Columbia University Press.
———. 2011. "Beauvoir on the Allure of Self-Objectification." In *Feminist Metaphysics*, edited by Charlotte Witt, 117–29. London and New York: Springer Verlag.
Beauvoir, Simone de. 1944. *Pyrrhus et Cinéas*. Paris: Gallimard.
———. 1945. "La phénoménologie de la perception de Maurice Merleau-Ponty." *Les Temps Modernes* 1, no. 2: 363–67.
———. 1966. "Must We Burn Sade?" In *Marquis de Sade*, translated by A. Michelson. New York: Grove.
———. 1972. *The Coming of Age*. Translated by P. O'Brian. New York: Putnam.
———. 1975. *Force of Circumstance*. The third volume of her autobiography. Translated by Richard Howard. London: Penguin Books. Originally published as *La Force des Choses* (Paris: Gallimard, 1963).
———. 1976. *The Ethics of Ambiguity*. Translated by Bernard Frechtman. New York: Citadel Press.
———. 2010. *The Second Sex*. Translated by Constance Borde and Sheila Malovany-Chevallier. New York: Alfred A. Knopf.
Bergoffen, Debra B. 1997. *The Philosophy of Simone de Beauvoir: Gendered Phenomenologies, Erotic Generosities*. Albany: State University of New York Press.
———. 2000. "From Husserl to Beauvoir: Gendering the Perceiving Subject." In *Feminist Phenomenology*, edited by Linda Fisher and Lester Embree, 187–203. Dordrecht, Boston, and London: Kluwer Academic Publisher.
Camus, Albert. 1955. *The Myth of Sisyphus and Other Essays*. Translated by Justin O'Brien. New York: Alfred A. Knopf.
Direk, Zeynep. 2011. "Immanence and Abjection in Simone de Beauvoir." *Southern Journal of Philosophy* 49, no. 1 (March): 49–72.
Hegel, G. W. F. 2018. *The Phenomenology of Spirit*. Translated by Michael Inwood. Oxford: Oxford University Press.
———. 2010. *The Science of Logic*. Translated and edited by George Di Giovanni. New York: Cambridge University Press.
Irigaray, Luce. 1985b. *This Sex Which Is Not One*. Translated by Catherine Porter with Carolyn Burke. Ithaca, NY: Cornell University Press.
Kant, Immanuel. 1997. *Critique of Practical Reason*. Translated and edited by Mary Gregor. Cambridge: Cambridge University Press.
Kruks, Sonia. 1990. *Situation and Human Existence: Freedom, Subjectivity, and Society*. New York: Routledge.
———. 1995. "Teaching Sartre about Freedom." In *Feminist Interpretations of Simone de Beauvoir*, edited by Margaret A. Simons, 79–95. University Park: Pennsylvania State University Press.

Langer, Monica. 2003. "Beauvoir and Merleau-Ponty on Ambiguity." In *The Cambridge Companion to Simone de Beauvoir*, edited by Claudia Card, 87–106. Cambridge: Cambridge University Press.

Lundren-Gothlin, Eva. 1998. "The Master-Slave Dialectic in *The Second Sex*." In *Simone de Beauvoir: A Critical Reader*, edited by Elizabeth Fallaize, 93–108. London: Routledge.

Merleau-Ponty, Maurice. 1973. *Adventures of the Dialectic*. Translated by Hugh J. Silverman and Joseph J. Bien. Evanston, IL: Northwestern University Press.

———. 1990. *Humanism and Terror: An Essay on the Communist Problem*. Translated by John O'Neill. Boston: Beacon Press.

———. 2012. *Phenomenology of Perception*. Translated by Donald A. Landes. London: Routledge Classics.

Moi, Toril. 1999. *What Is a Woman? And Other Essays*. New York: Oxford University Press.

Sandford, Stella. 2006. *How to Read Beauvoir*. London: Granta Books.

Sartre, Jean-Paul. 2003. *Being and Nothingness*. Translated by Hazel E. Barnes. London: Routledge Classics.

———. 2004. *Critique of Dialectical Reason*. Vol. 1. Translated by Alan Sheridan Smith. Edited by Jonathan Rée. London New York: Verso.

Tidd, Ursula. 2004. *Simone de Beauvoir: Gender and Testimony*. Cambridge: Cambridge University Press.

Ward, Julie K. 1995. "Beauvoir's Two Senses of 'Body' in *The Second Sex*." In *Feminist Interpretations of Simone de Beauvoir*, edited by Margaret A. Simons, 223–42. University Park: Pennsylvania State University Press.

Wilkerson, William. 2017. "Beauvoir and Merleau-Ponty on Freedom and Authenticity." In *A Companion to Simone de Beauvoir*, edited by Nancy Bauer and Laura Hengehold, 224–35. Hoboken, NJ: Wiley-Blackwell.

Chapter Two

Georges Bataille

Erotic Experience

In the late 1940s and early 1950s in France, which is the epoch in which Simone de Beauvoir's *The Second Sex* denounced patriarchal sexual oppression by offering the first remarkable ontology of sexual difference, Georges Bataille was pursuing what I call an *ontology of erotic experience*. Although Beauvoir was interested in the question of ethics of eros, which she interpreted in terms of generosity, she did not deeply reflect on erotic experience as an ontological issue. Bataille's way of elaborating the question might have seemed as a "new mysticism" to her, as it did to Sartre. Her political and cultural criticism did not license a philosophical discourse on *life* as erotic energy in relation to the profane and sacred realms; she was content to uncover sexism as it manifested itself in these realms.

Bataille affirms, as much as Beauvoir, the body in flesh and blood over and against the abstract subject and its cosmic time. However, he does not consent to an ontology of freedom understood in terms of the temporality of the project. He gives a different account of incarnated freedom as sovereignty. One of the experiential sites of sovereignty is erotic experience. Unlike Beauvoir, Bataille did not focus on the experience of the body as sexed. He would not be satisfied by a reflection on how the situated body is lived in culture; he wanted to go deeper into the natural forces that, from his point of view, ontologically precede culture. I devote this chapter to Bataille because I believe that ontologies of erotic experience belong to ontologies of sex. In the unfolding of this book, in the fifth chapter, I argue that Jean-Luc Nancy takes seriously this project of the ontology of erotic experience and gives it a new form.

Georges Bataille's notion of erotic experience is ontologically grounded in his political economy, which not only concerns human existence, but also takes into account the totality of the biomass and life energy circulating on the globe. On the one hand, human existence belongs to the general economy of life, and on the other, human species' enrootedness in the totality of the biomass, which is the condition of its possibility, also threatens its survival. Bataille suggests that the survival of humanity required the invention of another economy, which separated humans from other living beings. This is an economy specific to human beings: a restricted economy of give and take, governed by reciprocity. As a consequence of its condition of belonging to a double economy, human existence is conceived by Bataille as made possible and continually disturbed by economical paradoxes, which function as existential paradoxes. The human world is irreducible to the natural world because its economy is different. Bataille is more concerned with the way natural life energy contests human constructions; he considers the tension between these double economies without really raising the question of whether the human-restricted economy harms the general economy of nature.

In the human world, conventional rules and laws regulate the economic and political realm, enabling people to make contracts with each other. In fact, these rules and conventions are of two kinds. First, there are the conventional rules of the restricted economy, which serve to accumulate surplus value to secure our future existence. The purpose of inventing a restricted economy is to guarantee our survival and constitute the reserves to satisfy future desires. Second, there are the conventional rules of the general economy, which point to the presence of another economy beyond the restricted economy. These are the conventions of the sacred realm that organize and regulate human conduct in ceremonies and rituals, structuring the important events of human life such as birth, marriage, death, and religious festivals. Bataille, like anthropologists such as Claude Lévi-Strauss and Marcel Mauss before him, perceives a tension between the general economy of life and the restricted economy of human existence in the world of work. Erotic experience, too, bears the tension that originates in that duality, for it lies at the intersection of both economies. It is an experience in which two dimensions of human existence play against and undermine each other.

Bataille argues that we should not study Eros by separating it from the sacred realm, because human sexuality is based on prohibitions and taboos, and hence is subject to laws and conventions of the sacred realm. In religions' organization and regulation of sexuality, erotic experience is structured as transgression, which means breaking of the law. There is nothing erotic in sex understood as a natural activity, not subject to any limit or norm. The law (sexual prohibitions) is logically prior to human sexuality and getting rid of it would be to get rid of the erotic element in human sexuality.

Transgression must be understood with a focus on its existential and economic effects; it gives an outlet from the restricted to the general economy. Erotic experience suspends the world of restricted economy, which is subordinated to utility and gives access to the impersonal ground of our incarnated existence, to the communication in the life of immanence. Bataille conceives erotic experience as *inner experience*: the transgression of desire culminates in the experience of sovereignty in which the Self is experienced in relation to the other. This is described as a destruction of rigid social identities and an overcoming of separate individuality. Subjectivity in the realm of restricted economy cannot be sovereign insofar as by economic and social status it is separate from the others. Neither the egoist subject seeking to maximize benefit for itself, nor the utilitarian subject attempting to maximize pleasure and reduce pain for the greatest number of people, can find access to general economy, for both calculate in accordance with the rules of the restricted economy. Subjectivity, beyond the circular economy of economic and social relations, goes back to that expenditure of energy in a shared space of incarnated openness.

Although Bataille's main issue is not sexual difference, I think the experience he names "communication" can be the very space of sexual differentiation. Whether or not this is compatible with queerness is an open question. Bataille invites us to a radical reflection on a new economy that takes seriously the biological nature of our existence. As I interpret him, he would not deny that that which is biological or material in the body never appears as such, but historico-social structures can be destabilized by its effects. Elaborating a Nietzschean idea, he views the body in the restricted economy as open to the challenge of the natural forces.

The controversy about interpreting Bataille's work in terms of feminist and queer theorist questions has not yet been settled; whether we should read him as a heterosexist or a critic of heteronormativity is debated. Bataille speaks from the male position in his fictional works, and it is possible to read him as a sexist. I side with the interpretations that see Bataille as affirming female desire. He deems feminine sexuality, especially in the mother, not as something to negate but as divine. In my view, Bataille attempted to think of female sexual difference beyond the logic of abjection he pointed to. Moreover, I agree that his general economy of sex is not based on the binary division of sex and that he paves the way for a reflection on queer pleasures. The sacred laws that are transgressed are made up of heterosexual norms. Whether or not the understanding of the erotic experience as transgression is worth retaining remains open as an important question. The transgression model adheres to the norms it transgresses to be able to transgress them. Hence, it keeps old patriarchal norms as part of the sacred realm.

At the end of the chapter, I turn to the question of violence in Bataille's erotic experience and inquire if it can give rise to an ethics of Eros. I argue that Bataille is not concerned with an ethics of Eros based on principles and prohibitions; however, his search for intimacy in violent sexual encounters is not the same as a sadism that dominates over the other and does not care for the other's life. In Bataille's literary works erotic violence is not provoked by hatred—it has ontological significance and does not exclude care for the other. Bataille has a very interesting ontology of sex, which rests on ontologico-economical paradoxes and the negativity of sexual desire; however, he does not sufficiently reflect on what it means to be in an erotic relationship from an ethical point of view.

BATAILLE'S ONTOLOGY OF SEX: THE ECONOMIC AND THE EROTIC

In *The Accursed Share*, the term "general economy" refers to the exuberance of living matter as a whole. The problem of the general economy, which can be seen by a macroscopic gaze, concerns the excess rather than the lack of resources (Bataille 1991a, 39). Bataille insists that the economic problem needs to be conceived as an existential one. Such an attempt would leave behind the "classical economy" that concentrates on the pursuit of surplus to be invested in growth, thereby missing the general existential problem: that the essence of the biomass is such that it "must constantly destroy (consume) a surplus of energy" (Bataille 1991a, 182). Here I think that Bataille responds to existentialism by raising the question of the economy of existence. The existence of a human being cannot be explained only by the restricted economy of the world—by concentrating solely on the way the individual is situated in facticity as a member of a class, race, and sex. We must also take into account the subject's rootedness in the general economy of life.

The body as a living organism, as an impersonal part of the biomass, is always to be found in a situation determined by the "play of energy on the surface of the globe, [which] ordinarily receives more energy than is necessary" for surviving (Bataille 1991a, 21). The general economy of life presses us to squander energy, whereas the restricted economy of the world of work urges us to accumulate surplus in order to survive. Bataille conceives of human existence as caught up in this tension between life and the world. We are also caught up in two temporalities; the cosmic time of life and the time of the project constantly interrupt each other. In "Truth and Lying in a Non-Moral Sense," Nietzsche argues that we are creatures who, in order to survive, construct a world by way of schematizing life according to our practical needs (Nietzsche 1999, 85). Nietzsche's view implies that the chaotic energies of life continue to surround, penetrate, and constantly challenge us through our bodies and threaten our stability in our personal lives. On the macro scale, our scientific, conceptual, legal, and moral commitments make up our worldly nest, analogous to a spider's web. Nietzsche acknowledges the superiority of the standards of the human architectural genius:

> Here one may certainly admire man as a mighty genius of construction, who succeeds in piling up an infinitely complicated dome of concepts upon an unstable foundation, and, as it were, on running water. Of course, in order to be supported, his construction must be like one constructed of spiders' webs: delicate enough to be carried along by the waves, strong enough not to be blown apart by every wind. (Nietzsche 1999, 85)

Without our worldly constructions we cannot survive, yet how permanent are they going to be? Life can always take them back from us and throw them to oblivion, leaving us bewildered in the midst of chaotic forces. The modern capitalist world submits man's activity to use for the purpose of constant development and growth of economic forces. In the first volume of *The Accursed Share*, Bataille is concerned with the way restricted economy (constant development of economic sources) poses the general problems that are linked to the movement of energy in the globe (Bataille 1991a, 20–21).

Erotic experience in the modern world, the acknowledgment and transgression of prohibitions at the same time, is an economic play between life's forces and worldly powers that necessarily reaches a limit in the investment of surplus in growth and development. Eroticism is the "unproductive glory" of life energy. Bataille makes clear that erotic desire does not originate in a need or a lack in our being-in-the-world; it is a surplus, luxury, and frivolity in our being. Not only does the erotic belong fundamentally to luxury, but sexuality, too, is in its very essence luxurious. He writes: "Under the present conditions, independently of our consciousness, sexual reproduction is, together with eating and death, one of the great luxurious detours that ensure the intense consumption of energy" (Bataille 1991a, 35). In animal sexuality, the squandering of sexual energy "goes far beyond what would be sufficient for the growth of the species. It appears to be the most that an individual has the strength to accomplish in a given moment" (Bataille 1991a, 35). Bataille emphasizes that "the excess energy (wealth) can be used for the growth of a system (e.g., an organism)," and further that "if the system can no longer grow, or if the excess cannot be completely absorbed in its growth, it must necessarily be lost without profit; it must be spent, willingly or not, gloriously or catastrophically" (Bataille 1991a, 21).

The restricted economy of the world is self-destructive, and life's energy cannot be captured and domesticated by the schemas and limits of an ever-growing system. "In a sense, life suffocates within limits that are too close; it aspires in manifold ways to an impossible growth; it releases a steady flow of excess resources, possibly involving large squanderings of energy" (Bataille 1991a, 30). The limit of growth being reached, life, without being in a closed container, at least enters into ebullition: without exploding, its extreme exuberance pours out in a movement always bordering on explosion" (Bataille 1991a, 30). The general economy at the impersonal layer of existence bears in itself destabilizing virtualities. *Erotism* highlights the explosive nature of life:

> We refuse to see that life is the trap set for the balanced order, that life is nothing but instability and disequilibrium. Life is a swelling tumult continuously on the verge of explosion. But since the incessant explosion constantly exhausts its resources, it can only proceed under one condition: that beings given life whose explosive force is exhausted shall make room for fresh beings coming into the cycle with renewed rigour. (Bataille 1986, 59)

Erotism and death are luxuries of life, the greatest squanders, which give rise to new beings or clear the space for fresh beginnings in the world. They destroy the authority and power of the previous generations that rigidify life to maintain their privileges. Erotic activity is not productive; it is one of the fundamental ways of squandering the excess energy of life that challenges us from within the impersonal, general ground of our incarnated existence. War and eros call the self and the world into question and pave the way for a reorganization of worldly structures. Both the necessity of the modern wars and Eros exceed teleology. They are never means of growth and development, but ways of squandering the excess that, without an outlet, would explode the whole system of production. They are also transgressions that put us in contact with life and death and make us return to the impersonal ground of existence.

In *Theory of Religion*, Bataille establishes an opposition between that which is personal and the impersonal existence (existence *apersonnelle*). On the one hand, there is the clear consciousness of the world of objects and of persons, and on the other hand, there are the inner experiences of the world of immanence, which reveals the impersonal, indistinct, and intimate existence (Bataille 1992, 56). Although Bataille does not talk about that, my proposition is that the impersonality of existence can be conceived as an ontological plane of sexual differentiation. On this plane, the body is affirmed in its generality as a communicative, non-separate being, embedded in the dynamic life of the cosmos. This is not a sex that is given at birth; it is not limited to the binary. It is in differentiation in the realm of immanence in communication with the other. If we go in that direction sexual differentiation becomes a matter of erotic experience, which is communication and sovereignty.

In my reading, Bataille is a radical thinker of subjectivity in its ontological, energetic dimension. For him, subjectivity does not chiefly mean the clear consciousness of objects. It is foremost the body, corporeality at the impersonal layer of subjective existence, beyond mineness, in its limitless, dynamic fluidity. *Inner experience* is an experience of sovereignty, a subjective experience of freedom, of selfhood, which is not the same as the experience of the I or ego. In the experience of sovereignty there is an interlacing of subjectivities, such that the other's experiences confound with mine, making us have a common experience of the Self. Bataille explains in a footnote: "I cannot in fact ascribe to subjectivity the limit of the I or of I's, not because I could apperceive it elsewhere but because without being able to limit it to myself, I could not limit it anyway" (Bataille 1992, 32 translation modified) ("*Je ne puis en effet prêter à la subjectivité la limite du moi ou des moi humains, non que je puisse l'apercevoir ailleurs mais parce que, n'ayant pu la limiter à moi même, je ne puis la limiter d'aucune façon*" (Bataille 1974 VII, 300). I find this interesting because it seems to me that it is an ontological perspective that does not lead to the impasses of identity politics. Coming from a Nietzschean background, Bataille's approach does not endorse a sexual politics that reclaims equality based on the evocations of feelings of resentment, shame, and guilt. In this framework, the self appears to be fluid and relational. It may embrace queer, non-binary ways of embodying—as much as a materialist feminist perspective, according to which biological sex is not a construction and is indispensable for feminist political struggles.

An account of sexual difference requires that the double economies are taken into consideration. Restricted economy pervades the social and economic institutions in which erotic relations are lived. Sexual division of labor in the heterosexual patriarchal family subordinates women to men. However, a fair organization of the restricted economy is helpful to liberate women from their imprisonment in the domestic sphere. As I have already hinted, the sacred laws also intervene to gender the erotic relationship in its accommodation in the restricted world of work. These laws support the sexual division of labor in the restricted economy by delineating gender roles in sacralizing symbolic language. This is why people can feel approved by God by playing their traditional gender roles. This framing of Eros by the laws of the general and restricted economies does not, of course, diminish its subversive potential. Without doubt, erotic experience is schematized by contracts that, in the encounter of gendered human beings in particular social, cultural, historical, racialized contexts, are made in oppressive power relationships. History of sexual repression, inherited structures of power, and various forms of oppression may force individuals to erotically relate to others for self-preservation, supportive partnership, productive growth, and acquisition of power.

Bataille teaches us that sooner or later, life will suffocate in those contracts and schemes that can hardly contain it indefinitely. All success understood in restricted economical terms will be taken over by anguish. According to Bataille, "Anguish . . . signifies the absence (or weakness) of the pressure exerted by the exuberance of life. Anguish arises when the anxious individual is not himself stretched tight by the feeling of superabundance" (Bataille 1991a, 38–39). "Anguish is meaningless for someone who overflows with life, and for life as a whole, which is an overflowing by its very nature" (Bataille 1991a, 39). Anguish is here the feeling triggered by the forces that work against those internal and external forces that function to maintain stability and order in an individual's life. They hold in check the destructiveness and creativity of our erotic energy. Erotic energy is in quest for differentiation. It is the drive that brings about change. As such, it shakes the relations and structures that eliminate sovereignty and overcome suffocation. Bataille is interested in this ontological event of Eros's destruction of the old world and the creation of the new.

In his philosophical framework, the corporeal subject is pressed by the primary existential condition of spending energy. Erotic experience is communication; it brings into being an openness in which bodies co-incarnate and differentiate. The question arises if this openness can be a space of sexual differentiation beyond the cis-heteronormative order. Bataille thinks that the inner experience of eroticism gives access to the originary, impersonal ground of our existence. He is foremost interested in the erotic act that has a sacred sense. Take the orgy in pagan festivals as the example of such an erotic act that interrupts the continuity of the world of work. It not only transgresses sexual prohibitions, it also ignores the borders between different sexes, genders, classes, races, cultures, and ages. It brackets and effaces the personalities of the profane realm. In that scene, the erotic experience bears an emancipatory potential. It liberates subjects from the social and economic positions they occupy in the restricted economy of the profane world. Erotic experience in its outburst can go as far as to interrupt gender identities. A reflective dimension accompanies this: in erotic experience, being calls its own existence into question by losing itself in the very experience (Bataille 1986, 31).

The de-rigidification of fixed difference and the dissolution of personality in the playfulness of the erotic experience are conducive to a realm of immanence, a level of existence where we come into contact with the continuity of the impersonal layer of existence. This is well known to the phenomenological tradition of Merleau-Ponty, Sartre, Beauvoir, and Levinas. This is not a solid ground at all; it is fluid; it consists of communication in the life of immanence, beyond separate, unrelated subjectivities. The suspension of the absolute discontinuity of the world reveals the abyss of impersonal existence. Both the erotic experience and the experiences of laughter, of tears, of love are interesting from this point of view when they are considered not as separate moments but in terms of their unity: "we are referred back, provided, we attain it, to deep subjectivity" (Bataille 1991b, 234). Bataille refuses to think of the subject as a knowing subject or as "person," the subject of ethics and politics in the existentialist sense. Subjectivity for him "is never the object of discursive knowledge, except obliquely, but it is communicated from subject to subject through a sensible, emotional contact: it is communi-

cated in this way in laughter, in tears, in the commotion of the festival"
(Bataille 1991b, 242). No doubt, intersubjective communication presupposes
separate personalities, but at the same time, it requires the interruption of
rigid personal boundaries. In his fictions, Bataille's subjects can connect and
communicate through interrupting acts of violence that shatter the illusion of
coincidence of the subject with itself.

By "inner experience," Bataille understands the interruption of the world
of utility, action, production, and possession. Such an interruption, because it
is both the loss of the subject and of the object, is a destruction of the world
in which human existence is submitted to projects in the temporality of
which the primacy of the future determines the significance of the present.
We tend to believe that we create ourselves by our projects, deeds, and
achievements, but also suffer the loss of the feeling of self and intimacy with
the other. When relations with the others are determined by goal-oriented
contexts, it can never lead to "communication" in the specific sense Bataille
gives to this term. He denies that selfhood is a future project and that true
communication between the I and the other can be accounted by the teleolog-
ically oriented contexts of utility. On the contrary, the sense of the self is to
be found in "religion" in the sense of being connected, related again to the
immanent continuity of Being. In order to understand how such a possibility
of "religare" is opened up by radical or "inner experience," we must first
recognize that Bataille's use of the "interior" and "exterior" is quite extraor-
dinary. What is at stake is not the interiority of an isolated subject, but the
outside of the interior/exterior divide that draws the limits of that subject.
Inner experience is a relation of communication with the other and it is for
the other. And Bataille insists that its temporality is that of the present. We
can further elaborate that temporality by taking the erotic experience as ex-
emplary of inner experience: erotic experience breaks the ordinary time of
the world submitted to the primacy of the future and productivity, thus rein-
stituting the absolute value of the present moment. The time of the erotic is
the reevaluation of the present moment, the affirmation of beyond being-in-
the-world in a return to an amplified contact with the immanent energy of the
universe. Erotic extasis—being outside one's self in passion and desire for
the other is *in-stasis*—is a stance in the present moment. The instant of *Eros*
is the moment of sovereignty. The presence of sovereignty is revealed only
through interior communication (Bataille 1991b, 245). It does not mean "independence" in the sense of not living in a dependency relationship to the
other. Even though erotic desire is consumption, this is a consumption of a
surplus rather than of the other or of the erotic relationship. All this discourse
about dependent/independent relationships belongs to a reorganization of the
world in terms of individual growth and productivity. For Bataille, such a
setting of one's self as a separate, independent being would be the destruc-

tion of the erotic, the loss of the sovereignty of the present, its submission to an economy of survival and growth and the primacy of the future.

The release and the dynamic flow of the erotic energy animating our incarnated existence require that one does not close off the possibility of risk and loss by taking precautions and setting defense mechanisms for protecting one's average emotional stable being-in-the-world. According to Bataille, "desire demands the greatest possible loss" (Bataille 1991b, 141). We restrict our own erotic affects by setting ourselves up as independent things, i.e., objects of seduction, presupposing that the dialectic of Eros should be one of conquest, worldly possession, and utility. From Bataille's point of view, this is indeed the reversal of the erotic dynamic into a logic of "extreme poverty." The loss of previous erotic experiences by their transformation into worldly gains, past failures to control the logic of desire, and the inability to avoid the harmful consequences of the inversion of love to hate may limit our future capacity to go beyond erotic beginnings. One may argue that erotic experience as intersubjective communicative denuding is also impeded by cis-heterosexist roles and prejudices which prevent us from living up to the erotic dynamics in our bodying forth with the others.

Even though the telos of animal sexuality is reproduction, it is still an expenditure of the animal's being. In the human realm, reproduction is not the telos of erotic desire but one of its possibilities. The movement of erotic desire goes beyond being in the sense of persisting and acquiring more and more power in our worldly survival and self-preservation. Bataille nowhere denies that we desire to survive and struggle to satisfy our needs. However, erotic luxury transcends the needs of self-preservation. The movement of desire goes beyond the urge to self-preserve, in attempting to open up life possibilities. Despite the fact that life has many possibilities that cannot be realized indefinitely, the concern for survival is not sufficient to account for our being: being must be rethought in terms of sovereignty, that is, the desire to open life possibilities beyond utility, to enjoy what the world has to offer us by going beyond an existence subordinated to the necessities of subsistence and labor, what Bataille calls *slavery*. He believes that the natural resources of the world are sufficient for all. People who lack the means to satisfy even their basic needs are the victims of human-made economies and of their accursed share. So, in principle, we can imagine a Bataillian new anti-capitalist economy in which there is a fair distribution of wealth and in which the main problem concerns the expenditure of the excess energy in Eros, art, and science. Sovereignty is not a telos; it is the denial of all telos in wasting and squandering the excess of being.

There is a tension in Bataille between the positivity of desire and the imaginary and affective return to animality. Bataille is not mourning or regretting the loss of our animal intimacy with the world; he does not want human animals to renounce their humanity to become animal again. Having said that, I would also note his fascination with the ways in which we can relate to animality, this forgotten origin, without falling back into it. There is no humanity before the delineation of the sacred and the profane worlds. The restricted economy of the profane world stems from a negation of nature, it is a product of culture. The profane world and the sacred world are co-originary. The sacred world operates with the general economy; hence in a dialectical manner it is a sublation of nature, in a signifying realm. Humanity results from this double negation: at first, nature is negated, from which the profane world follows. A second negation, the negation of negation, immediately follows; the sacred world comes into being from the negation of the profane world. The sacred world relates back to animality by way of double negation (Bataille 1991b, 51–60). Bataille finds self-consciousness and the truth of deep subjectivity in the movement of man's return to the intimacy of his being. Isn't that nostalgic metaphysics? In nostalgia, we have a melancholic sadness. In Bataille, although dialectic movement signals the impossibility of return, eroticism gives us a sense of the origin in "intimacy." "Intimacy is not expressed by a *thing* except on one condition: that this *thing* be essentially the opposite of a *thing*, the opposite of a product, of a commodity—a consumption and a sacrifice. Since intimate feeling is a consumption, it is consumption that expresses it, not a *thing*, which is its negation" (Bataille 1991a, 132). Our desire is to regain an intimacy that was always *strangely lost* and the intimacy we have the consciousness of having lost is our own *animality* (Bataille 1991a, 133). How can we be conscious of our lost animality? Even though Bataille believes, just like Nietzsche, that intelligence separates us from such a communication, he seems to affirm with Bergson that we can swim in the reverse direction of intelligence, use intelligence against itself to create the erotic possibility of finding an exit to an organic memory, i.e., a self-conscious experience of the internal relation of all living beings. Consuming of the excess energy enables us to overcome the intellect in not-knowing and touch the profound ground of our existence in life, nurturing and destructive at once. In Bataille's discourse, the materialization of the erotic desire is a way of negating the servile self, and this is why Bataille thinks that it can lead to the sovereign manifestation of the corporeal life. Indeed, Bataille's discourse may often lend itself to be misinterpreted in terms of the desire to return to an immemorial past. What stands as "the immemorial past" here is still in some sense present: at stake is not the recovering of a simple origin at all, but the acquisition of the self-consciousness of belonging together to an original immanence in differentiation. In other words, "return" means here the acquisition of the self-consciousness of what we already are in our historical forgetfulness. Bataille writes:

> The regret that I might have for a time when the obscure intimacy of the
> animal was scarcely distinguished from the immense flux of the world indi-
> cates a power that is truly lost, but it fails to recognize what matters more to
> me. Even if he has lost the world in leaving animality behind, man has none-
> theless become that *consciousness* of having lost it which we are, and which is
> more, in a sense, than a possession of which the animal is not conscious: It is
> *man*, in a word, being that which alone matters to me and which the animal
> cannot be. (Bataille 1991a, 133)

I believe there is another reason for being careful in qualifying Bataille's
notion of immanence as metaphysical. As *The Theory of Religion* makes
clear, this realm of immanence is also primarily the realm of the divine and
the sacred and hence prior to the apparition of the metaphysical oppositions
between humanity/animality and humanity/divinity.

TABOOS, TRANSGRESSION, AND SEXUAL DIFFERENCE

According to Bataille, animal sexuality is different from human sexuality
because the latter is marked by the presence of taboos in society. In contrast
to animal sexuality, which results from instincts, eroticism is proper to human sexuality. Eroticism cannot be explained on the basis of biological instincts; it presupposes desire, which is more complex than natural impulse in
its constitution. Human sexual desire is bound by taboos. Animals are more
"god-like" than human beings because they are not bound by taboos in sex
(Bataille 1986, 81). Why are there taboos in human sexuality? Taboos are
signs of the past threats of violence in the face of which human beings must
retreat to protect themselves. All taboos are traces of withdrawal in the face
of something that appeared as a cause of suffering and destruction. Bataille
says: "If a taboo exists, it is a taboo on some elemental violence, to my
thinking. This violence belongs to the flesh, the flesh responsible for the
urges of the organs of reproduction" (Bataille 1986, 93). If sex is taboo, and
taboo is about violence, sex is conceived either as inherently violent or as
leading to it (sex may create trouble, for it can incite competition, even blood
feuds, which may threaten societies with destruction). Sigmund Freud, too,
interpreted taboos as indicating the fear of violence. As he comments on the
taboo of virginity, he explains why defloration can be a burden for both
women and men (Freud 2001c, 194). Anxiety around virginity reflects a
primitive fear of blood because blood is believed to indicate the presence of
the maleficent forces in the woman's body that can hurt the husband. This is
why there were societies that maintained rituals of defloration by third parties or by the use of instruments before the wedding.

Although both Bataille and Freud inquire into the significance of the
taboos that relate to femininity, for Freud, sexual difference as we have it in

the society, is always something that calls for explanation. In Bataille, however, there is no clear account of the invention of sexual difference as a consequence of the institution of sexual taboos. The creation of taboos and the subordination of women to men are interrelated phenomena. Bataille accepts the anthropological claim that exogamy is based on the logic of the gift by relying on Claude Lévi-Strauss's thesis that the exogamous primitive societies considered women as precious gifts given by men to other men. Exchange of women between tribes cannot really be characterized as general economy if it is based on calculation and reciprocity. Freud accounts for the origin of exogamy in *Totem and Taboo*, with reference to the feeling of guilt that follows the act of killing the father who has sexual monopoly over all the females in the tribe. The male children's feeling of guilt after killing the father indicates that they can still identify with the father that they have killed to enjoy their own sexuality. The question remains open if guilt presupposes the acknowledgment of the father's law. For guilt to be possible, the law must precede guilt. However, Freud seems to derive the law from the feeling of guilt. Again, it is this feeling that hinders the sexual enjoyment of the females in an endogamous way. Bataille makes no reference to patricide as a trauma requiring some sophisticated legislation. However, he, too, like Freud, seems to acknowledge that it is the exogamical symbolic system that leads the species to make the leap from nature to culture. Bataille, too, commits himself to the view that it is the passage from nature to culture, from animality to humanity, that gives rise to sexual difference beyond nature. In the general economy of nature, sexual difference is not limited by the binary of male and female; the flow of life energy may allow for unlimited diversity. The restricted economy of the world of production, on the other hand, captures life energy to invest it on production. General economy resurfaces during the periods in which work is interrupted, allowing for the enjoyment that disregards calculation within the boundaries controlled by rituals. Bataille argues that these two economies are complementary; they form a system based on an ontological/anthropological sufficient reason: human beings cannot ontologically be reduced to their role in production for the sake of survival.

What is the violence in the face of which sexual taboos were created? According to Bataille, humans have violent urges in nature; they created taboos in order to control them (Bataille 1986, 55). Taboos are created by a negation of our animality, and they are the necessary conditions for the coming into being of the profane world. In general, sexuality is a taboo because it inheres in itself a natural violence. "All we can say is that as opposed to work, sexual activity is a form of violence, that as a spontaneous impulse it can interfere with work" (Bataille 1986, 49). However, human beings feel a desire for their depassed animality. The sacred world necessarily opens in response to this desire and gives imaginary and symbolic access to the general economy by way of the transgression of taboos.

Bataille explains the violence inherent in sexuality with reference to disgust and horror. In *Eroticism,* he claims that we feel horror and disgust when there is a dead body, and this feeling of nausea is similar to the feeling that we have about excreta. Sexual organs are seen as obscene because they are also used as "body sewers"; as Saint Augustine says, "We are born between faeces and urine" (Bataille 1986, 57–58). The perception of the sexual organs as obscene is because of their proximity to organs of excretion. And there is a connection between excreta and death. Unlike sexuality, feces and urine are not subject to taboos, but they are abject, excluded from the world, banned from the realm of social visibility. Bataille inquires into what excreta, sexuality, and decay signify for the primitive human mind and seeks to explain the associations it made between their significations (Bataille 1986, 58). It follows that sexuality is prohibited because of such primitive experiences, the senses of which are obscure for modern humanity.

Transgression is an act of invalidation that at the same time validates the prohibition that is transgressed. Prohibition does not abolish desire; on the contrary, it provokes it. Bataille insists that desire and horror go together in sexuality. Although taboo is something forbidden and avoided, it can be transgressed. "There exists no prohibition that cannot be transgressed" (Bataille 1986, 63). Every taboo comes with its permission. For instance, murder is a taboo, but it can be transgressed in a war (Bataille 1986, 63). Orgy is a taboo, but it can also be transgressed during festivals (Bataille 1986, 112). In a similar way, sex is a taboo, but marriage is seen as a transgression (Bataille 1986, 109). Therefore, transgression is, as Bataille says, "[a]t such and such a time and up to a certain point . . . permissible" (Bataille 1986, 65), a permission, so to speak, to break the rule that forbids something.

Why are women and not men taboo? According to Freud's account of virginity taboo, woman is thought of as mysterious and unknown for man because man sees her as an enemy. That woman is seen as hostile, and rejected, by man is part of the practice of the taboo. Another reason why man fears woman might be the relaxation and flaccidity of sexual intercourse. Man is afraid of being weakened by woman, and he believes she wears him down by her sexual acts. Freud even entertains the idea that the castration complex may arise in him because of her losing virginity by him, and because she is seen as a danger by him (Freud 2001c, 198–99). As Bataille argues, sex is associated with reproduction, and reproduction with menstruation. Thus, sexual activities allude to plethora, and plethora is linked with death and violence. Even though Bataille does not explicitly address the question of sexual oppression, the problem of sexual oppression cannot be separated, in his framework, from the economic problem. The institution of family is based on both the general and restricted economies. The political organization of the restricted economy presupposes the institution of family, which is grounded on marriage. In *The Accursed Share*, Bataille speaks of the economic value women have as objects of exchange among men. The domestication of carnal communication reveals how the restricted economy aims at controlling the general economy of sex and how the laws of the sacred realm license the exchange of women among men.

Both Bataille and Freud think that sexual taboos are based on the experience of fear, even though they have different conceptions of the object of human fear. Indeed, the fear arises for different reasons in their accounts. Bataille traces the fear to the proximity of the sexual organs with the organs of excretion. Freud similarly says, "Today we find taboos among primitive peoples already elaborated into an intricate system of just the sort that neurotics among ourselves develop in their phobias" (Freud 2001c, 200). In the taboo of virginity, the example is the deflowering of women's virginity during the wedding ceremonies, because the groom must avoid the blood shedding. In *Totem and Taboo*, however, Freud grounds the taboo character of femininity in the Oedipus and castration complexes. The first totem originates from the act of redeeming the dead father, whom the brothers had killed in rebellion against his sexual monopoly over all the females. And the incest taboo derives from the ambiguous feelings of love and guilt that male children have for their father.

While Freud tries to give a hypothetical, genetical account for the symbolic laws of the patriarchal system, Bataille is seeking to contest the law of the father. A law that he insists on disregarding even though the act of transgression acknowledges it. The existential rejection of the patriarchal symbolic system and its moral values gives rise to a surreal hedonism. Once the symbolic system is suspended, we no longer know the scene and the roles that characters are supposed to play. This is the world of Bataille's erotic stories: there is no way to know where an erotic encounter will lead and the extent of violence it will unleash. The subordination of women to men is undone, sex is spiritualized, multiple pleasures arise, and the subject is opened up to a general economy of generosity and conversion. However, we can doubt that this world has an ethics of Eros.

I pointed elsewhere that Bataille's reference to women in his account of taboos is closer to Beauvoir's way of describing women's status in agricultural cultures in *The Second Sex* (Direk 2011, 62). For Beauvoir, women were not slaves because they were protected by sexual taboos. Men associated women's reproductive powers with the powers of nature and projected their fear and respect of nature on them. The view that human sexuality is not natural, but organized by taboos and rituals is a major step on the way to the invention of the concept of sexual difference as culturally constructed. The point plays a pivotal role in Beauvoir as well. She argues that as soon as man took control over the forces of nature, he subjected women and her children not to slavery but to servitude. Man projected his possibilities on nature and built his world, produced the patriarchal culture that imprisons women into the realm of immanence. According to Beauvoir, men's possession of women who are exploited in an economy of the "gift" is a result of a historical development, which is dialectically decipherable. Man postulated her as the essential insofar as the natural forces were beyond his understanding and control, but as he soon as he became capable of dominating nature, his relation to her changed as well; she was now seen as the inessential. She does not enter into the Hegelian master and slave dialectic in which the slave can constitute itself as an independent consciousness, through the *fear of death, discipline* and *self-reflection* (which is made possible because the products of his labor could mirror him) (Hegel 1977, 111–19). At the end, Hegel leaves the way open for the slave to attain self-consciousness by achieving his independence from the master. This self-consciousness can reconcile with another self-consciousness, which is the condition of attaining freedom in a politically organized community.

According to Beauvoir, matriarchy is built on men's horror of women's reproductive powers. Patriarchy changes women's status by relegating them to immanence; this did not relinquish man's horror and anxiety in the face of woman's body. While the successful control of nature by means of production—transformed the profane world of work, the symbolism of the sacred realm underwent its own revolution. In the new symbolic instituted by the revealed religions, the prevailing fear of women is attached to a representation of her sexuality as the source of evil. The myth of the eternal feminine reflects the ambiguous, contradictory logic that constitutes woman as radical alterity. "She is an idol, a servant, source of life, power of darkness; she is the elementary silence of truth, she is artifice, gossip, and lies; she is the medicine woman and witch; she is man's prey; she is his downfall, she is everything he is not and wants to have, his negation and his raison d'être" (Beauvoir 2010, 162). By attributing contradictory properties to woman, man makes her an ambiguous and mysterious being. As the absolute unintellible, unsolvable secret, she was excluded from being party to a relation of mutual recognition. As I have elsewhere argued, Beauvoir holds that radical alterity imprisons women into immanence, and leaves no place for transcendence. This lack of transcendence reduces woman to being-in-itself, and takes away from her the possibility of being-for-itself (Direk 2011, 61). Man exploits her in satisfying his need to retreat in immanence, while unjustly; the patriarchal order prevents her from satisfying her capacity for transcendence. Beauvoir conceives human beings as constituted by their capacities of immanence and transcendence, and in her view, human flourishing requires that doble ontological belonging to both immanence and transcendence. It is unjust to force women to remain only in the realm of immanence, as that would be to deprive them of access to a sense of their being. In a world where women are oppressed, male transcendence, too, becomes part of oppression, for it is made possible by the repetition, internalization, and forgetting of abjection (Direk 2011, 71).

Beauvoir's argument explains sexual difference as a consequence of the constitution of patriarchy by an open-ended, contingent, historical dialectic. In Bataille such an account is missing. They both point to the contingent experiences of the primitive male to explain why women are taboo. Nonetheless, Beauvoir's effort to interpret the relation between eroticism, sexual difference, and abjection in an account of sexual oppression contrasts with Bataille's lack of interest in the problem of women's emancipation from sexual oppression. In the framework of the complementary double economies Batille introduces, what is the necessity that turns women's bodies to gifts that men give to other men? If this is just a contingent historical manifestation of human sexuality, why not replace it with another general economy of sexuality? Why not have an economy of erotic experience as sovereignty without sexual servitude? How to liberate sexuality from its patriarchal organization without naively secularizing and desacralizing it? I do not believe that for Bataille the patriarchal relegation of female sexuality to immanence as luxury for men should be the only manifestation of female sexuality in the sacred realm. He explores mysticism in the general economy of the sacred to talk about female sexuality as expenditure and generosity. In the third chapter, I shall talk about how that becomes an issue in the debate between Irigaray and Lacan.

Beauvoir's logic of the gift in the erotic relationship creates a world in which there is transcendence in immanence for both sexes. Corporeal generosity is based on mutual recognition and friendship. Beauvoir uses the term "conversion" in the sense of the overcoming of alienation to one's self. It is a related way of inhabiting the ambiguity in transcendence and immanence. "Mutual recognition," "conversion," and "generosity" are possible in the erotic relationship between women and men if sexual oppression is overcome. Sexual oppression does not automatically disappear with the emergence of new sexual practices. It is still there, insofar as it is not surpassed by a new symbolism; it still continues to provide for the concepts and norms in terms of which erotic encounters make sense. Second wave feminism has the important insight that the struggle for oppression requires a symbolic struggle and that it can be overcome with the creation of new symbolic forms. Bataille's affective negativity is perhaps part of such a quest.

HETEROSEXUALITY AND QUEERNESS IN BATAILLE

In my reading, Bataille contests a patriarchal interpretation of gender, and I suggest that we can find the evidence for that in his fictional works. He challenges the patriarchal culture by representing women figures, including the mother, as capable of sovereignty, and by disagreeing with the moral condemnation of these figures as monsters or criminals.

My Mother is notorious in representing the mother's sexuality not as abject but as divine. This text is a blow to the heart of Christianity, for it celebrates the mother as a subject of desire. Bataille challenges Christianity's effacement of sexual desire in mothers to promote the patriarchal value that women should behave altruistically and must be willing to sacrifice themselves for the well-being of the other family members. In *My Mother*, the protagonist is not ashamed of her mother for experimenting with her own desire and exploring herself through sexuality. A transgressive mother, who subverts motherhood as a traditional gender role, is adored. The mother figure that Bataille depicts in this text does not seem to be burdened by sexual prohibitions or penis envy; she is not hostile to men because of defloration by a man; and she does not resent men because she feels rejected by them.

From a psychoanalytical point of view, this is often diagnosed as perversion. Kristeva qualified the adoration the protagonist feels for her mother and Bataille's celebration of it as "psychotic" (Kristeva 1987, 365). Indeed, we can evaluate Bataille's position by taking into account Freud's strategy of explaining sexual difference through the Oedipus and castration complexes. According to Freud, all children desire their mothers. The male child represses his desire for his mother, given the incest prohibition and the threats of castration that the child imagines as coming from his father. The castration complex makes him recognize the authority of the father. In the pre-Oedipal phase, the little girl has her mother as the object of desire; however, when she discovers her castration, her desire shifts from the mother to the father (Freud 2001b, 229–30). Unlike the little girl, the little boy does not have to change his love object from the mother to the father. In Bataille's *My Mother*, the father figure is insignificant and even nonexistent and the mother is not castrated; she is powerful and even omnipotent. She is free and not a possession of the father. Is *My Mother* a narrative about what horrible consequences might result if the castration complex becomes ineffective or an attack on the idea that the castration complex is a necessary structure of human sexuality? The mother in Bataille's text has sexual desires, and engages in sexual practice by disregarding the classic gender norms that shape and regulate sexual behavior. His narrative explores a situation in which the mother is liberated from being an executioner of the law of the father. Bataille feels almost a religious fascination in the face of manifestations of female sexuality that are not controlled by the complex of castration.

Arguing against readings of Bataille's fictions as sexist and misogynistic, wherein the subject of erotic experience is always masculine or virile, Susan Rubin Suleiman argues that in the 1930s, at a time when "many European intellectuals were becoming politically concerned with political action, prompted by the rise of Fascism and a general historical unease," Bataille moves "from an action-oriented defition of virility to an inward one" (Suleiman 1995b, 34). In fascism, Bataille saw an explosition of the virility that bourgeois culture represses. What preoccupies him is less the desired end than its possible failure—not virility, but castration. The loss of the head, decapitation, is a figure of castration. Castration as the very ground of male potency is at the core of fascist masculinity. But after all, does not this quest for virility represent femininity as a dark continent, as a figure of absolute alterity?

The feminine approached in desire in Bataille's fictions can be castrating, like Dirty in the *Blue of the Sky*, Edwarda in *Madame Edwarda*, and the mother in *My Mother*. It is not the law of the father but the unscathed alterity of the other sex that undermines the male pretension of having the phallus. Arguably, this paves the way for a virility (masculinity) that differs from the virility fascism seeks to create, one that can subverse gender identity. Although Bataille has been criticized because of his heterosexist language in speaking of erotic experience in his fictional works, there is room to raise the question of whether or not he obeys the law of the heteronormative symbolic order. How does that desire function? Does it distribute subjects as male and female in the same way as the patriarchal symbolic?

I think Bataille is fascinated by the possibility of an insubordinate feminine sexual freedom. He does not privilege the moral traditional value of the sacrificial feminine as virgin, wife, and mother. He is interested in the figure of the woman who breaks up with the traditional morality. Bataille's characters do not seek to possess each other's desires, and this is precisely what exceeds the discourse and the norms of the heterosexual desire. For example, women in Bataille's fictions are never possessed beings—they are independent, disinterested, and free from monogamous heterosexual contracts that would alienate them and make them servile. A carnal act with them never relates to them as possessed objects. Bataille's notion of erotic experience is a refusal of the objectification of the female body by the male gaze. For him, women are impossible to know, possess, and domestically enclose.

He is particularly interested in female sex workers, whom he sees as incarnations of femininity beyond possession and objectification. Madame Edwarda is a prostitute whose presence opens a space for transdendence because, in her madness, she seems to be beyond possession, production, and reproduction. Even though prostitution is an institution that complements the patriarchal possession of women by men, Bataille approaches it as an outlet of general economy. In *Madame Edwarda*, femininity manifests itself as divine in all its horrifying queerness. For Bataille the subordination of women in heterosexual contracts is a socially and historically contingent form of restricted economy. The sex work that he describes is also a patriarchal contract. It gives men access to a general economy of erotic experience within the limits controlled by the restricted economy.

Bataille's fictions do not reaffirm heterosexual normativity; they reveal its contingency because heterosexuality in Bataille would always be under the destruction of a liberating communication that differentiates bodies as sexed beings. I disagree with the view that Bataille submits the logic of erotic desire to heterosexism. Even though he does not raise the question of sexual difference explicitly, his erotic experience operates as differentiation, through the transgression of the prohibitions that regulate and bring into being cis-heterosexual gender identities. Differentiation is not understood as deviation from an intrinsically heterosexual nature; it is conceived as the overcoming of the alienation and servility that restrict the possibilities of intimate communication between bodies that are dynamically and communicatively sexed.

Bataille's discourse on erotic desire makes the claim that erotic situations are often provoked by separation and distance. Desire aims at overcoming separation. Love may surpass the differences that are socially constructed and open a space for sovereign differentiation. Oneness in the immanence of carnal communication is quite different from the unity of a couple whose characters have merged in a "we" without difference. Sexual alienation constitutes our worldly factical situation as incarnated beings, and we recognize it as we find ourselves constantly challenged by the ways in which our erotic excess energy overflows our sexual identity. We find glory in letting that energy flow in transgression of the social restrictions of our bodily existence in communication with the other. We find the joy of sovereignty in the sharing of the incarnated freedom with the other.

By "incarnated freedom," I do not simply understand the letting of one's own and the other's body be alive, expressive, and responsive beyond all forms of oppression exerted by the norms that regulate gender, class, race, sex, age, and stylistic differences. Incarnated freedom is not just freedom from norms, but the creation of new norms and their negotiation in the process of our bodying forth as sexed beings. Arguably, Bataille's sovereignty fits with queer ontology and politics. His fundamental insight is that the transgression of borders sets us in intimacy with the others. It is in this intimacy that he finds sovereignty, friendship, truth, compassion, and the welcoming of differences. Sexual difference beyond identity politics can only be lived and expressed in the intimacy of transgressive erotic communication. When such an intimacy takes place in the world, it suspends gender identities and let the differences freely express their own excess energy in communication with each other.

I am sympathethic to the claim that transgression paves the way for queer styles of being. The dynamic space that Bataille's conception of Eros opens can be generative of new norms. Eroticism is expenditure in a domain marked off by the transgression of laws or rules. Nevertheless, as I have noted above, a transgression such as *adultery* complies with the transgressed law—this is why erotic experience can often be a paradox (Bataille 1991b, 124–25), for transgression violates and reinstitutes the law. The same claim can be made for the erotic pleasures that result from queer transgressions of heteronormative sexual practices. However, this fact does not close off the possibility that the play of transgression opens the way for transformation of the laws, thus giving rise to new norms. Although the world may be structured by a binary understanding of sexual difference, the erotic life energy subverts these constructions and makes existence queer in its dynamic, subversive pleasures.

The fluidity of the erotic existence allows for the transformation of the bodies, which Bataille locates in the dialectic that takes off from the animal immanence and culminates in contemporary interpretations of monotheistic religions as religions of sharp transcendence. His notion of erotic experience may reinvoke a new interpretation of pagan spirituality. For him, human sexuality in its most creative forms can never be only a profane matter. In all the configurations of erotic relationship, there is an experience of intimacy that opens a queer space for a dynamic play of life's forces.

In her "Bataille's Queer Pleasures: The Universe as Spider or Spit," Shannon Winnubst proposed to read Bataille's fictions as queer narratives. Bataille focuses on the drives that subvert and substitute for the real, and in sexual enjoyment make the body go beyond a framing as object of desire. As the anal drive presents itself in the figure of the solar anus or anus as an eye, the organ disappears as an object of satisfaction and acquires metaphysical and surreal value. The world seen by the anus, as offering a spectacle of exterior objects, including bodies, is a metaphor of perception. Sexual drives give rise to new experiences of Being. It is thanks to the sexual drives that the world emerges in an original sense. Bataille explores the world as it appears in enjoyment, rather than in satisfaction by way of the appropriation of an object of desire. *Story of the Eye* presents a series of transgressions that makes the world show itself as a new realm of beings and relations. According to Winnubst, sex is about transition into a new way of being together (Winnubst 2007, 89–90). I think that Bataille celebrates sexual violence insofar as it can be an instrument for the creation of the new. He does not see violence as leading necessarily to a new system of sexual subordination. Sexual violence shakes resilient values and schemata that prevent different drives to explore the self and the world. Violence does not discipline; on the contrary, it aims to make bodies unlearn gender norms. The queer element in Bataille is a transgression of the norm that channels sexuality through socially prominent drives, prohibiting the imagination, narration, and repetition of other sexual drives. In Bataille's framework the experience of queerness by a violent exploration of the drives leads to the immanent realm of communication in which the subject meets a self from which the other is not excluded.

IS THERE ETHICS OF EROS IN BATAILLE?

In the introduction to the first volume of *The Accursed Share*, Bataille argues that the transition from the restricted economy to a general economy calls for an *ethical revolution*. Indeed, this is a radical subversion that reminds Bataille of the Copernican Revolution: "The extension of economic growth itself requires the overturning of economic principles—the overturning of the ethics that grounds them. Changing from the perspectives of *restrictive* economy to those of *general* economy actually accomplishes a Copernican transformation: a reversal of thinking—and of ethics" (Bataille 1991a, 25). As growth reaches a limit in the restricted economy of capitalism, capitalism will undergo a large-scale crisis, which will bring about an ethical change in our lives. The crisis can lead to war and the destruction of life on the planet, or give rise to a new ethos—a new caring relation to nature, and a new approach to Eros.

In *Eroticism*, war and Eros are contrasted. War is violation by force without consent; it is conquest, domination, exploitation, and refusal of the respect for difference, whereas Eros is based on transgression of taboos with permission. War is the expenditure of the excess invested in a military organization aiming to defeat and destroy an enemy. In contrast, the expenditure of the excess in Eros is not teleogical. Both war and Eros feed from the dynamic forces of life. The primary problem with Eros is that it is based on the transgression of the taboos, which belong to the patriarchal Ethos in which women circulate as luxurious gifts in the sexual market. But this is not the only problem; compulsory heterosexuality and cis-heterosexuality should be problematized as well. Bataille believes that the crisis of capitalism will break into a general economy, which calls for a new understanding of Eros based on communicative openness, sovereign differentiation, and corporeal generosity. This access to the general economy of generosity by way of the repudiation of norms, comes with, in my understanding, a de-rigification of sexual identities and roles that prevailed in the restricted economy.

Bataille believes in the revolutionary potential of the erotic relation. By insisting on the inseparability of the economic from the erotic, he reveals that the economic problem does not simply reduce to class struggle. Erotic forces can find only limited expression in social life and are often restricted, domesticated, and exploited for the accumulation of a capitalist surplus. Not only the society but also the individual himself/herself is urged to control or repress the erotic forces in the transgressive movement of bodily expression, for they can destroy the conditions of self-preservation for the individual and harm the economical foundations of the society of growth.

Is there room for the family, in the patriarchal sense, in the new general economy? Marriage provides a framework for sexuality that protects the couple from the risks of the violent forces. But marriage and sexual desire can also be incompatible: stable relationships and marriages in the modern world often start as erotic encounters and turn into partnerships in economies of growth. When growth comes to a limit and the life energy is completely captured by the restricting schemes and structures of the world, the pressure of the excess energy that we cannot squander in other erotic encounters will produce negativity in the sense of restlessness, irresolvable conflict, depression, and unhappiness and shall ultimately lead to the destruction of the worldly stability that constitutes the emotional and material conditions of self-preservation. At times, people intuitively struggle to hold such stable structures in place precisely by being unfaithful, for that can be a way to make a suffocating marriage or relationship last longer than it otherwise would. In other words, the moment comes to face with the tension between the search for stability and the demands that excess energy make on us.

Although he is critical of utilitarianism for failing to understand the economy of existence, Bataille agrees with utilitarianism on the principle that all meaningful discourse on ethics must acknowledge that lesser forms of violence are preferable to greater or worse violence. If violence is inevitable, we should choose for the action that leads to lesser violence. The worst violence is the extermination of human civilization in wars and genocides. The growth of capitalist surplus will widen the unequal distribution of resources and wealth. An insistence on the production of surplus at the same rate may provoke a general economy of the destruction of populations. Hence, either a fair distribution of the accumulated surplus will be made or humanity will undermine its civilization in excessive violence. Given the conditions of vast inequality created by contemporary capitalism, Bataille adopts a consequentialist ethics that recognizes the possible positive and negative outcomes of an outbreak of general economy. What is the lesser violence then?

The lesser violence option for all humanity is based on the rejection of the enslavement that the capitalist mode of production imposes on human beings. Moreover, we need to change our mode of consumption. The capitalist mode of consumption commands the possession and enjoyment of a greater number of material objects, at the cost of constraining the free expenditure of corporeal energy spent in intimacy. Capitalism substitutes the consumption of things for the sovereign experience in Bataille's sense. How is the erotic related to lesser violence? Does he recommend a new communism, a communism of sovereignty with a new philosophy of Eros and of the sacred?

Unfortunately, Bataille does not say that the transition from the restricted to the general economy must suspend the patriarchal sexual market that is regulated according to the intricate logic of gift. Even in societies in which this kind of market no longer exists, gender norms that prevail can undermine the achievement of incarnated freedom. Bataille understands human carnal communication as a relationship to the impure, the accursed, the evil, the expenditure of agonizing excess, the confusion, and disorder threatening the profane order of things. Can this be the source of a civilization that is less violent to all beings?

Let me try an answer: the general economy of Eros can be a queer economy because it is based on sexual communication beyond sexual identities. Carnal communication dislocates identity, makes corporeal becoming a shared process, brings about a contact with the alterity within the self via an ecstatic being in the other. Indeed, immanence means being inscribed in the flesh of all beings, and to inhabit with the elemental powers of the cosmos itself. The cosmic nature of the embodiment in question contrasts with how sexuality is socially and historically organized. Restricted economy is based on possession, whereas the general economy of Eros makes possible the generous sharing and consumption of both corporeal energy and the material and spiritual resources we have. In Bataille's fictions, different bodies connect through their shared excessive life energy and bring into being different pleasures. It follows that the erotic experience as an embodiment undermining social hypocrisy and sexual oppression is conducive to a different political economy. There can be a way of loving that lets beings flourish in their differences. How religious elements fit in the picture is an interesting question. We can speculate that the transition to the general economy can bring with it a return to some form of paganism. This is supported by the conception of erotic relationship as a doorway to the sacred, the possibility that Eros can pave the way for a mystical experience of the immanent oneness of the human, the divine, and the animal.

Let me raise the question of ethics of Eros in Bataille at this point. Although he speaks very little of ethics, he is widely read as challenging the bourgeois traditional morality. What is the ethical problem that pertains to erotic experience understood within the general economy of the erotic? Bataille is seeking for sovereignty achieved in the erotic communication in which excess energy is spent. Erotic communication inheres violence, a violence that belongs to the realm of immanence. Moreover, Bataille explores the ways in which erotic violence disturbs the restricted economy. He does not exclude violence from the dynamic space of the erotic because he believes *negativity* is a leading force of carnal communication. Nadine Hartmann writes: "Eroticism demands that one give oneself away and abolish the imaginary wholeness of the being, a process that demands a great deal of violence. The idea of a continuity to be approached in eroticism should not be mistaken for the phantasmatic ideal of a fusion between two individuals. It is rather an affirmation of the violence of the act described as "frenzied desire to lacerate and to be lacerated" (Bataille 2011, 141; Hartmann 2016, 140). Negativity does not only show itself in the transgression of prohibitions that set the norms for acceptable behavior. First of all, erotic communication as such takes place through the negation of the separation that makes us individual beings, which implies the overcoming or the interruption of artificially constructed borders. Such a negativity does not lead to fusion, but to an intimacy in which the truth of corporeal being is shared.

Although the lived experience of eroticism can be understood as a site in which the values of good and evil undergo reevaluation, it is hard for a third party to judge the experience in terms of objective moral values, from the outside. This being said, we evaluate erotic violence in respect of equality and justice. Sexual violence cannot be part of general economy, if it reproduces the sexual hierarchies and power relations. What norms organize erotic immanence? Whether or not immanent violence is structured by the subjects' social status in the restricted economy is a meaningful question. And one must also question what and how gender norms are performed, because norms can be perverted in their very performance.

It is clear that Bataille's erotic affirmation of violence does not come with an ethics of Eros based on the respect for bodily borders. However, it does not resemble the sadism that keeps intact the enjoying subject while piercing the borders of the others' bodies. Nothing in erotic experience shelters me from my own death; death is as much a possibility for me as it is for the others. Ethical problems proliferate also because this literature effaces the consenting subject based on free will and prefers to talk about sovereignty. For example, the question arises if rape, too, which ignores consent, may not be described as a radical experience of a renewed contact with immanence. But rape is at the same time an exercise of power that objectifies and reifies the other's body. Arguably, insofar as Bataille's erotic experience, as an inner experience, aims at the liberation of the body from being a thing by destroying the thing in it, it excludes rape. This argument will work only if rape is defined as domination and not as an expression of sexual desire. And erotic experience by definition excludes domination.

If Erotic is a contact with the kernel of the living being by breaking the alienating shell, erotic experience cannot be conceived as a transition from erotic subjectivity to objectivity and vice versa. Bataille rejects that conception of the erotic as an experience of an object by a subject, to replace it with a different model: the communication of two or more beings in the unlimited impersonal subjectivity of existence. Nonetheless, the following question remains: If sovereign experience "is the power to rise above the laws of the society," where can erotic experience find the normativity that would make us take a refusal or rejection seriously? If violence and evil give us momentary access to immanence, how is the other's life, difference, and sexed being to be respected in the erotic experience? Bataille is equivocal at this point, to say the least. He offers no norms or principles that would make the erotic relation ethical. But ethics does not reduce to principles and norms. Bataille can be envisaged as imagining the possibility of respect without norms. It is true that he does not think that human sexuality is possible without norms and he conceives the erotic as based on the regulated transgression of norms. The world without sexual norms, for example, during times in which society has collapsed, can be an excessively violent world. In such a world, people may also resort to using excessive violence whenever they believe they are in danger. If the excessive violence that may follow from the destruction of the society is not at all desirable for Bataille, should we try to preserve social spheres by keeping in reserve the permission for their partial negation, which implies the suspension of some of their prevailing norms under well-controlled limits? What kind of sexual norms should there be in the new general economy? And how to set them without also setting taboos? Bataille's understanding of eroticism as transgression should perhaps be modified in the attempt to answer such questions.

A brief comparison between Bataille and Marquis de Sade can be illuminating in explaining the specificity of Bataille's appeal to erotic violence. In Sade's narratives the body is ontologically represented from a scienticist perspective, as a mechanical object of nature. The insertion of the body in nature as an entity that is subject to the laws of nature serves to rip apart the social and moral constructions that cover over the body's natural reality. Sade thinks that we can get rid of all social construction and reach a natural sexuality, which is morally alienated and kept under control by such constructions. Bataille does not share Sade's mechanistic view of nature and does not embed the body in problematic hierarchies of natural strength.

Sade justifies naturally strong individuals' transgression of moral norms to sexually exploit and harm the weak. Bataille, on the other hand, is not interested in making a defense of strong individuals' natural rights over the weak. A distinction between "immanent violence" and "transcendent violence" may help us to better express the difference between Bataille's and Sade's positions. First of all, for Bataille, immanent violence is a condition for the overcoming of the separation that sets the stage for transcendence and the struggle for power that accompanies it. For Sade, erotic violence is about sovereignty as transcendence. This transcendence challenges the ethical foundations of the society, and as a consequence, it socially isolates itself. In *The Accursed Share*, Bataille refers to Sade's system as "the most consistent and the most costly form of erotic activity" whose condition of possibility is moral isolation, denial of solidarity, and freedom from the respect for others. Sade challenges the ethics of respect in the world of restricted economy that subordinates human beings: "solidarity keeps man from occupying the place that is indicated by the word 'sovereignty': human beings' respect for one another draws them into a cycle of servitude where subordinate moments are all that remain, and where in the end we betray that respect, since we deprive man in general of his sovereign moments (of his most valuable asset)" (Bataille 1991b, 178–79). Secondly, expenditure of energy is a negation that, as Blanchot says, becomes apathy in the sovereign man (Bataille 1991b, 179). However, there is a limit to Bataille's approval of Sade. Bataille thinks there is an ethics to general economy; Sade refuses that.

In Sade, negation becomes the negation of the partners' interests and existence. In contrast, Bataille does not want to deny the affections of pity, gratitude, and love, which are part of the genuine corporeal energy. He writes: "There is no doubt that the way of individual love obliges us to limit ourselves not only to those possibilities that make allowance for the partner's interest, but also those that the partner herself can bear" (Bataille 1991b, 174). Bataille's notion of individual love designates the relation to another individual whom the subject loves and is interesting for ethical reasons. Nonetheless, it is unclear if individual love can define relations with all partners and if it ensures that an erotically active subject would respect the bodily boundaries of all erotic partners. Sade passes beyond the obligations of the individual love by denying the interests of those who are subjected to erotic torments and by putting their very lives at risk. Bataille is ambiguous about Sade. On the one hand, he says Sade opens "a new domain to eroticism," for he believes Sade is denying the social link that attaches someone to its fellow human beings to liberate sexuality from the limits community imposes on its free reign—and on the other hand, he argues that Sade, in setting the crime as the condition of sensual pleasure commits himself to the isolation of the individual, which Bataille seeks to overcome in erotic communication. The negation of the individuality and of communality when it leads to communication sexed beyond sexual identities dissolves "the close connection between criminal destruction and sensual pleasure" (Bataille 1991b, 176).

In my reading of Bataille, in immanent violence communication beyond identities leads to impersonal existence, which is the destruction of individuality and public personality. The connection between sensual pleasure and crime dissolves if the other is not distinguished from myself. Immanent violence does not set me against the other in a power position and does not make me higher than him or her. Negation in eroticism negates the separate being; however, here denial does not serve some transcendent affirmation. I do not achieve a human or godly transcendence or fulfill a natural essence by denying the other's individuality. We can still ask the question if it is not wrong to expose the other to immanent violence in carnal communication without asking for consent. Does it make sense to ask a person's consent for a communal depersonalization? The notion of immanent violence does not preclude the possibility of harm in erotic communication. If no personal responsibility is taken, can anyone be blamed for harm?

In *Story of the Eye*, Bataille's characters do not come together for orgies to go back to their own lives after the carnal confusion is over. Erotic communication connects their lives in infinite desire and compassion. The violence that they exert with each other is different from the violence they direct to those who pretend to coincide with their social roles. The release of the abject to the effect of overcoming worldly separation and hygienic hypocrisy is never the end of care and friendly compassion for them, but "religare" in the sense of being reconnected. The compassion here is, first of all, respect for the way the other incarnates in erotic pleasures and to support and welcome these pleasures. Negation at work in the erotic experience also paves the way for the impossibility of being indifferent to the other from whom I am not absolutely separated.

Andrea Dworkin contests this reading in defending her thesis that pornography harms women, and gives a reading of the character Simone in *Story of the Eye* as a sadistic whore with a murderous and insatiable sexuality, a figure of the pornographic male imagination (Dworkin 1981, 176). Susan Sontag takes the opposite position by arguing that Bataille's narratives, such as *Story of the Eye*, *Madame Edwarda*, etc., go beyond works of pornographic imagination, because pornographic imagination tends to destroy irreplaceability by making people easily substitutable by others (Sontag 1969). In this kind of communication, partners become irreplaceable for each other. Simone in *Story of the Eye* is designated as the sister soul of the narrator, and as Susan Rubin Suleiman remarks, she is different from a Sadean character: "transgression in Sade occurs when a sovereign subject defies an external Law. In Bataille, the Law is internalized; the drama of transgression occurs within the subject" (Suleiman 1995a, 324). Sontag notes that, unlike Sade's character Justine, Bataille's female characters do not appear as the victims of male fantasies; they are not exposed to experiences in which they are expected to learn, suffer, and transform themselves. The violent characters of *Story of the Eye* experience sex as "profoundly scandalous." Their erotic consciousness destroys the profane bourgeois morality and its category of personhood, which obstructs and stiffens life.

It is true that Bataille's way of thinking about our incarnated existence is quite different from Sade's. He knows that the body can be only an object or a thing at the limit and that erotic experience negates the thing in the body. Indeed, Sade and Bataille are concerned with quite different things in sexuality. Sontag is right in emphasizing that Sade's orgies consist of an inventory of a great number of different configurations of mechanical bodies and that he neutralizes the sexuality of all personal connections in order to represent an impersonal, pure sexual relationship. Bataille, too, wants to neutralize the personal, but he does that in order to experience the impersonal fluid ground of our existence. In the erotic experience, life relates to itself by overcoming the separation and distribution in beings, and it uses its excess energy to go beyond the profane world of intelligence and work. This is why I think the erotic experience in Bataille cannot just be a thirst for annihilation. Attempts to go beyond the bourgeois morality by liberating sexuality can perhaps create new societies in which people lead more sovereign lives. But how these societies should organize themselves in the ethico-political sense remains an open question.

For Bataille, we do not come into erotic encounters as self-made, self-coinciding subjects who seek to objectify the other through the master and slave dialectic of the struggle for power. He explores the powerful insight that the erotic relationship opens a new space for subjectivity. What he calls "the profound subjectivity" overlaps with the immanence of the divine, the human, and the animal (Bataille 1991b, 234). In other words, he is not interested in the subject who is an effect of the power struggles, experiences of hardships of life and past traumas, but in our subjective capacity to take the step in an erotic encounter to renounce generously and luxuriously all struggles for power. Insofar as erotic communication is concerned, "winning over the other" may amount to losing a conversation, for winning in love may result in the destruction of further possibilities of genuine communication. Erotic communication may involve playing roles in fantasies in which people wear masks to explore themselves in a trusting relationship. One comes into contact with one's self in different modalities of the erotic relation to the other. Erotic experience by setting us in a communicative relation to the other can saves us from falling prey to an unreflective repetition of our drives. Eros in its truth, which does not exclude play, exceeds contracts and promises. Even though intimacy can be bound by promise making, it can also become something more truthful, and more profound than promising in the sense of making contracts. Bataille knows that "betrayal" is also included in the erotic experience. He writes: "In eroticism there is ordinarily an impulse of aggressive hatred, an urge to betray. That is why a feeling of anguish is connected with it, and also why, on the other hand, when the hatred is a powerlessness and the betrayal an abortive act, the erotic element is ludicrous" (Bataille 1991b, 178). This can be due to an impulse to separate, the human incapacity to persist too long in the longed-for profound intimacy with the other. If erotic truth is found in participation in the unlimited, there is also an element of finitude, that which reveals itself in the feeling of its overwhelmingness, in the longing for separateness and solitude.

Erotic truth in communication is an opening to the profound subjectivity of our sexed being experienced in pain and pleasure. Sovereignty is not mastery over the other; it comes with fragility because it is always open to violence, betrayal, and loss. The distinction I make between "transcendent" or "immanent" violence can be useful in drawing an ethical boundary. Violence is *transcendent* if the subject uses violence to control and dominate the other; to establish one's self as independent and superior, and if it involves sexism, classism, and racism. However, it is *immanent* if it is used for exploring the possibilities of incarnation with the other within the limits of individual love.

To conclude, Bataille gives us an ontology of erotic experience based on his notion of sovereignty. This approach is worth comparing with the phenomenological ontology of freedom, for it has a different understanding of what it means to be erotically free. Sovereignty is the experience of an incarnated being capable of sexual differentiation in intimate communication with others. Bataille's ontology of sex differs from Beauvoir's, for the former analyzes human existence by making a threefold ontological distinction between animality, profane existence, and the symbolic realm of the sacred. Beauvoir's analysis depends on the notion of existence understood as being-in-the-world. She does not offer a philosophy of nature and refers to the religious symbolism in her critique of the patriarchal culture. Neither the nature nor the sacred are for her necessary to understand the being of the erotic. Bataille disagrees with Beauvoir: he claims that the problem of Eros should be addressed by considering the interrelation between the three layers. He misses the feminist perspective: he gives no account of sexual oppression, and fails to do a critique of patriarchy. Against the feminist critiques, I have argued that there are elements that contest patriarchy in his fiction. In this chapter I tried to approach him as doing an ontology of sex rather than a philosophical anthropology. I think Bataille helps us understand the scope of the ontological problem better than alternative theories. Beauvoir's and Bataille's ontologies are very different, but not necessarily incompatible. Bataille is not just doing a philosophical anthropology; he thinks of Being as generosity. For Beauvoir, generosity is an ethical value: eroticism in a relationship of equality, and reciprocity is also generosity.

Bataille reflects on the erotic experience in its relation to horror and violence; however, he does not make sufficient effort to delineate an ethics of eros that ensures safety. The phenomenon of violence he is interested in is not domestic violence; he is not looking at poisonous intimate partner relationships. He does not attempt to think through the cyclical violence in the couple, whose members might be violently entangled with each other such that either one torments the other or they both engage in controlling and injurious behavior. In the cyclical violence of intimate partner violence (domestic violence) people keep suffering, often without being able to escape. In contrast, Bataille's erotic texts, harm, destruction, and violence are presented as the hazardous events of the desire in the encounter with the other. Violence does not target people to whom the male subject is attached or closely related. Indeed, this is a world in which caring acts do not flow from personal attachment and nourish individual love. In a stage set by detachment and alienation, acts of erotic violence enact the fantasy of being in proximity with all living beings in carnal communication with the other. The absence of care in the world of the separated subject is, so to speak, compensated by the desire for fusion in the realm of immanence. A feminist ethics of care can be of use in evaluating Bataille at this point. Care ethics rests on an ontology that affirms the fundamental relationality of human beings. The denial of relatedness is often associated with male gender with its overtones of individual separation from others and ontological independence. Indeed, from a feminist care ethicist perspective Bataille would look like striving to cope with masculinity structured by independence and separatedness. He is seeking and reaffirming relationality, and he seems to confuse it with fusion.

Even if we grant that his violent, sovereign erotic experience does not involve domination over the other, even if we hold that the violence he has in mind may not reduce to sexism, the attempt to extrapolate a normative ethics of eros from Bataille's writings would be in vain. Respecting norms and boundaries would always be a problem, because, for Bataille, norms and boundaries provoke transgression. Although excessive violence is something to avoid, it is unclear how it can be avoided. One may invoke the postulate that erotic violence is ethically permissible on the condition that there is no coercion. Nonetheless, this postulate is problematic given the difficulties in establishing that coercion is really nonexistent. The individual who is giving explicit or tacit consent may not be in the possession of the kind of concepts and terms that would enable her to make an adequate judgment of her situation. For example, a woman may not object to marital rape because she believes that the marriage contract gives her husband sexual rights over her body. The situation one is in may shape one's freedom. Moreover, coercion can be subtle and manipulative. Racial, gender, and class inequalities may make coercion invisible. There is room to wonder if sexual violence is not unethical even in cases in which it is exercised with "consent." Despite all of this, one can in principle imagine a situation in which freedoms are equal and acts of erotic violence can be reciprocal. Take a case in which power relations are sufficiently balanced in a given encounter or specific relationship. Of course, that kind of balance can only be the necessary condition for not objecting to violence. I think that erotic violence can be permissible if the erotic relationship keeps open a space for a critical re-evaluation of its terms, and if the partners in the relationship sufficiently care for each other.

I have so far emphasized that Bataille sees in erotic acts of violence an incarnated consciousness that transcends the world of power struggles and contests the hypocrisy of the bourgeois morality, but none of these metaphysical and political reasons exempt it from ethical evaluation. The fact that a violent act puts me in an intimate relation with the other who consents to it does not make it automatically permissible in the ethical sense. An ethical relation is grounded on caring for the other. Even though Bataille does not use the term "care," "individual love" can be his term for the same thing. I, personally, do not think that care is the same as individual love. In an erotic relation, individual love may or may not accompany care. It is possible to imagine that one cares without feeling love. One can imagine people who are attracted to each other without being in love; not being in love does not mean not caring for the other.

Bataille is right in suggesting that the tenets of personalism are not fit to describe erotic experience. In his writings violence destroys personalism and the ethics that comes with it. Meanwhile, he acknowledges the importance of individual love and, perhaps, of care. If human sexuality is based on norms and transgression of norms, erotic experience is a limited experience that involves risks. We need good reasons to worry about the consequences of violence that I or the other may experience in sex. Women all over the world lose their lives because of sexual violence. A care ethical point of view requires that sexual violence for pleasure be limited by the caring attitude. Although no pre-given norms are imposed, a care relationship is capable of introducing the bodily boundaries that foster the well-being of the related beings. Care ethics can dispense with principles and rules. Nel Noddings writes:

> Any mode of thought that lays out complete and final answers to great existential questions is liable to dogmatism. A great attraction of care ethics, I think, is its refusal to encode or construct a catalog of principles and rules. One who cares must meet the cared-for just as he or she is, as a whole human being with individual needs and interests. [. . .] At most, it directs us to attend, to listen, and to respond as positively as possible. [. . .] It recognizes that virtually all human beings desire not to be hurt, and this gives us something close to an absolute. (Noddings 2012, 109)

A care ethics approach is based on individual needs and interests of the other cared for, rather than respect for the preexisting normative standards. I think Bataille can acknowledge a care ethics of eros in that sense. Care serves to reduce and control the risk. Whether we can do without setting norms at the face of sexual violence and how care ethics can accommodate deliberate hurt or pain in the realm of Eros is a problem of the normative ethics of sex that I am not going to discuss further.

Bataille's ontology of sex speaks of the importance of the symbolic of the sacred, but it does not really discuss the role that the symbolic system plays in the constitution of sexual difference. The symbolic constitution of a phallocentric economy of sexual difference has very much to bear on what it means to be a woman or a man and shapes the way the erotic experience is lived. In the third chapter, I turn to Luce Irigaray's reading of Freud and Lacan to explore how she understands the "phallocentric economy of signification."

REFERENCES

Bataille, Georges. 1970. *Œuvres Complètes I*. Paris: Gallimard.
———. 1974. "Théorie de la religion." *Œuvres Complètes VII*, Paris: Gallimard.
———. 1986. *Erotism: Death and Sensuality*. Translated by Mary Dalwood. San Francisco: City Lights.
———. 1987. *Story of the Eye*. Translated by Joachim Neugroschel. San Francisco: City Lights Books. (Georges Bataille. 1970. *Œuvres Complètes I*, 12–78. Paris: Gallimard.)
———. 1988. *Inner Experience*. Translated by Leslie Anne Boldt. Albany: State University of New York Press.
———. 1991a. *The Accursed Share*. Vol. 1. Translated by Robert Hurley. New York: Zone Books.
———. 1991b. *The Accursed Share*. Vols. 2–3. Translated by Robert Hurley. New York: Zone Books.
———. 1992. *The Theory of Religion*. Translated by Robert Hurley. New York: Zone Books.
———. 1995. *My Mother, Madame Edwarda, The Dead Man*. Translated by Austryn Wainhouse. New York: Marion Boyars.
———. 2011. *Guilty*. Translated by Stuart Kendall. Albany: State University of New York Press.
Beauvoir, Simone de. 2010. *The Second Sex*. Translated by Constance Borde and Sheila Malovany-Chevallier. New York: Alfred A. Knopf.
Direk, Zeynep. 2011. "Immanence and Abjection in Simone De Beauvoir." *Southern Journal of Philosophy* 49, no. 1 (March): 49–72.
———. 2015. "Kristeva and Bataille: On Religion." In *Negative Ecstasies: Georges Bataille and the Study of Religion*, edited by Kent Brintnall and Jeremy Biles, 182–201. New York: Fordham University Press.
Dworkin, Andrea.1981. *Pornography: Men Possessing Women*. New York: Perigee.
Freud, Sigmund. 2001a. "Totem and Taboo: Resemblances Between the Psychic Lives of Savages and Neurotics." In *Standard Edition of the Complete Pyschological Works of Sigmund Freud*. Vol. 13. Translated by James Strachey. London: Hogarth Press and the Institute of Psycho-Analysis.
———. 2001b. "Female Sexuality." In *Standard Edition of the Complete Pyschological Works of Sigmund Freud*. Vol. 21. Translated by James Strachey. London: Hogarth Press and the Institute of Psycho-Analysis.
———. 2001c. "The Taboo of Virginity." In *Standard Edition of the Complete Pyschological Works of Sigmund Freud*. Vol. 11. Translated by James Strachey. London: Hogarth Press and the Institute of Psycho-Analysis.
Hartmann, Nadine. 2016. "Eroticism." In *Georges Bataille: Key Concepts*, edited by Mark Hewson and Marcus Coelen, 136–47. London and New York: Routledge.
Hegel, Georg Wilhelm Friedrich. 1977. *Phenomenology of Spirit*. Translated by Arnold V. Miller. Oxford: Oxford University Press.
Heidegger, Martin. 1991. *Nietzsche*. Vols. 3 and 4. Translated by Joan Stambaugh, David Farell Krell, and Frank A. Capuzzi. San Francisco: Harper.
Irigaray, Luce. 1993. *An Ethics of Sexual Difference*. Translated by Carolyn Burke and Gillian C. Gill. Ithaca, NY: Cornell University Press.
Kristeva, Julia. 1987. *Tales of Love*. Translated by Leon S. Roudiez. New York: Columbia University Press.
Lévi-Strauss, Claude. 1969. *The Elementary Structures of Kinship*. Translated by James Harle Bell and John Richard von Sturmer. Edited by Rodney Needham. Boston: Beacon Press.
Nietzsche, Friedrich. 1999. *Philosophy and Truth: Selections from Nietzsche's Notebooks of the Early 1870s*. Translated by Daniel Breazeale. New York: Humanity Books.
Noddings, Nell. 2012. *Peace Eduation: How We Come to Love and Hate War*. Cambridge: Cambridge University Press.
Sontag, Susan. 1969. *Styles of Radical Will*. New York: Vintage.

Suleiman, Rubin Susan. 1995a. "Transgression and the Avant-Garde: Bataille's Histoire de l'Oeil." In *On Bataille: Critical Essays*, edited by Leslie Anne Boldt-Irons, 313–34. Albany: State University of New York Press.

———. 1995b. "Bataille in the Street: The Search for Virility in 1930s." In *Bataille: Writing the Sacred*, edited by Carolyn Bailey Gill, 26–45. London and New York Routledge.

Winnubst, Shannon. 2007. "Bataille's Queer Pleasures: The Universe as Spider or Spit." In *Reading Bataille Now*, edited by Shannon Winnubst, 75–93. Bloomington and Indianapolis: Indiana University Press.

Chapter Three

The Problem of Phallocentrism

In her book *Speculum of the Other Woman*, which dates from 1974, Luce Irigaray discusses Sigmund Freud's writings on femininity and denounces the presence of a masculine signifying economy in Freud's psychoanalytical account of sexual difference. Her claim is that this economy cannot signify feminine alterity, that is, female sexual difference as such, or in itself, without reducing it to a necessary means or support for male subjectivity. Therefore, Freudian psychoanalysis does not allow for the discovery of a plurality of fluid sexual differences, which are not the instances of essences that pre-exist existence.

To understand Irigaray's notion of sexual difference, we need to explain her notion of "phallocentrism" and the way she problematizes it. According to her, both Freud and Lacan are theorizing within a phallocentric economy of signification. In *This Sex Which Is Not One*, which she published in 1977, she challenges patriarchy in the psychoanalytical tradition by returning to female morphologies in which she explores the drives in women's bodies, which would help her to signify female sexual difference. She uses fiction and philosophy to undermine the patriarchal and phallocentric domination in the sphere of representations, and to open the theoretical space for a mode of representation for women as women. In this chapter, I shall first explain the difference between Freud's and Lacan's reading of sexual difference and explain the reasons that justify Irigaray to designate both accounts as phallocentric. Secondly, I shall clarify the ontological commitments implicated in her hermeneutical strategies. Finally, I shall argue that *essentialist realism* is not an appropriate characterization of her ontological position because the psychoanalytical and phenomenological presuppositions of Irigaray's thought imply that although for her sex is real, the real remains unapparent without the imaginary and symbolic representations that open the space for its manifestation.

PHALLUS: THE PRIVILEGED SIGNIFIER

What is phallocentrism? To begin with, the term "phallus" necessitates that we really start with Lacan rather than Freud, for it plays a central role in Lacan, not in Freud. Irigaray was a follower of the Lacanian school of psychoanalysis when she took up Freud's discussion of sexual difference to criticize it as phallocentric. "Phallocentrism," in the broad sense, is related to the understanding of sexuality as a development that accomplishes itself in phallic sexuality—in which genitals are the privileged sexual organs and reproduction is seen as the aim of the genital sex. It follows that the traditional, patriarchal conception of sexual difference is phallocentric. Of course, Irigaray's study of phallocentrism aims to reveal the extent to which Freud's discourse is traditional. However, this frame is not sufficiently narrow to understand Irigaray's argument in *Speculum*, which becomes more explicit only if we read Freud as informed by Lacan.

IRIGARAY'S READING OF FREUD

In *Speculum of the Other Woman*, Irigaray takes up Freud's treatment of femininity, and although Lacan's name is absent, Lacanian concepts and distinctions (such as the threefold distinction between the real, imaginary, and symbolic) shape Irigaray's discussion of sexual difference in her commentary on Freud. Let me begin by saying a few things on Irigaray's methodology: "The Blind Spot of an Old Dream of Symmetry" concentrates on the role of the imaginary in the articulation of the symbolic. Freud first captures the girl's sexual being in an image, which paves the way for his symbolic articulation of female sexual difference. Irigaray's relation to the psychoanalytic tradition of Freud and Lacan is subversive mimesis. Elizabeth Grosz argues that rather than aiming at producing a universal truth, this is a psychoanalytical work that recodes the readers' imaginary and symbolic structures (Grosz 1989, 117). For Irigaray, psychoanalytical knowledge contributes to sexual oppression, which we should overcome by a revolutionary poesis that transforms the imaginary and symbolic realms.

Irigaray wants to subvert the existing organization of the realm of representation; she destabilizes it to reach at the femininity that it excludes. This can be designated as the *real* sexual difference. However, Irigaray makes the underlying assumption that the real does not automatically or by itself appear. Its apparition depends on the presence of enabling images and the symbols. Some images can block the way for the apparition of the real;

others can facilitate its self-expression. Irigaray's close reading of the psychoanalytic discourses manifests their blind spots, which means they produce images that only help male self-affection and symbolization and obstruct female self-affection. The term "blind spot" suggests that the subject of such discourses is blind to its own operation. By *subversive mimesis*, Irigaray finds the gaps in these discourses in which she could re-inscribe images of women's bodies. She positively reconstructs female morphologies, and thus creates new positions, which can be inhabited by women as women, as desiring female subjects. Irigaray takes a feminine position in writing, as posited by Freud and Lacan: a masquerade, the mimesis of mimicry, the textual enactment of hysteria to make the point that the representational systems at hand represent women in man's terms and leave no place for self-determined femininity.

In "The Blind Spot of an Old Dream of Symmetry," Irigaray is interested in developing accounts of subjectivity and knowledge that acknowledge the existence of two sexes, two bodies, and two ways of knowing. For her, the questions of sexual specificity and multiple sexualities are bound up with the first opening of a symbolic space for the two sexes. Whether or not two would be sufficient to do justice to the indefinite, indeterminable plurality in the realm of sexual difference is a legitimate question that has been asked of Irigaray by feminists and queer theorists. There are feminist readings of Irigaray, which conceive the binary as opening to plurality, and feminist interpretations that argue that she fails to accommodate sexual plurality. The thesis concerning the irreducibility of the two sexes provoked the view that Irigaray holds an essentialist realist position. If by "essentialist realism" is meant that the real naturally exists and appears by itself, independently of the locking/unlocking power of the images, which release or obstruct it, the characterization of Irigaray as an essentialist realist would at least contradict the ontological position she takes in this early text we shall discuss.

Let me now turn to Irigaray's reading of Freud. At the first reading, "The Blind Spot of an Old Dream of Symmetry" can be a very puzzling text because it is not very clear why Irigaray describes Freud's discourse as *phallocentric.* Freud's explanations of femininity are centered around and related to the male sex organ, rather than the *phallus*. Does Irigaray equate the real organ with the symbolic phallus? Does she aim at revealing the organization of Freud's signifying economy by the leading signifier "penis"? In other words, is Freud's explanation of sexual difference phallocentric because the penis figures as the privileged signifier organizing the narrative of sexual development? If this is the case, Irigaray would be disregarding the fact that the *phallus* in Lacan does not have to stand for the male sexual organ; it is veiled as a signifier, making sexual desire enigmatic. As I shall explain in the next section, the *phallus* is severed from the penis by way of an *Aufhebung* in the dialectic of desire. In Lacan, women are not characterized by penis envy though they are characterized as not-all; and as being the *phallus*, i.e., as objects of desire who may "resent" or "envy" the privileges men enjoy as desiring subjects in the symbolic system.

Irigaray's use of the term "phallocentrism" can only be less puzzling if we focus on how she redefines it. In the *Speculum*, phallocentrism is described as an economy in which women are spoken of and represented by men, without having their own voice in signifying their own being. This comes with a lack of role in the creation of a world to inhabit. Women cannot fulfill their transcendence because reality is organized by the phallocentric symbolic system that do not let them manifest themselves without being caught up in the oppositions of the system. "Phallocentrism" is the name for the male-dominant economy of sexual difference in which men are the speaking beings and women are the objects, targets, and stakes of a masculine discourse (Irigaray 1985a, 13).

The feminine alterity, the alterity in a female being as such does not have a place in this economy, which signifies the feminine in terms of the masculine. How should this alterity be understood? The alterity in question is natural and real, but must also be envisaged as realizing itself by self-expression. However, this self-expression is not an effect of teleology but a symbolic event that is enrooted in virtual multiplicity. Irigaray shows that Freud's narrative of sexual development in *"Femininity"* (Freud 2001d) effectively impedes self-manifestation of female alterity, by an imaginary understanding of the being of sexual difference in terms of sameness. An image of original sameness assures a symbolic articulation by constant comparison between the children of different sexes. Freud makes the claim that a girl child has to go through a much more difficult period of development in comparison with the boy, to become a heterosexual woman. The sameness argument is not based on Freud's belief of the precedence of sexually undifferentiated life to sexual division. The ontological grounds of Freud postulation of sameness are vague. Sameness is here a way of imagining, seeing, fantasying. Freud attributes it to children, implying that they all take a male position in their pre-Oedipal fantasies.

According to Irigaray, the image of the little girl as a little boy does not solicit her own sexual difference. Freud is setting the terms of the apparition of sexual difference in a manipulative way. The sameness claim confers on the little girl an original masculinity. The little girl, at the beginning, is comprehended as, in fact, a little boy, because Freud decides to see her clitoris as a penis equivalent. This makes the little girl a "disadvantaged little man" (Irigaray 1985a, 26). How to make sense of that? Does Freud mean that in nature the clitoris is an undeveloped penis? As one could call, for example, the testicles in the male body vaginal lips that did not properly develop? Even if in nature sexual division could give rise to different genital organs, the ground of priming one sex in understanding the other can only be the founding, schematizing act of imagination.

Freud's narrative is well known: both children go through the phallic phase, in which they play with their sexual organs and experience pleasure. The boy plays with his penis, while the girl plays with "the penis equivalent," her clitoris. Soon the little girl will realize that the boy possesses something that she does not have. She begins to undergo her experience of castration. The little boy, on the other hand, discovers that the girl does not have a penis and, assuming that she is castrated, he begins to fear losing his own. Thus, he suffers the fear of castration. Irigaray says that this is dogmatic and arbitrary. She points to how very focused Freud is on the fact that the boy has a penis and the girl does not. The girl "exposes, exhibits the possibility of a *nothing to see*" (Irigaray 1985a, 47), as if this absence, "*this nothing to be seen is equivalent to having no thing. No being* and *no truth*" (Irigaray 1985a, 48). In Freud's logic, there does not exist a girl, as an other, whose sexual difference can manifest itself to an open-ended phenomenological investigation. The gaze that is directed at her takes the little boy as a model. The comparison of the little girl with the little boy presupposes that they are basically the same, though the girl is a deficient instance of that sameness. The measure being the boy, she turns out to be the inferior, because instead of having a penis, she only possesses the much smaller, and therefore less valuable, clitoris.

What makes this narrative phallocentric? It could be that Irigaray thinks that the penis functions here as the "phallus" because it serves to define the feminine in relation to the masculine. For her, phallocentrism is a normative system. This normative system is not based at all on the real but gives rise to social reality. Freud, too, acknowledges that the real nature may not at all work according to these norms. This distinction into "male" and "female" is not of psychological nature; it is rather brought into being, by "anatomy and conventions" (Irigaray 1985a, 15, quoting Freud). Anatomical difference prescribes a mental life (Irigaray 1985a, 15) only because of this normative system. The opposition between active and passive may shed light on this. To speak of women's sexual life in terms of "passivity" in relation to men's "activity" and of the female activities such as breast-feeding, by way of grammatical reversal, as if they were passivities, can be seen as the effects of phallocentrism on us because phallocentrism exercises a "monopoly of productive activity of man." "Man is *the* procreator," and only due to his activity, his "production reproduction" is succeeded (Irigaray 1985a, 18). Women are merely the receivers of men's product. "He will mark the product of copulation with *his own name*" (Irigaray 1985a, 23), while woman is the "anonymous worker" (Irigaray 1985a, 23). Irigaray describes the maternal function as subservient to the ends of male cultural production. A child, too, is a cultural production. Man labels his cultural products to show that they are originally his. The child is his "pro-ject" (Irigaray 1985a, 18). But this is not merely a matter of fecundity as the prolongation of family in time. As Whitford puts it in *Philosophy in the Feminine*, "woman (the maternal feminine) provides the unsymbolized basis of masculine theoretical constructions" (Whitford 1991b, 7).

Irigaray asks a set of questions to exhibit phallocentric logic: (1) "Why does Freud, against all rhyme and reason, want the little girls' masturbation to involve only the clitoris?" (Irigaray 1985a, 29). Given that the little girl is conceived as in fact "a little boy," she would be in the *phallic stage* when she explores her genitals. But why speak of a phallic stage and not a "vulvar stage" (Irigaray 1985a, 29)? What makes Freud focus only on the pleasure coming from the clitoris by disregarding the possibility that the little girl's masturbation may involve touching the other parts of the female genital organs, such as the vulva and lips? The answer is that Freud concentrates only on the clitoris because he sees it as the penis equivalent. Even the assumption that the vaginal sensations are not yet present is another symptom of the phallocentric definition of sexual pleasure in terms of the penis. (2) Why must women shift their erotogenic zone from the clitoris to the vagina? They have various erotogenic zones in their sex organs, and they do not have to exchange one for the other. Irigaray remarks that this shift must happen in Freud's discourse because vagina becomes "the indispensable instrument of male pleasure" (Irigaray 1985a, 30). Freud instrumentalizes the female sex for male pleasure. "After all the two organs [talks about the clitoris and the vagina] are in no way interchangeable, but rather contribute, along with others, and with specific sensitivities, to woman's sexual pleasure" (Irigaray 1985a, 30). According to Irigaray, Freud has the fear of "*her*" having other desires, of a different nature from *his* representation of the sexual and from *his* representations of sexual desire" (Irigaray 1985a, 51). In order to suppress this fear, he needs the girl to envy his penis. Both questions help the reader remark that Freud's discourse on female sexuality is "phallocentric," because it takes the unjustified step of effacing the plurality of her desires to reorganize all desire with a view to his sexual satisfaction (which implies the reduction of the non-phallic desires to the phallic).

Irigaray's reading of Freud's discussion of castration points to how female castration amounts to a radical break with the origin without any possibility of return. Freud says that the girl, like the boy, has the wish to represent and reproduce herself in the origin, in the first object of love, which is the mother. At the beginning of her castration complex, the little girl realizes that the little boy has different genital organs. When she realizes that not only herself, but all other women, including the mother, lack a penis, she feels "wronged" and blames the mother for not giving her a penis. The mother is held responsible because the mother is the creator of life. She is guilty for bringing to life a penis-lacking, inferior being like the little girl. "The little girl does not forgive her mother for not giving her a penis" (Irigaray 1985a, 47). Penis envy and blaming the mother are inseparable; the presence of these feelings indicate that the little girl is facing with the reality of castration. If this psychic pain leads her to switch her object of love to her father, she becomes a heterosexual female. The girl has to turn away from her mother to her father in order to become feminine, whereas the boy continues to love his. If the mother represents the place of origin and the child desires to return to the origin, this switch implies that the girl will not be able to reproduce and represent herself in her origin. She has to accept that she has to reproduce and represent someone else's origin, her later partner's, by bearing him a child. She can achieve happiness if "the baby is a *little boy* who brings the longed-for penis with him" (Freud, cited in Irigaray 1985a, 74). In Freud's account the boy can return to his place of origin by penetrating a woman, while the girl can only become a "new" place of origin. This assumes that "[n]o return to, toward, inside the place of origin is possible unless you have a penis" (Irigaray 1985a, 41). It is unclear why the little girl's masturbation or lesbian sex should not count as return to the place of origin. If all children fantasize about a return to the origin through penetration, why this remains only as the boy's privilege is unanswered.

This narrative is too well known. It is the story of a woman who "*becomes into being*" (Irigaray 1985a, 84) as if there is a predestined path to femininity. If sexes result from becomings, there should be different processes of becoming. Freud describes the path the little girl has to follow as first being a little boy who then has to become a man, minus certain attributes. According to Freud, the little girl's desire is only to remain a man. It is this desire for the same that sets her to become what she is supposed to be, her gender. Although Freud recognizes the little girl's assets that make her superior to the boy (she is more intelligent, can control the production of feces, of language, and social relationships earlier), these positive characteristics are only valuable insofar as she will be an object of the male desire. Freud's question about becoming, by way of a psychic evolution, a man or a woman from a bisexual disposition to start with at the beginning, could have been a fair question, if Freud's answer to this question had not come within "an economy of representation" (Irigaray 1985a, 22) in which the "phallic currency" sets the standards of meaning. This economy of signification resonates with the patriarchal economy of the gift by means of which patriarchal kinship bonds are created. "Man is the procreator" (Irigaray 1985a, 18), and "he will mark the product of copulation with *his own name*" (Irigaray 1985a, 23); woman is there only as a condition for the reproductive necessity. Her worth is subordinated to and reduced by the "phallic currency." The value in this economy is determined in terms of masculinity.

Structurally speaking, we have here a system of oppositions in which femininity is captured. The function of the negative (woman's "not having it") ensures that she is captivated in such oppositions as being/*becoming*, having/*not having* sex (organ), phallic/*non-phallic*, penis/*clitoris* or else penis/*vagina*, plus/*minus*, clearly representable/*dark continent*, logos/*silence* or idle chatter, desire for the mother/*desire to be the mother*, etc. The idea that females suffer from a lack is the key for women's representation in this system. The system does not make room for the non-phallic; it converts it to the phallic. Thus, it forms the hierarchy that subordinates women to men. In patriarchal cultures, women are born into this phallocentric system of signification; they find themselves caught up in it before they can seek ways to release themselves from it. According to Irigaray, this system gives men mastery, power over the other sex. There he projects what he pretends to know. She will have no part in this, due to her remaining off-stage, that is "beyond representation, beyond selfhood" (Irigaray 1985a, 22).

According to Freud, women "have only one desire—that of being *as much as possible like man's eternal object of desire*" (Irigaray 1985a, 32). By making such a claim, he denies that women have their own desire. As a result, only a male desire is left, and this undermines the possibility of the relation between two desiring beings. How can the little girl have her own desire for her mother, if desire is masculine? When Freud talks about women's libido, he makes clear that there cannot be a specifically female desire: "the libido is masculine, or at any rate neuter" (Irigaray 1985a, 43). If the female libido cannot be represented, the strength of woman's sexual impulses must be reduced.

Irigaray questions the status of Freud's claim that women have penis envy, that this determines all their "instinctual economy" (Irigaray 1985a, 92), and their behavior at the time of and after "the discovery of her castration" (Irigaray 1985a, 51). Assume the contrary, that a woman does not have penis envy, how would a man deal with the fact that she has her own desires and representations of sex that pertain to a non-phallic economy? This would, according to Irigaray, also put in question unity, and the mirror function woman seems to fulfill for man. Penis envy assures man by buttressing his "narcissistic construction" (Irigaray 1985a, 51); if this envy is not there, the assurance might also disappear. Irigaray implies that if the assumed penis envy does not exist, the whole phallocentric economy would collapse.

The phallus acts in psychoanalysis as the ultimate signifier; it was predominant already in ancient metaphors and remains in control in the psychoanalytical "new signifying economy" (Irigaray 1985a, 44). Clearly, Irigaray remarks how continuous psychoanalysis is with the patriarchal tradition of Western civilization. In this civilization there is an economy of representation which is regulated "by paradigms and units of value that are in turn determined by male subjects" (Irigaray 1985a, 22). In this economy of signification, femininity is expected to serve "a function of the (re)productive necessities of an intentionally phallic currency" (Irigaray, 1985a, 22). Indeed, she is assigned a complementary role without being recognized as the other in an equal partnership relation. She is not taken in her difference on her own terms and considered as equally worthy of respect but represented as man's opposite. Irigaray lists a whole set of attributes that are set in a relation of opposition, to be used to explain the pair man/woman: to be/become; have/ not have sex; phallic/non-phallic; penis/clitoris; penis/vagina; plus/minus; representable/dark continent; logos/silence; desire for the mother/desire to be the mother; etc. These pairs serve to define woman in relation to man and as his opposite; they thus efface what she can be outside of this matrix. Freud knows that the biological sex cannot explain why and how people play the sex roles in the ways they do; the social world is not determined by human biology. People identify with gender roles depending on how they react to their unconscious experience of the complex structures that shape the history of human psyche, given the patriarchal organization of human civilization. This history takes a particular shape depending on what sex we have been assigned on the basis of the anatomy of the genital organs. The "anatomy is destiny" formulation concerns sexual development because how children go through the castration and Oedipus complexes depend on what sex they are assigned at birth.

Phallocentrism is a system that does not simply make women secondary; it effaces their being, to give rise to a substitute in the position of the second sex. To subvert phallocentrism means to create another system of representation, in which women can relate to each other and to the male sex without being complementary. Phallocentrism is a burdening problem for Irigaray because it suppresses sexual difference. By setting the female always in relation to the masculine and by comparing them, it suggests that both come from the same. Indeed, Irigaray speaks of the "a priorism of the same" because this discourse does not start from the female body and its experiences. With respect to the phallocentric economy of signification, the feminine is absolutely Other. This is not the Lacanian Other that begins to impose its desire to us as soon as we act as desiring beings in this phallocentric economy. It is the Other that can never be accommodated in this phallocentric economy. Indeed, it haunts the phallocentric economy and leaves its traces there.

Irigaray's use of language aims to create a new symbolic that accommodates sexual difference. This implies a "revolution," the overcoming of the existing symbolic order. The phallocentric economy of signification functions as the *a priori* register that organizes, regulates, and justifies the empirical, factual relations of subordination of women to men. The symbolic system is like a theology that expatriates, expropriates, and excludes difference (Irigaray 1985a, 27). Female libido is expatriated and cut off from access to signifiers. Irigaray argues: "Access to a signifying economy, to the coining of signifiers, is difficult or even impossible for her because she remains an outsider, herself a subject to their norms [. . .] which all surely keeps her deficient, empty, lacking, in a way that could be labelled 'psychotic'" (Irigaray 1985a, 71). In neurosis, the subject relates to signifiers that can substitute for one another—in psychosis, on the other hand, there is a signifier that is irreplaceable. It is the presence/absence of the irreplaceable, ultimate signifier in the phallocentric system that sets the stage for the outside as psychotic. "[H]ysterical miming will be the little girl's or the woman's effort to save her sexuality from total repression and destruction" (Irigaray 1985a, 72). Freud finds a way of not taking women who react to sexual oppression seriously by diagnosing them as "hysterics" and "psychotics." In fact, the symptoms of psychosis and hysteria could be women's response to the system of sexual oppression. They can be part of women's attempts to free themselves from it. The phallocentric economy Irigaray is talking about is discursive, symbolic, a site of power, and women are not allowed to inhabit it as speaking subjects. In order for them to become speaking subjects, we need to subvert the phallocentric economy of signification and create a new symbolic language. This is the same as creating a new culture; in short, Irigaray's symbolic revolution gives rise to a cultural revolution.

Finally, phallocentrism does not only neglect feminine otherness, it disregards other modalities of otherness as well. In a system in which its relation to the phallus defines every sexual difference, can the position of woman be expanded to include people who desire to identify as woman? What about non-binary, gender-fluid people? How can they have access to the signifying economy if the economy of signification remains phallocentric? And how does this framework respond to transfeminist claims that some females can be born with male genital organs? Do people need the endorsement of biological science to be woman? Do we have to take into consideration the personal history as narrated by the individual, the individual's narrative identity, which begins with the sex assignment to a body for that individual to count as woman in the symbolic system? What are the conditions of identifying with the feminine alterity that the phallocentric system excludes? I believe Irigaray starts with the male/female binary, takes her departure from the biological reality of being born with female sexual organs, and considers how the bodies that fall in this category are inscribed in the phallocentric economy of signification. Is it necessary to be born with the constitution socially recognized as "female biology" in order to be woman in the economy of signification? Inspired more by Beauvoir than by Irigaray, my answer to this question would be negative. I believe that, rather than expanding the category of the female to make it inclusive, we should go back to Beauvoir and insist that being born female or not does not in fact explain "being a woman." Being seen as feminine or declaring oneself as woman would be sufficient to include one in the history of sexual oppression. We can perhaps make room for heterogeneity in woman's symbolic position in Irigaray's framework. However, we cannot dispense with sex because Irigaray defends women's sexed rights. Creating diversity in the symbolic position of woman to respect the rights of trans women should not result in undermining women's sexed rights. In a framework that maintains the fundamental tenets of the Irigarian framework, a defense of trans women's sexed rights can be made without a clash between women's sexed rights and trans women's sexed rights. One may object that Irigaray talks only about the non-phallic female sexual difference, which may not so easily escape from being opposed to the phallic male sexual difference. Isn't the new symbolic that Irigaray called for already here? Has not phallocentrism been overcome by the revolution that expands the symbolic to include positions as diverse as non-phallic masculinity, phallic femininity with ambiguous relation to castration, phallic femininity that rejects castration to take the place of the father and to command others and ask for absolute obedience, non-binaries that reject the symbolic opposition of the phallic masculine and the phallic feminine, non-binaries that demand the right to transition from one position to another? Aren't these positions still defined with reference to the phallus? If this is indeed the case, there would still be only one sex. The question arises if the presence of the penis in the woman's body would make the economy of signification less phallocentric?

"Psychoanalysts often complain ironically about women being unanalyzable" (Irigaray 1985a, 44), Irigaray says. This is true when thinking in Freud's terms, and this is a direct consequence of phallocentrism. The phallus is used to describe the woman. Due to woman only being described in relation to man, in relation to the male notion of the phallus, one can only analyse the male and *his* relation to what is also *his, part of him*. Freud's account therefore only analyses males, and how females *relate to these males*.

According to Irigaray, Freud's discourse on women on grounds of the history of the male psychic development is inspired by the "one-sex" theories of his time and his inability to think of another perspective, one which regards women's experience in order to extrapolate the structures that give rise to its own possibilities for being. Freud contrives to understand women as complementary others to men at the same time as the deficient instances of the masculine original. These are the terms of heterosexual desire, which is based on a monosexual analysis of specularization. Although Freud presents himself as giving an objective psychoanalytic response to the question of sexual difference, there is an ingrained dogmatism about sex in his discourse, which prevents it from being scientific in the sense of maintaining a "sexual indifference." If Freud's were a sexually unbiased approach, even the declarative address to women that "you are yourselves the problem" (Freud 2001d, 113) must have sounded strange and inappropriate.

I conclude this section by coming back to my original question: why designate Freud as phallocentric? The term phallus is used to refer to an economy with phallic currency that describes *femininity* only in relation to *masculinity*. This economy leaves no space for *independent* femininity. I think Irigaray points to how the male sexual organ functions as the privileged signifier, the phallus of this economy. Insofar as the female sexual difference is characterized by the absence or the presence of the penis, the being of women would be submitted to a phallocentric economy which subordinates women to men.

IRIGARAY AND LACAN

Irigaray argues in *Speculum of the Other Woman, This Sex Which Is Not One*, and *An Ethics of Sexual Difference* that Western culture's symbolic and imaginary systems are monosexual. There is only one sex, the male sex; the female is defined in relation to the male. She aims to show that Lacan's psychoanalytical account of sexual difference is not an exception to that. She makes the claim that Lacan erases feminine sexual difference. What are the reasons that lead her to make such a claim?

In "The Signification of the Phallus," which is a text that dates from 1958, and included in *Écrits* (Lacan 2006), Lacan provides a reading of Freud's 1932 text entitled "Femininity" (Freud 2001d). In addition, the Seminars XVIII and XIX shed light on the phallic function and the essays on The Seminar XX (*Encore 1972–1973*) takes up the question of woman's *jouissance* beyond the phallic function. Let me start with a brief summary of Lacan's response to Freud's account of feminity. In Freud, male and female sexual difference is marked by the presence and absence of the male sexual organ. Having seen the genitals of his younger sister the little boy thinks of her as having lost it and imagines himself as vulnerable, that is as threatened by the deprivation of his penis as a punishment for the sexual desire he feels for his mother. The little girl, on the other hand, seeing that her little brother has a penis, imagines herself as having lost it. Lacan complicates Freud's account of castration by locating the function of the phallus in the symbolic order rather than focusing on the phallus as real and imaginary entity. Lacan transforms Freud's theory of sexuality in some important ways: for instance, castration is not understood as an imagined threat of a real father, it is interpreted based on the dialectic of desire that involves a reversal of the demand at the face of absence, a reversal that gives birth to the desire by the recognition of the Other's desire. In other words, it is the inevitable absence of the mother who fails to satisfy the child's infinite demand for her presence and the name of the father as the cause of her desire that set the conditions for the constitution of a castrated subject of desire who would enter the symbolic system by recognizing the law of the father. And, of course, the law belongs to the father, but it is the mother who recognizes it at first and implements it in the child's world. In Lacan's version, the father can be absent or even dead. His name alone is sufficient for the child to go through castration. Lacan argues that we all enter the symbolic system as castrated subjects, and this is the condition of being a subject of desire, a speaking subject. In other words, rather than being autonomous subjects we are split subjects, marked by loss, split by the signifier, lacking self-possession, vulnerable all through the process of subjectivation.

Lacan's reading of the phallic phase of sexual development is grounded on becoming a being of language by an entry into the symbolic system. He conceives of the symbolic system as a phallic system. The phallus is said to be a product of an *Aufhebung* that severs all ties with the body as a living being with organs and parts. Just like the penis is imagined as an organ severable from the body, the phallus appears as the operator of linguistic division. Such a division is necessary for desire to be signifiable and express-ible in language, and its being expressible is an essential property of desire. For Lacan, desire is demand minus need; hence it is always more than the satisfaction of desire by its object. He thinks phallus as the "master signifier" because one's relationship to it defines one's social existence. One is intro-duced to the world by the signifier as such, which he thinks we need to separate from its meaning effects. In his view, the signifier does not only call for a signified in the mental realm, it opens being-in-the-world, the world in which we are with the others.

How does the *phallus* manifest itself in the dialectic of desire? In "The Significance of the Phallus," there is a dialectic movement that goes from the need to the demand and gives birth to desire from the demand. The need looks for satisfaction. The demand is for the presence of the mother who satisfies the need. Needs are alienated in demand. Lacan's writes: "The de-mand for love can only suffer from a desire whose signifier is foreign to it" (Lacan 2006, 582). It is possible to go from the demand to the desire by a radical reversal (repression). Desire is the power of pure loss, for it gave up the demand for the satisfaction of needs. That repression results from the recognition of the other's desire, which gives rise to the desire for being the reason of the other's desire. For the fulfillment of the demand, for the mother to be there, she must desire the baby. The baby desires the desire of the mother, whose signifier is unknown and thus veiled. It can never know why the mother desires what she desires. The infant who experiences the absence of the mother wants to be whatever the mother desires—the phallus—in order to regain her attention. The infant's realization of the impossibility of the fantasy of mastering the mother's desire will make him enter the symbol-ic system in which it becomes a symbolic subject—a speaking subject. In Lacan's account, the *phallus* is not the sign of the penis. However, Irigaray sees it that way. She may be objecting to Lacan's choice of the word "*phal-lus*" to designate this veiled signifier, given that the term in ancient myths is the sign for the male sexual organ. This might seem arbitrary if there is no necessary connection between the *phallus* as a signifier of desire and the penis. According to Irigaray, this is a decision to keep the phallic currency and as long as we conserve it, we will continue to convert the non-phallic to the phallic and fail to free ourselves from the phallocentric economy.

Lacan says that the castration complex manifests "in the subject of an unconscious position without which he could not identify with the ideal type of his sex" (Lacan 2006, 575). We now call "gender" what he designates as "the ideal type of one's sex." One is assigned a biological sex at birth; however, one will not automatically be a woman or a man because one's body has female or male biological organs. To become woman or man one must assume the ideal type of one's biological sex, and that does not happen if the subject does not take an unconscious position in the symbolic order, which the castration complex makes possible. One becomes a man because one takes a position in the unconscious, that is, because a male unconscious is produced in the aftermath of the castration complex. And one becomes a woman because a female unconscious is produced due to penis envy. Lacan appreciates Freud because he has seen that disturbance is essential to human sexuality. The implication is that the *aporia* of gender cannot be solved just by looking at the biological data or by studying culture. The experience of becoming sexed or gendered is nothing biological; one must look at the way desire is structured. Lacan, as a reader of psychoanalysis through the lenses of modern linguistics, rejects a historical and cultural account that invokes gender norms as explananda. Although he is quite distant to the kind of analysis that Simone de Beauvoir makes in *The Second Sex*, the function of the mythological Other in *The Second Sex* can be compared to the Other in the Lacanian sense, understood as the language of the unconscious.

That Lacan is far from naturalism is clear in his interest in "a relation between the subject and the phallus that forms without regard to the anatomical distinction between the sexes" (Lacan 2006, 576). The relation with the phallus constitutes us as woman or man. Hence, one can be assigned male sex at birth and be a woman. The phallus is, in Lacan's terminology, the privileged signifier of the Other's desire, the key to it. The signifiable (meaning) appears as an effect of the relation between the signifiers. The phallus is the veiled signifier that organizes the play of the signifiers to give rise to some meaning effects, in accordance with which bodies are materialized as gendered. Lacan claims that woman occupies the position of "being the phallus" and man of "having the phallus." Hence, sexual difference is not natural or real, it is symbolic. We are symbolic beings: man's nature is woven with the effects of language—he is the "structure of the language of which he becomes the material" (Lacan 2006, 578). And the same can be said for woman. This is another confirmation of the claim that one is not born a woman or a man, but one becomes woman or man. Although we are in the grid of the heterosexual matrix here, Lacan does not say that there are only two possible ways of becoming corporeal (materialization).

In "The Signification of the Phallus," he takes up the fate of the sexual relationship in the "closed field of desire" (Lacan 2006, 580). Desire is wedded to logos, but the Other mediates all relation to the other (the sexual partner), in other words, messages alienate to the speaker and become as if they are emitted from the site of the Other. More importantly, in a relation of desire we do not know how the other's desire is organized and what its reasons are. I can neither know my own desire (why I desire this individual rather than somebody else) nor the privileged signifier of the desire of the person by whom I want to be desired. This is the reason why the desire of the other is indistinguishable from the desire of the Other. The upshot is that the Other scene in which the sexes encounter each other involves irreducible ambiguities, ambivalences, pretensions. The relation to the specific other cannot not be a relation to the Other. It follows that the possibility of sexual relation is at the same time its impossibility. Because there is an irreducible aporia here, any ethics of Eros would have to be aporetic as well.

From a Lacanian point of view Irigaray's critique of phallocentrism implies a refusal to recognize the necessity for symbolic castration (see Rose [1986] and Ragland-Sullivan [1986]) as a condition for the entrance into the symbolic system, on which women's symbolic subjectivity depends. On this account, Irigaray would also be depriving women from being subjects of desire. Margaret Whitford highlights the contradiction that has been at the center of the feminist readings of Lacan in *Feminism and Psychoanalyis: A Critical Dictionary*. As Elizabeth Wright puts it: "Lacan's theory paradoxically suggests at one and the same time (a) that sexual identities are the result of a process of construction and are not naturally or biologically given, so that identities formed in patriarchy are a construct, and thus, in theory, modifiable; and (b) that each individual has to insert him-or herself into a Symbolic order which already exists, so that the possibility of modifying patriarchy is so minimal as to be virtually non-existent" (Wright 1992, 302). Irigaray can accept that sexual identities are sexually constructed and that some symbolic system must always be there for bodies to manifest their sexual difference. The pressing problem is that she must come up with a different account of the speaking subject, which is not based on castration understood in the Lacanian sense. But how is the feminist subject possible at all? Must not she accept and take seriously the history of castration and challenge and wish to change it at the same time? Is this only Irigaray's problem?

Irigaray shares some common tenets with Lacan. For example, she would accept the Lacanian psychoanalytic idea that desire is a signification that is made possible by the displacement and condensation of signifiers, and only as such it is attached to the bodily drives. Desire for an object is accompanied with the unconscious investments and projections onto the object of desire, which represent it as desirable. Moreover, desire is bound to the laws that sexually position people and structure their interactions, making possible evaluations of behavior as meaningful, acceptable, appropriate, and intelligible, or as meaningless, awkward, inappropriate, and unintelligible. Hence the symbolic sets the stage, imprecisely specifies possible scenarios, and opens and closes possibilities of anticipation. This is how the world appears as meaningful to desiring subjects, even though the sphere of sexual relations has its own structural impasses and impossibilities. I think that it is perfectly possible that one commits one's self to the truth of these statements without having to accept that we enter the system as marked by the phallus. Why not imagine a symbolic system in which sexes are represented in relation to themselves and in ethical relations with each other? To be able to introduce signification to the body, in order to make the body a signifying body we need absence, plurality, and self-relation. Now, even if Irigaray can create images of female bodies that meet these conditions without being castrated, she would still need the Other in relation to which the subject signifies.

How does Irigaray deal with this problem? "The Other" is the name Lacan gives to the unconscious system of symbolic laws. It is the structuring alterity in language, which precedes the selves and contributes to their formation. It traverses selves, and orchestrates their social relations. The Other means radical alterity, irreducible to the conscious I and to the social contracts of the individuals. The Other is a collection of the conventions, which individuals have not consciously agreed to, but found themselves as presupposing. The Other is there like a custom, a social practice people do not have to justify. Thus, to speak of the "Other" is appropriate because what is at issue is neither a product nor an object of consciousness. It is an unconscious sedimentation. The moral world—which is a gendered world—is an effect of the operation of the radically Other. If we speculate about what gendering might be in a Lacanian context, we can say that it is not only about the symbolic setting up of the individuals in roles that they will play as sexed, it is also about how the Other enables them to make sense of events, future presumptions, and inferences about acts from where they stand. Although the source or the ground of the Other is radically unknown, it traverses the way people understand and evaluate, incites them to imagine, expect, give reasons, and make judgments. As in Simone de Beauvoir, in Lacan as well, the Other can have many faces and God is designated as a face of the Other.

Both in "The Signification of the Phallus" and in "God and the Jouissance of the Woman" the Other figures in puzzling ways. In "The Signification of the Phallus," the mother appears to be the first figure of the Other insofar as the formation of her desire is unknown to the infant. In fact, the Other cannot be identified with any other. If we take the statement "the Unconscious speaks the language of the Other," we can envision the Other as consisting of the structures, laws, and norms of language of which the Unconscious is constituted. The Other is also the mother's unconscious. In Lacan's account, the Other in whom the subject finds its signified place prior to any relation to the signified, does not recognize a desire or a pleasure that would be expressed independently of the phallus.

> The fact that the phallus is a signifier requires that it be in the place of the Other that the subject have access to it. But since this signifier is there only as veiled and as ratio [*raison*] of the Other's desire, it is the Other's desire as much that the subject is required to recognize in other words, the other insofar as he himself is a subject—in other words, the other insofar as he himself is a subject divided by the signifying *Spaltung*. (Lacan 2000, 582)

For Lacan, the phallus is veiled because of the *Aufhebung* that lets it operate, by severing all possible connection to a signified. This is the reason why the phallus has no reference to a body part. In the dialectic of the desire which passes from the need to the demand and from the demand to the desire, the phallus first signifies the reason for the mother's desire, it then spreads to structure all the desire of the impersonal divided subject, which operates in accordance with the laws governing the other scene, the Unconscious. This is how the Other intervenes in concrete sexual relations, to give rise to enjoyment and to suffering. Irigaray should be quoting Lacan when she says: "In other words, what we are saying is that love is impossible, and that the sexual relation is engulfed in non-sense, which doesn't diminish in the slightest the interest we must take in the Other" (Irigaray 1985b, 91–2).

Lacan articulates sexual difference according to a logic of "being" or "having." When the phallic phase is completed, x is woman if x took the position of being the phallus. She *is* the phallus, while he *has* the phallus (Lacan 2006, 582–83). Lacan's transcription of Freud is remarkable here: according to his symbolization, woman who lacks the phallus (because she does not know how the other's desire is organized) is the phallus (she may pretend that she is the phallus). And the man who lacks the phallus because he does not know how her desire is organized may pretend he has what she desires. The only difference here is that he thinks she wants something he has (other men may have it, too, because these are properties or things that people can possess) whereas she desires to be the unique cause of his desire. The fear of losing the organ in Freud's story is translated into the Lacanian symbolic as "having it," and the suffering for not having it as "being it." This symbolization establishes that woman and man belong to the logic of desire as castrated and pretending beings. They are in a relationship of desire as immersed in assumptions, pretensions made in the absence of understanding. She acts as if she is the phallus, for she tries to convince him that she is the unique cause of his desire, and he pretends that he is capable of satisfying her desire.

Lacan teaches us that it is not as simple as one is male if one has a penis and a female if one has a vagina. Being male means to enjoy male pleasures and being a female means to enjoy female pleasures. But enjoyment does not reduce to the pleasure of the body as a biological entity; it does not exist without being enfolded by imaginary and symbolic elements and structures. By making subjectivity a question of desire and by acknowledging that sexuality is an integral part of the imaginary and symbolic stages of the development of subjectivity, Lacan refuses to treat sexual difference as a biological matter. The body is first unified at the mirror stage; a narcissistic ego is formed, before the signifier divides it and it is the latter that makes possible the subject's sexual differentiation in the symbolic order. In Lacan's theory this happens through one's relationship to the master signifier, the phallus. The inscription of the signifier into the desire introduces an immanent division in it, which is first felt in the desire of the Other.

The *phallus* is the signifier which is the currency of desire in the in the economy of heterosexual world. Even though non-heterosexual relations cannot escape from it either. In fact, in the Lacanian framework, a woman who occupies the male position of having the phallus is in fact a man no matter how we have identified her at the first sight. And a person who is socially identified as man can occupy the place of a woman in the symbolic system and would be a woman. The Other in language forces infants to take this or that position in the symbolic order. In the symbolic of the patriarchal culture, male children are invited to take the position of having the phallus and female children the position of being the phallus. In the life of a gender non-conforming male child, the social coercion to take the privileged position of being man may result in pain and suffering if the child identifies with woman's position. In such a case, the advantages and disadvantages in the exercise of speaking subjectivity are hard to assess, because in the Lacanian framework, woman's relation to self-expression seems to be engulfed in shame or masquerade. Demands that the Other makes on gender non-conforming people will certainly make life difficult to live for them, and this may vary from person to person depending on the specific position the individual takes. Indeed, some positions can be more unimaginable and unintelligible than others given how the symbolic system is in the present.

The value of the phallus is determined in this phallic economy by the one who has the phallus. Being the site of substitutions, the phallus is inseparable from power constituted by whatever is desirable. Whoever possesses an erotic power based on whatever valuable assets one possesses in a sexual economy, be it a person who is socially identified as woman, the power in question is constituted in accordance with the logic of male domination. Lacan is offering an account of gender in terms of psychoanalysis and linguistic structuralism, which is very different than a notion of gender based on social construction. The symbolic precedes and grounds the social and cannot simply be reduced to the sociocultural. What does that imply? The symbolic is like a quasi-transcendental structure that underlies and sustains all cultural interaction. We cannot change culture at will or by convention without making significant transformation in the imaginary and symbolic.

In Irigaray's reading of Lacan the stress is on the phallocratic logic of the Lacanian Other. Irigaray asks why there is no female/feminine radical alterity in the symbolic system. She sees the question of otherness as an imaginary and symbolic matter. *Speculum of the Other Woman* established that the question of the alterity of the female, the "otherness" of women (Irigaray 1985a, 52) cannot manifest itself because of the a priorism of the same: feminine alterity that might be spoken of in the phallocentric symbolic system is no more than a symbolic and cultural construct because the system derives the female sex from the male sex. This is another way of saying that the phallocentric system is centered on one sex (male sex) and presents all the other sexed bodies in terms of the male sex.

Although in 1974, Irigaray made that point about Freud's articulation of sexual difference in *Speculum*, a year later she will argue that Lacan's account of sexual difference suffers from the same problem. In "Così Fan Tutti" (Irigaray 1985b), which was first published in 1975,[1] Irigaray gives a reading of Lacan's *Encore*, Seminar XX, this time problematizing the phallocentric approach in Lacan's discussion of women (female/feminine sexual difference). According to him, the sexes are constituted in and through language. Sex is nothing before discourse; the sexed body as real prior to the discourse is an imaginary and symbolic construct. As Lacan puts it: "There is no pre-discursive reality. Every reality is based upon and defined by discourse" (Lacan 1999, quoted in Irigaray 1985b, 88). Feminists can object, "this discourse is perhaps not all there is"; to this objection his response will be "that it is women who are not-all" (Irigaray 1985b, 88). Feminists are asking about the non-phallic reality of women's sexual enjoyment. Lacan responds:

> There is jouissance that is hers (*à elle*), that belongs to the "she" (*elle*) that does not exist and does not signify anything. There is jouissance that is hers about which she herself perhaps knows nothing if not that she experiences it— that much she knows. She knows it, of course, when it comes (*arrive*). It doesn't happen (*arrive*) to all of them. (Lacan 1999, 74)

Lacan does not think that all women have some sexual excessive enjoyment, but he acknowledges that there are women who admit to having an excessive experience of it. If by "excessive" is meant the excess over the symbolic and the imaginary representations, to admit its possibility is an acknowledgment of the existence of the real that cannot be spoken of, and that remains outside the system, as a lived experience of sexuality. Lacan accepts that there is reality prior to enjoyment, but he also suggests that reality can be approached with the apparatuses of enjoyment (language) (Lacan 1999, 55). If this enjoyment cannot be known and become an object of signification, women would only live it when it arrives.

But the point could be that whatever is lived is structured by language in the unconscious. Let's take the claim that women are "not-all": it is possible to misunderstand this expression by taking it to mean that women are lacking. Lacan is not saying that because women are represented in the order of discourse as lacking, an excessive sexual enjoyment (*jouissance*), which is not representable within the symbolic system, is possible for them. By "not-all" he means the separation of a woman from her own sex (women) by being designated as unlike them. As an object of love a woman is symbolically individuated by distinction from other women. Being like other women is equivalent to being disvalued, degraded, and marked in language as unworthy of being loved. But there is nothing non-phallic in this; on the contrary, this purports to be a description of women's phallic sexual enjoyment. What makes the experience of enjoyment "supplementary" or "excessive" may be the unconscious jubilation of being preferred to other women. Hence she does not excessively enjoy sexual pleasure in relation to him, because of what he gives, but in relation to her own sex—a relation of rivalry and competition.

So is there really female excessive non-phallic pleasure outside of the sphere of representation? Lacan invokes art works (more specifically, Bernini's sculpture *The Ecstasy of Saint Theresa* in Santa Maria della Vittoria in Rome) that represent women mystics' experiences of ecstasy in the yearning to unite with God, as evidence. He considers the facial expression of Saint Theresa as an indication of an excessive female sexual pleasure in its transfiguration into a form of religious experience. I think that Lacan should be familiar with the association between the erotic and the mystic experiences from his acquaintance with Bataille's *Erotism*, which was first published in 1957. In "God and Woman's Jouissance," he speaks beyond an exegetical style in response to the feminist concerns about his previous texts on feminine sexuality. He says that any speaking being whatsoever that lines up under the banner of women is placed within the phallic function by being constituted as not-all (Lacan 1999, 72). He concludes that this prevents us from speaking of her as the woman insofar as the definite article stands for the universal, and of attributing an essence to women. The constitution of woman's being as "not-all" by the phallic function comes with a supplementary jouissance (which is not complementary) (Lacan 1999, 73). "God and Woman's Jouissance" considers women's jouissance, which the system cannot contain, as represented by the ecstatic experiences of women saints.

In Bataille's *Erotism*, Saint Theresa's mystical experience had already been considered, though his interest had a different aim: to explore the connection between the religious signification and the erotic experience. Lacan's point is different: In a symbolic order in which women are constituted by the phallic function, non-phallic jouissance would still be a relation to the Other. Religious ecstasy in a female mystic is referred to as the concretization in a representation of the female supplementary or excessive sexual enjoyment. At issue here is an image of a possible non-phallic real, which calls for a philosophical discussion of the role of the imaginary in relation to the real and the symbolic.

In "The Blind Spot," Irigaray invokes the mirror stage in order to make sense of Lacan's theory of subject formation as sexed. Lacan himself does not speak of the mirror stage in terms of sexual difference. At the mirror stage the infant acknowledges the inseparability of the I from his or her bodily existence, through the mediation of an image in the mirror. The problem concerns the articulation of the conditions of possibility of the infant's ability to relate to the image as its own. For that to happen, the image has to be mediated by the other's gaze. The mirror stage makes the infant accede to the reality of its own corporeal being through the imaginary. The mirror stage implies that both the perceptibility and the intelligibility of the subject's body are bound by the organization of the image and the linguistic signs and symbols, and that sexual difference belongs to the formation of subjectivity. The symbolic order does not only make speaking subjects possible, it also assigns the body the meaning it is supposed to have. Even the choice of regarding bodies as embodying created essences or as the natural products of evolutionary processes is a symbolic decision. Theoretical commitments about bodies depend on how they are going to be represented. How we live and enjoy our bodies is a different matter. Lacan gives a dialectical account of the transition from nature to culture, which has to do with becoming a subject of desire. The desiring subject is caught up in an economy of sameness, to which it is conveyed by the dialectic of desire, that constitutes it in the unconscious relation to the Other. The upshot of Irigaray's critique of the Lacanian model of desiring subjectivity is that it perpetuates the culture that is negatively biased against women. As this system cannot allow for the self-expression of feminine alterity, it has trouble representing women's sexual enjoyment.

Elizabeth Grosz in *Volatile Bodies* shows in detail the sources of Lacan's imaginary anatomy with reference to neurophysiologists, neuropsychologists, and psychoanalysts (Grosz 1994, ch. 2 and 3). The imaginary anatomy is an internalized image or map of the meaning of the body for the subject, for others in the social world, and the symbolic order conceived in its generality (that is for a culture as a whole) (Grosz 1994, 39–40). Imaginary anatomy is first produced through the mirror stage (Lacan 2006, 75–81), which refers to the event of the infant's first identification with itself through an image, which is its own and deceiving at the same time. Margaret Whitford argues that Irigaray's use of the term the "imaginary" does not only refer to Lacan's use of the term; it also converses with Sartre's *L'Imaginaire* (Sartre 1940) and Gaston Bachelard's *L'Air et les Songes* (Bachelard 1943) (Whitford 1991b, 54–56). The imaginary schemes a culture projects to produce itself should be the ground for a moral evaluation of that culture. Western culture auto-affects and produces itself via the mirror image of male body. Fields such as philosophy and psychoanalysis are clearly dominated by the image of masculine body. What about female bodies beyond their representations as objects of the male gaze?

In Lacan's mirror stage, at issue are the first formation of the I, giving rise to the feelings of jubilation in case one successfully identifies with one's self through the gaze of the other, and the feelings of aggression, in case the identification fails. The deception involved in identifying with an image and the other's gaze, which makes such a relation possible for the first time, is pivotal to Lacan's narrative. The first formation of the ego is narcissistic, and this narcissism rests on a self-relation through the relation with the other, from which deception and alienation cannot be eliminated. For Lacan this primary narcissism is a necessary step toward the symbolic formation of subjectivity. In *Speculum* Irigaray emphasizes that in Freud's discourse on femininity, femininity is distorted by a specularization through the male gaze. The Freudian imaginary does not allow for genuine duality or plurality of the sexes because it presupposes the same. It imposes a monosexual differentiation: the "differentiation" into two sexes derives from the *a priori* assumption of the same. Since the little girl was originally a little man, when she grows up she must become a man minus certain attributes. The morphological properties of the female body are evoked in accordance with the logic that assures the specularization, which is the reproduction of the same. Irigaray's interpretative strategy is based on highlighting that the imaginary specularization and the symbolic designation support and complement each other. In the case of the girl, the coherence between the imaginary and symbolic orders guarantee that she goes through the primary narcissism as fragmented. The lack inserted into her body turns her to a being for him. In *Speculum* Irigaray criticizes Freud in a Lacanian interpretation of him. This reading is at the same time a criticism of Lacan, because Irigaray's call for a new feminine imaginary and symbolic goes completely against the core of Lacan's theoretical account of sexual difference.

How does Irigaray approach the Lacanian threefold distinction between the real, the imaginary, and the symbolic? Does she commit herself to the view that the real is accessible only through the imaginary and the symbolic? This is an important question because the well-known accusation of essentialism directed to Irigaray's thought of sexual difference cannot be adequately answered before one manages to clarify the obscurity about how she welds the three orders together. Before one responds to this concern, one should remember that, as Margaret Whitford argues, Irigaray is not a theorist. "She is writing both/neither theory and/nor fiction, since she wishes not merely to state or claim, but also to show, manifest in her writing a different kind of parole" (Whitford 1986, 8). This writing has the double function of destruction and resignification. On the one hand, Irigaray pursues a method of destruction to attain the traces of the effaced or unrepresented real, and on the other hand, she underscores the importance of creating new imaginary and symbolic vocations so that this real becomes present. The double strategy of destruction and resignification approximates a phenomenological hermeneutics of the unapparent (that which does not, cannot yet appear).

> [E]ven with the help of linguistics, psychoanalysis cannot solve the problem of the articulation of the female sex in discourse. [. . .] What remains to be done, then, is to work at "destroying" the discursive mechanism. (Irigaray 1985b, 76)

What is exactly meant by destruction here? The destruction of the discursive mechanism includes an exposition of the conditions under which utterances are produced such as the matter of which the speaking subject nourishes itself in order to produce and reproduce itself, the constitution of the scene of representation, the architectonics of the scene, the framing of space and time, the actors, their positions, roles, dialogues, relations with each other, and the mirror, "most often hidden, that allows the logos, the subject, to reduplicate itself, to reflect itself by itself" (Irigaray 1985b, 75) Resignification is a return to the female morphology, the female body and its specific drives, to feminine pleasures.

Nonetheless, Irigaray sounds sometimes as if her pre-discursive real has already been a site of meaning in an immemorial past; even though the patriarchal and phallocentric system suppressed its imaginary representation and symbolic signification. This is interpreted as an element of fiction in Irigaray's performative texts. Even though female/feminine alterity with her own imaginary and symbolic would be inaccessible in its ancient form, this fiction sets up the imaginary and the symbolic as sites of repetition and invention. Irigaray fashions a female imaginary by exploring the morphological traits of the female body and thus substantiates her claim that the imaginary is sexed. The male imaginary and its cultural creations bear the marks of linearity, teleology, self-coincidence whereas the female imaginary would unfold in cultural creations that are characterized by plurality, fluidity, non-coincidence. Whitford reminds us that Lacan's "imaginary" may not be the only source of Irigaray's use of the term "imaginary":

> The imaginary, for Lacan, tends to be presented in rather pessimistic terms as a kind of trap, since imaginary identifications are essentially illusory and imprisoning, images of the self, which are alienating insofar as the subject does not

> realize that they are no more than images. Irigaray, in contrast, is seeking to
> make the emergence of a female imaginary possible and so has a more positive
> attitude towards the imaginary. (Whitford 1986, 4)

For Lacan, imaginary is the domain of the pre-linguistic specular identifica-
tions and the identity that these imaginations give rise to are unstable and
flimsy because they are dependent on the gaze of the other that may shift its
perspective at will and become mercilessly negative or even cruel. In
contrast, identity in the symbolic order depends on language and symbolic
representation. Signifiers can infinitely substitute for each other to mediate
an identity crisis and even make a new identity possible. Indeed, Lacan
seems to argue that in the course of the formation of identity, imaginary
identification will be superseded by symbolical identity. Irigaray thinks differently than Lacan: the imaginary passes over to the symbolic or at least,
culture takes up some imaginary objects to translate them into the symbolic
and ignores others. The phallocentric symbolic order does not translate the
female imaginary creations. How are we going to know about that which
does not get translated? Irigaray remarks that the female imaginary manifests
itself as *"those components of the mirror that cannot reflect themselves"*
(Irigaray 1985b,151).

For Irigaray, an exploration of the feminine imaginary is necessary in
order to open the possibility of another desire, another subjectivity. Desire in
psychoanalysis is ultimately desire for the self-identical, the self (as) same,
and of the similar, the alter ego, the desire for the auto, homo. The differentiation of the two sexes derives from the *a priori* assumption of the same. Both
Freud and Lacan posit a sexual difference based on the *"a priori* same." They
understand difference, understood as opposition and binary division, by the
presence or absence of a single term. At the beginning, the little girl was a
little boy. As Irigaray says, "she must become a man minus certain attributes
whose paradigm is morphological" (Irigaray 1985b, 27). This construction
assures the reproduction of the same by way of specularization. Woman = a
man minus the possibility of representing one's self as a man. Thus, psychoanalysis is one example among others of male specularization: a body of
knowledge inscribed with perspectives and interests relevant to men; the
investments of masculinity via a denial of the alterity outside of the specular
subject's self-definitions. The masculine can speak of and for the feminine
largely because it has emptied itself of any relation to the male body, its
specificity, and socio-political existence. This process of evacuating the male
body from (an Oedipalized) masculinity is the precondition for the establish-
ment of the "disinterested" neutered space of male specularization. Within
this (virtual and imaginary) space, the space of the ego, and its double in the
mirror, the male can look at itself from the outside, take itself as an object
while retaining its position as a subject. It gains the illusion of self-distance,

the illusion of a space of pure reflection, through the creation of a mirroring surface that duplicates subject at the imaginary order. In contrast, psychoanalysis forces the female imaginary to constrain itself to the creation of a mirroring surface that duplicates, represents everything except itself.

Although Irigaray addresses the reality of the real, which is deprived of its imaginary and the symbolic through fiction, she does not commit herself to unchanging, eternal structures or natural essences. In "The Eternal Irony of Community," she analyzes Antigone's speech with reference to a matriarchal symbolic, which has been defeated and obliterated by the patriarchal symbolic. In Antigone, Irigaray sees the symptoms of a historically repressed difference. In her reading of Sophocles's tragedy, she grounds the feminine irony (mascarade) of patriarchal cultural domination as a consequence of the effacement of sexual difference. Undoubtedly, symbolic struggles belong to concrete power struggles and new social and political orders survive if they can legitimate themselves by discourse, by building their own symbolism. Although Lacan saw nothing political in his choice of the phallus as the master signifier, for Irigaray this is compliance with the existing relations of power. Even though he strongly emphasizes that the phallus as a purely symbolic category of subjectivity is independent of an anatomical connection with the male body, Lacan's preference of that symbol already suggests a commitment to a unilateral model of interpreting the social dynamics between the two sexes. Irigaray thinks that the choice Lacan makes confirms Freud's male-centered theory. She rejects Lacan's treatment of the symbolic order by giving it the status of an ahistorical transcendental scheme; in her approach, the symbolic order and its laws are constructs based on the reversal of the concrete power dynamics, expressions of cultural revolutions.

Let us return to our question of the reality of sexual essences. The real can only appear if the imaginary can pass it into the symbolic. In case the imaginary creation is impeded, the pre-discursive real can only be posited even though nothing can be said about it. Lacan notes that in psychoanalysis a living body means a body, which is capable of sexual enjoyment. And sexual enjoyment implies "corporealization in a signifying manner" (Irigaray 1985b, 92). The body is neither a material substance, *partes extra partes*, nor an organism with an environment as in the case of animal life. People have desires in contrast to animals that have instincts. The erotic body is an enjoying body; a body that enjoys itself precisely as the Other symbolizes it. The Other determines how male and female bodies are supposed to enjoy their bodies. Thus it turns them into enjoying substances. The question thus arises if there can be an enjoying body without relation to the Other? In Irigaray's view, Lacan speaks here of a projective machinery from which no corporeality can escape, and which transforms the body and the way the body lives its own sexual pleasures (Irigaray 1985b, 88). She argues that this machinery, the necessary laws of which are fantasy constructions, chops up and mortifies the real body. This is what Lacan's phallocentrism does to women's bodies. The phallocratic structures do not reveal any scientific truths. Men inscribe women as not-all into these structures to design a way to pursue her; however, women do not exist because language, as the master, positions them in a certain way. Men, too, are aware that she is not wholly there in language, and that her pre-discursive reality continues to threaten to disrupt his order (Irigaray 1985b, 89).

The Other, which we cannot identify with any other, and which appears to approximate the objects of negative theology produces sexed bodies by gendering them. As Irigaray remarks: "It is the Other that makes the not-all, precisely in that the Other is the element of the not-knowledgeable-at-all in this not-all" (Irigaray 1985b, 93). And here gendering would be a process of bringing a reality into being through imaginary and symbolic means. Women and men are different, because Lacan notes that the Other takes women one by one. Because women are not-all, they do not form a universal category. In Irigaray's view, what Lacan calls "The Other" is the unconscious place in which the male fantasies or imaginary constructions are inscribed. These fantasies are powerful and must be wrestled with in the symbolic sense. The prediscursive corporeal reality Irigaray refers to is the irreducible remainder she designates, by using Antonine Artaud's term, as "body without organs" (Irigaray 1985b, 90). This implies that the prediscursive body can challenge the mastery of the phallocentric system over women's bodies by refusing to use its organs in accordance with the functions the system assigns to them.

Irigaray argues that, for ethical reasons, there ought to be two different models of sexual difference, which enable us to symbolically position the two sexes independently of one another. These models would produce and reproduce the symbolic expressions. In my view, such expressions may turn into essences that last in being or fall depending on the ethical reasons for their existence. But even if Irigaray rejects the existence of the non-linguistic essences in the domain of sex, the limitation of the symbolically created essences by two is an ethical problem. If there are two models, two symbolic systems, people will have to be categorized by two. And an individual who objects to being classified as male or female shall still have no place in sexed existence.

Let me recapitulate: first of all, Irigaray takes both Freud's and Lacan's accounts of sexual difference to have opened important paths of reflection into the materialization of sexual difference. Secondly, she distances herself both to Freud's monosexual, unilateral, or reductive view of femininity and to Lacan's positioning of the phallus as the master-signifier of the symbolic order as an ahistorical transcendental system that specifies the default categories and norms of the becoming present of a sexed subject. Freud's discourse represents a particular social and cultural economy, the political economy in which Sex is One. Freud's reduction rests on an organistic argument that assimilates women's sex to a lack. Did Lacan surpass the phallocentrism in his reinterpretation of psychoanalysis by way of the structuralist linguistics? Did he not arrive at the same conclusion, by designating women as not-all? Irigaray argues that this is indeed the case. Thirdly, Irigaray adopts a mimicry which she believes can at once destroy the old system and re-inscribe there the alterity that that system ignores. She allows for the possibility of alterations and normative inventions in the symbolic system, which would require psychoanalysis to be more than a discourse with scientific pretensions that reproduce the patriarchal forms of subjectivity.

Although both Freud and Lacan pretend that psychoanalysis speaks a sexually neutral language (like other dominant discourses), which is universal and disinterested, Irigaray argues that this language is in fact a product of men's self-representations. Psychoanalysis cannot really include women unless it leaves the monosexual model behind. This would be to open it to sexual difference beyond the patriarchal fantasy dictates; the institution of a symbolic that makes room for genuine sexual alterity and plurality. If Freud's psychoanalysis represents the pre-Oedipal/Oedipal and the imaginary/symbolic pairs of structures from the point of view of the boy; the new task should be to re-interpret them from the girl's perspective. Irigaray focuses on the under-represented pre-Oedipal forms of mother/daughter relations and explores a feminine imaginary. It is also worthwhile to note that, although she is presupposing the male female duality, she made significant contributions to lesbian symbolism. "It seems that the phallic instinctual script is never written out so clearly as in the case of *female homosexuality* [Irigaray's italics]" (Irigaray 1985a, 99). She remarks that Freud's entire analysis on female homosexuality is actually about male homosexuality.[2] Surely, Irigaray holds a dualist position, however, that does not imply that she opts for heterosexuality as a better choice than homosexuality. The critiques coming from queer theorists are nevertheless valid. The theorists of sexual difference who came to Irigaray's defence against such critiques have responded that even if sexual difference is unlimited, all possible differentiations result from the two (Grosz 2012, 72). The binary is for them the ground of plurality. In the last analysis, Irigaray's notion of sexual difference rests on the duality of male and female sex as biologically real even though she is less interested in explaining what that reality consists of than whether the imaginary and symbolic economies of signification are sufficiently fair to allow that the female sex, which is fluid and plural, express itself in the culture.

THE REAL AND THE IMAGINARY

In contrast to the realist readings of Irigaray that seek to reach the real, Whitford sees Irigaray's fundamental question as being about the possibility of a feminine unconscious. Her interpretation primes the imaginary rather than the real. Irigaray follows Lacan in refusing to talk about women, sexuality, and desire in terms of the real, natural essences. Freud argued that the libido is male. This is not a statement about the real, but rather a determination concerning the imaginary character of psychic life. Are there in what has been designated as the "unconscious" some censored, repressed elements of the feminine? The working hypothesis is here the following: We cannot interpret psychic life without images and the language that symbolizes them. Both the unity and the cohesion of the ego, and the parameters and the structures of the body as it lives and enjoys itself depend on signifying practices and symbolic representations. Although I agree with Elizabeth Grosz that Irigaray sees in nature dynamic forces, multiple tendencies, and potentialities, and that she envisions a nature that rises itself to the cultural and spiritual, I would also stress that she reads such forces psychoanalytically, as drives, in need of images and symbolic representations to give rise to a self-affecting body, a body that enjoys itself in relation to the other. Irigaray returns to female morphologies because our primary imaginary and symbolic significations are derived from our body, and in turn our bodies think and act, become materialized and real within imaginary and symbolic structures. When Irigaray seeks to invent a feminine imaginary based on female morphology, she does not appeal to biology or anatomy; she focuses into images of self-affection, which can give rise to the expression of social/ psychical relations. Margaret Whitford says that in the creation of the new symbolic by way of imagining the unimaginable "what is at stake is the ethical, ontological, and social status of women" (Whitford 1991b, 22).

Irigaray does not think of difference as an essence; she considers difference in the way sexes exist, in their self-relation, relation to the other, and relation to the world. She goes in the direction of a phenomenological/existentialist ontology rather than of an ontology of essences. Hence, she should also reject an ontology of substances, attributes, and properties. Why are there differences between the worlds the sexes create? To talk about bodies by comparing them to other bodies, to designate some as lacking or deficient, and others as endowed with superior properties and complete is morally unacceptable because it leads to a moral inequality in which some bodies appear in terms of the way of existing of the other bodies. And this obstructs their world creating possibilities. Freudian economy substituted the capacity to give birth for lacking the penis, without objecting to the existence of an economy that defines the value of one sex in terms of another. The birth of difference in the way different sexes inhabit the world depends on the cultivation of drives, which is a matter of imagination. As Alison Stone recognizes in the book review she wrote for *The Way of Love*, "Each subject must 'cultivate' his or her natural drives by practising 'negativity' towards him or herself, restraining his/her desire to appropriate the other in order to listen to the other, to allow the other to speak" (Stone 2004b, 318).

In *This Sex Which Is Not One*, Irigaray postulates that there is a different form of self-affection for each sex. The image of two lips is not just a sexual image; it indicates a drive, an orifice made of mucous and skin that connects the outside and the inside. The two lips that touch each other represent a female erotogenic zone as a zone of self-affection, as a site of communication and recognition of the other's self-affection. The two lips is a metaphor of a force of subjectivation. As Whitford notes: "The importance of the mucous as a symbolic term is that it offers a way of representing the imaginary body as non-phallic, without recourse to the concept of castration, and therefore proposes a different symbolic economy . . ." (Whitford 1991a, 104). It is possible to see here an "imaginary anatomy," which constitutes the foundation of a symbolic representation of the female body as not One, beyond pure identity. Thus, Irigaray attains an understanding of female sexual difference as "pure difference," difference without positive terms. In other words, this difference should not be understood as a relation to man, but as an altogether different space for women, the female body as a site of differences. As such a place, the feminine body is conceived as a mediation of relations; it is always already matter animated by a language, always already sexuate flesh. My contention is that to interpret this body as involving a real essence would be to misrecognize the ontological commitments Irigaray makes. When Alison Stone recontextualizes essentialism in the context of feminist philosophy to give an interpretation of Irigaray's late work in terms of realist essentialism, she tends to forget that Irigaray is far from metaphysics of object and property. Stone writes:

> Recontextualized within feminist philosophy, "essentialism" becomes the view that there are properties essential to women, in that any woman must necessarily have these properties to be a woman at all. So defined, essentialism entails a closely related view, *universalism*: that there are some properties, which are shared by, or common to, all women—since without these properties they could not be women in the first place. Essential properties, then, are also universal. "Essentialism" as generally debated in feminist contexts embraces this composite view: that there are properties essential to women and which all women therefore share. (Stone 2004a, 8)

Even if we agree with the claim that Irigaray wants to think the real (in fact just like Lacan did at the end of his career), it is too far-fetched to presume that her quest for the real lends itself to an interpretation in terms of object ontology. To ponder on the real in an ontology of flesh and to address the real in an object ontology are very different undertakings. How convincing would it be to substitute the Anglo-Saxon philosophical discussions of realism for Irigaray's post-psychoanalytical and post-phenomenological relation to the real? Are we ready to admit that Irigaray, when she calls for a return to the real, is renouncing to her early project altogether to commit herself to an ontology of present-at-hand? Alison Stone sees what Irigaray does in *Speculum* and *This Sex Which Is Not One* as "reimagining symbolic femininity" (Stone 2004a, 7) and *An Ethics of Sexual Difference* as a turn to the real as capable of expressing itself vis à vis some symbolic structures, which may have positive or negative effects on bodies' self-expressions. I grant that Irigaray's own language can be misleading or open to misinterpretation: "I start from reality, from a universal reality, sexual difference. . . . This reality of the two has always existed. But it was submitted to the imperative logic of the *one* . . ." (Irigaray 2000, 146–47).

What does it mean to start with the real? Do we know how to start with it? If it means taking the real as a source of the imaginary and the symbolic, over against the existing traditional symbolic of the *one*—this would still be to relate to nature imaginatively. Natural differences signify if our imagination lets them do so, if it does not foreclose this space for self-affection. The position that natural differences signify by themselves, in virtue of their natural essences or principles, is plain naturalism. The real appears as signifying in virtue of imagination, and our capacity to imagine it differently is the only way to liberate the real from the yoke of the symbolic that distorts its self-manifestation. To think of the real as *pure difference* implies that the states of masculinity and femininity are ultimately indeterminable, always as stemming from self-affection, therefore in a state of becoming. Indeed, this accords with Irigaray's statement that there are no fixed positions and that we are all becoming together (Irigaray 2001, 55). I think this sharply contests the attempt to think the real as an essence, if essentiality implies the precedence of some unifying principle in the nature of a being. Alison Stone agrees that in Irigaray's early work nature has no determinate character prior to cultural development, however, she denies that this is true for her late work: culture has agency vis-à-vis nature only because culture arises from an internal division *within nature itself* (Stone 2003, 417). It is fine to think of nature as internally divided; I think there is room for arguing that in her late work Irigaray tends to conceive nature as capable of rising to the imaginary and to the symbolic. But what does that mean? It means that nature can inspire us into a new way of being-with, a new manner of inhabiting the earth. Human beings have the preference to embrace some images rather than others, and this is part of what is meant by the self-affection of nature. Irigaray tries to create a new symbolic by choosing to elaborate on some images rather than others that are given to us in our experience of nature. This is to take nature as a model, to view it as a source of ethics, which does not have anything in common with the essentialist realism as Alison Stone defines it.

To conclude, in the early work Irigaray remakes the speculum by creating a female imaginary. As Margaret Whitford argues, she substitutes instead of the flat mirror, the curved, distorted medium of women's self-observation and self-representation. Her "mirror" surrounds, and is surrounded by, the contours of the specificity of the female body. It is not a device of self-distance, but of self-touching. In the late work, Irigaray becomes interested in the phenomenon of reversibility that is the landmark of an ontology of flesh, for which the problem is no longer how to reach the real by stripping out the imaginary and the symbolic layers, but to see what new images and symbols nature can offer us. Nature is interpreted as a site of self-affection, and as already productive of the symbolic.

REFERENCES

Bachelard, Gaston. 1943. *L'Air et les songes*. Librairie José Corti.
Freud, Sigmund. 2001b. "Female Sexuality." In *Standard Edition of the Complete Pyschological Works of Sigmund Freud*. Vol. 21. Translated by James Strachey. London: Hogarth Press and the Institute of Psycho-Analysis.
———. 2001d. "Femininity." In *Standard Edition of the Complete Pyschological Works of Sigmund Freud*. Vol. 24. Translated by James Strachey. London: Hogarth Press and the Institute of Psycho-Analysis.
Grosz, Elizabeth. 1990. *Jacques Lacan: A Feminist Introduction*. London and New York: Routledge.
———. 1989. *Sexual Subversions. Three French Feminists*. Sydney: Allen & Unwin.
———. 1994. *Volatile Bodies: Towards a Corporeal Feminism*. Bloomington and Indianapolis: Indiana University Press.
———. 2012. "The Nature of Sexual Difference: Irigaray and Darwin." *Angelaki* 17, no. 2 (July): 69–93.
Irigaray, Luce. 1985a. *Speculum of the Other Woman*. Ithaca, NY: Cornell University Press.
———. 1985b. *This Sex Which Is Not One*. Translated by Catherine Porter with Carolyn Burke. Ithaca, NY: Cornell University Press.
———. 1993. *An Ethics of Sexual Difference*. Translated by Carolyn Burke and Gillian C. Gill. Ithaca, New York: Cornell University Press.
———. 2000. *Why Different? A Culture of Two Subjects: Interviews with Luce Irigaray*. Edited S. Lotringer. Translated by C. Collins. New York: Semiotext(e).
———. 2001. *To Be Two*. New York: Routledge. 2001.
Lacan, Jacques. 1999. *Encore: The Seminar of Jacques Lacan: On Feminine Sexuality, the Limits of Love and Knowledge, 1972–1973*. Book 20. Edited by Jacques-Alain Miller. Translated with notes by Bruce Fink. New York and London: W.W. Norton & Company. Originally published as *Le Séminaire, Livre XX, Encore* (Paris: Éditions du Seuil, 1975).
———. 2006. *Écrits*. Translated by Bruce Fink. New York and London: W.W. Norton & Company.
———. 2008. *The Seminar of Jacques Lacan: The Ethics of Psychoanalysis*. Book VII. Edited by Jacques-Alain Miller. Translated with notes by Dennis Porter. New York and London: W.W. Norton & Company.
Nancy, Jean-Luc and Lacou-Labarthe Philippe. 1992. *The Title of the Letter: A Reading of Lacan*. Translated by François Raffoul and David Pettigrew. Albany: State University of New York Press.

Rose, Jacqueline. 1985. "Introduction II." In *Feminine Sexuality: Jacques Lacan and the école freudienne*, edited by Juliet Mitchell and Jacqueline Rose, 27–58. Translated by Jacqueline Rose. New York and London: W.W. Norton and Pantheon Books.

Sartre, Jean-Paul. 1940. *L'imaginaire*. Paris: Gallimard.

Stone, Alison. 2003. "Irigaray and Hölderlin on the Relation between Nature and Culture." *Continental Philosophy Review* 36, no. 4 (December): 415–32.

———. 2004a. "From Political to Realist Essentialism: Re-Reading Luce Irigaray," *Feminist Theory* 5(1): 5–23.

———. 2004b "The Way of Love, by Luce Irigaray, translated by Heidi Bostic and Stephen Pluháĉek," *Journal of the British Society for Phenomenology* 35, no. 3: 318–20.

Sullivan, Ellie Raglan. 1986. *Jacques Lacan and the Philosophy of Psychoanalysis*. Chicago: University of Illinois Press.

Whitford, Margaret. 1986. "Luce Irigaray and the Female Imaginary: Speaking as a Woman." *Radical Philosophy* 43, no. 4: 3–8.

———. 1991a. "Irigaray's Body Symbolic." *Hypatia* 6, no. 3: 97–110.

———. 1991b. *Philosophy in the Feminine*. London and New York: Routledge.

Wright, Elizabeth. 1992. *Feminism and Psychoanalysis A Critical Dictionary*. Oxford and Cambridge: Basil Blackwell.

NOTES

1. Originally published in *Vel*, no. 2, 1975.
2. He constitutes the female homosexual to reflect masculinity—a lesbian rebels against castration. Freud had female homosexual patients during his work as psychiatrist. One of them, which Irigaray discusses, is described by Freud as having "her father's tall figure, and her facial features were sharp rather than soft and girlish, traits which might be regarded as indicating a physical masculinity." Her intellectual talents were likened to masculine characteristics. The title of this section reveals Irigaray's stance on Freud's account of female homosexuality: "Female Hom(m)osexuality." The "(m)" testifies the "Homme"-relatedness of the so-called female sexuality, "homme" being the French word for "man." Because even though the homosexuality is female, it is as if it was male to begin with. The lesbian is considered, by Freud, unsuccessful in achieving normal sexuality, normal femininity. She has become narcissistic; she takes her own sex as the object of love. The linguistic choices that Freud makes in representing the lesbian's sex presents another understanding of a modality of femininity in term of masculinity.

Chapter Four

Different Ontologies in Queer Theory

This chapter focuses on the debate over the "real" in different ontologies of sex. I shall first talk about how Butler offers rather distorted interpretations of Beauvoir and Irigaray in *Gender Trouble* to accentuate her own ontology of the gendered body. Then I turn to her notions of "performativity" and "agency" to explain how her ontology differs from existentialism. Finally, I compare Butler's ontology of gender with the naturalist ontologies of sexual difference, notably with those of Elizabeth Grosz and Claire Colebrook, to show how these ontologies of the body differ from each other.

Naturalism, broadly conceived, is the position that the sexed body is a natural reality. Feminist materialist naturalism rejects the essentialist version of naturalism on which the patriarchal account of sexual difference that justifies male domination has traditionally relied. In contrast to a teleological and essentialist conception of nature, feminist materialism conceives nature in terms of dynamic forces, as consisting of open-ended and nonteleological processes. In this view, sexual difference appears as a contingent product of nature, which is not limited by the male-female binary.

The central question from the ontological point of view is the following: are there bodies prior to the systems of power which materialize them? For Butler, the natural real is not only inaccessible independently of discourse; the presupposition that there is a natural reality of sex is part of gender. This sounds non-persuasive and counter-scientific to most people. For example, most practitioners in medical science can tell you that there is a female body and male body for medical science. To these scientists, a Butlerian queer theorist should respond by insisting that the male body and female body are socially constructed categories. Whether or not it makes sense to define sex as a gradation or spectrum, non-essentialist naturalists argue that nature has more varieties than we allow for. How nature is "in itself" becomes irrelevant once we hold the Butlerian view that both sex and gender are constructions of discourse/power regimes, although there is still an ongoing debate over the question whether gender identity, binary and nonbinary, can be natural, biological, and real.

In my reading, Butler makes the strong claim that that there is a natural reality of the body is a presupposition of gendering. The body as a being of nature is always already cultural, a constructed category. Reality for Butler means social reality, the constitution of which she tries to explain. Butler's anti-naturalist line of argument formulates itself in response to Beauvoir's and Irigaray's ontologies of the body as sexed. Her theory is still very important for the contemporary political questions around gender. I focus mainly on Elizabeth Grosz and Claire Colebrook as the proponents of the naturalist ontologies in which sexual difference undercuts the notion of gender identity understood as "performance." I conclude my chapter by highlighting the problems naturalist and non-naturalist ontologies are confronted with.

BUTLER'S CRITIQUE OF BEAUVOIR AND IRIGARAY

Gender Trouble is a philosophically very intense book; the reader must have a philosophical education in the twentieth-century philosophy to understand the concepts borrowed from thinkers such as Michel Foucault, Louis Althusser, Sigmund Freud, Jacques Lacan, Jacques Derrida, J. L. Austin, Simone de Beauvoir, Julia Kristeva, Luce Irigaray, and Monique Wittig, to name just a few. This is the book that transformed feminist studies and inaugurated queer theory as a philosophical field in the English-speaking world. Butler's major question, the question of "gender," is a philosophical question about the constitution of the social reality of the body. Given that *Gender Trouble* is written in the continental philosophical style of doing philosophy, to strip Butler's ontology of its entanglement with thinkers such as Beauvoir, Irigaray, Foucault, Lacan, and Althusser for an analytical exposition is neither easy nor fair because such a strategy will reduce the philosophical intensity of her text.

In *Gender Trouble*, Butler clarifies her theoretical position from within a critique of Beauvoir and Irigaray (besides other theorists). Her position with respect to Beauvoir is controversial because she reads the sex and gender distinction that she finds in Anglo-American feminism into *The Second Sex*. Moreover, she accuses Beauvoir of mind and body dualism. This accusation does not recognize that the phenomenological tradition attempts to overcome this duality in the notion of the "body as situation," even though a fair objection can be made that the phenomenological notion of body as a situation fails to overcome the dualism that it attempts to overcome. Arguably, Butler's reading of Beauvoir is superficial. Sara Heinämaa documents the problems of Butler's reading in her interpretation of *The Second Sex* as a phenomenology of sexual difference (Heinämaa 1997). I agree with most of what she says, even though my interpretative strategy is different.

I explained in my first chapter why Beauvoir's ontology of freedom is different from Sartre's and how the question of freedom leads her to make a complex phenomenology of sexual difference in which the voluntary is both limited and articulated by the involuntary, and how the involuntary does not necessarily annul the possibility of an open situation. I stressed that Beauvoir is against any kind of determinism—naturalist, psychoanalytical, and histori-cal. In *Gender Trouble*, Butler does not seem to understand in what ways Beauvoir departs in her account of freedom from Sartre. She misses the experience of being my body, which involves different significations, and the ontological account of the body as an ambiguous and complex source of motives. My sexed body is not facticity, not just a background necessity for my acts; it is the polemic bond of the voluntary and the involuntary. The affirmation of the capacity of transcendence implies that this living bond that reunites the voluntary and the involuntary can be actively conquered. Hence, it is unfair to read Beauvoir as a voluntarist, as Butler did. It is true that Butler's early texts offered a different approach (Butler 1988, 1992, and 1994). For example, she wrote: "No longer understood as a product of cultu-ral and psychic relations long past, gender is a contemporary way of organiz-ing past and future cultural norms, an active style of living one's body in the world" (Butler 1994, 131). However, this more nuanced reading is given up in *Gender Trouble* in favor of a less hermeneutical reading that makes Beau-voir a foil for the exposition of Butler's own views.

In *Gender Trouble*, Beauvoir is presented as contradicting herself. On the one hand, she argues that sexual difference is not natural and that the sexed body is a product of history, in which case sexual difference in the biological sense would be irrelevant: "If 'the body is a situation,' as [de Beauvoir] claims, there is no recourse to a body that has not always already been interpreted by cultural meanings; hence, sex could not qualify as a prediscur-sive anatomical facticity. Indeed, sex, by definition, will be shown to have been gender all along" (Butler 2008, 12). Again, "Nothing can be found in Beauvoir that would justify the presupposition that one should be born fe-male in order to be a woman" (Butler 2008, 11). On the other hand, Beauvoir holds that there are some real bodies with natural properties to which female sex is assigned at birth and that these bodies are constituted as women by patriarchal culture. And Beauvoir sometimes talks about women's bodies as if there are natural facts of sex.

The contradiction appears because Butler ignores that in *The Second Sex* corporeal existence is lived in a drama of the voluntary and the involuntary, and in woman's existence the involuntary may appear as a hostile force of contingent organic life, of unconscious, of social and historical structures.

For Beauvoir, being woman is a situation. She works with a phenomenological method, which inquires into the constitution of the lived experience of
corporeality. Stella Sandford makes a good point when she writes that "the
notion of 'woman' in *The Second Sex* is not simply translatable into the
category of 'gender,' indeed that it cuts across or problematizes the traditional sex/gender distinction" (Sandford 1999, 21). I do not think it is wrong to
read Beauvoir as working toward a notion of gender, but she does that with
the means of her existentialist ontology. To read *The Second Sex* as a phenomenology of sexual difference makes more sense, though this phenomenology should be conceived broadly, as including a hermeneutics that shows
how the essence of sexual difference is historically constructed by a play
between the forces of production and reproduction.

There are three important moments of Butler's critique of Beauvoir: first-
ly, Butler's critique of the feminists' use of *woman* as a category applies to
Beauvoir as well. Beauvoir too, subsumed all women under the category of
"woman" when she raised the question of a situation specific to woman.
Nevertheless, for Beauvoir, "woman" did not refer to an unhistorical essence
that precedes existence, which is historically constituted. Woman's essence
lies in her existence. She also acknowledges that existence is not unique.
Existence can be the site of various intersecting forms of oppression. There is
nothing that prevents us from thinking existence in this way. Sexual oppression can take different forms depending on what other forms of oppression
cuts it across. Beauvoir also stresses that the oppressed participates in her
oppression and that to achieve higher reflective consciousness is a goal.
There are resources in *The Second Sex* to defend Beauvoir against her own
universalism. Secondly, Beauvoir argued that the female bodies as sexed are
constituted by the history of patriarchy. Butler gives a different analysis of
constitution, by pointing to the way in which compulsory heterosexuality
genders heterosexual and non-heterosexual bodies. Beauvoir appeals to patriarchy as a universal logic of oppression, which is a strategy to which Butler
objects. The appeal to an overarching form of power can prevent us from
understanding how power operates and effectuates subjects in contexts in
which different forces intersect to give rise to singular configurations. That
being said, the appeal to compulsory heterosexuality serves to construe a
hierarchy of oppression which is as problematic as the overarching account
of oppression based on patriarchy. Thirdly, Beauvoir relies on an existentialist ontology, which is humanist and personalist. Butler rightly perceives personalism as deriving from the ontology of modern subjectivity. Beauvoir's
problem is that women are not persons, are not moral and political subjects
because of sexual oppression, which deprives them from the possibility of
fulfilling some of their ontological possibilities. Butler suspects that "the
person" itself is an effect of power. And we may wonder if this should make

us disregard the possibility of subjectivation which we can find in existentialist ontologies.

Already in her essay on Beauvoir, which was published in 1986, Butler brings forth the question of agency as she writes:

> It is usual these days to conceive of gender as passively determined, constructed by a personified system of patriarchy or phallogocentric language, which precedes and determines the subject itself. Even if gender is rightly understood to be constructed by such systems, it remains necessary to ask after the specific mechanism of this construction. Does this system unilaterally inscribe gender upon the body, in which case the body would be a purely passive medium and the subject utterly subjected? What is the role of personal agency in the reproduction of gender? (Butler 1998, 31)

From Butler's point of view, although Beauvoir starts with an insight into the construction of sexual difference, she does not have the means to show in what way the category of sex as natural and given is a product of gender. Beauvoir appeals to the myth of the eternal feminine to argue, in the structuralist manner, that the patriarchal male imaginary assimilates woman to nature. Butler's reading of Beauvoir does not give any weight to her notion of the Other. The constitution of women as radical alterity points to a symbolic position that remained continuous through the history of patriarchal culture. Butler is not interested in reading the myth of the eternal feminine as a power discourse regime. In contrast, she is interested in looking at how the juridical and scientific discourses invented the biological category of sex. Foucault's thesis in *The History of Sexuality* that sex is a product of scientific and juridical discourses on sexuality is central to Butler's argument. The important point is that these discourses were not based on an investigation of how nature in itself is; they constructed nature in accordance with norms about sexual difference, which imposed the binary division into male and female. This is to say that the system of compulsory heterosexuality brings into being through discourse/power regimes the natural category of sex—which limits sexual difference by two.

Finally, we can remark that both Butler and Beauvoir object to naturalism, and both understand naturalism in a rather limited manner. For both philosophers, even if naturalism is conceived as accommodating unlimited difference, it would not be clear how naturalism can contest power and why in its new forms it would cease to legitimate and disguise various forms of oppression. The theory of gender as self-identification adopted by contemporary transfeminist doctrine seems to me more naturalist than Butlerian. The claim is that sexual difference/gender identity binary, nonbinary, fixed and not fluid, comes from nature. According to this theory, the female in nature is not unique and does not depend on the internal and external organs of the body. One can be born female even if one is not so categorized by the science of biology (Bettcher 2014). This view implies, a rejection of the second wave feminism, Irigaray's understanding of the natural femininity as a category of the real, and the naturalisms that inspire from her.

In the third chapter, I have argued that the real in Irigaray cannot be spoken of independently of the imaginary and symbolic, even though it is irreducible. Let me now turn to Butler's interpretation of Irigaray: in *Gender Trouble*, Butler provides a critique of Irigaray as well. According to Irigaray, there is only one sex, which is male. The female sex, which is not "one" but multiple, is excluded from the phallocentric signifying economy that she attributes to the patriarchal culture. Butler does not designate the feminine excluded by the phallocentric system as the Other (in the sense of radical alterity). She is right in her remark that the Other in Beauvoir's sense would be the other inscribed within the phallogocentric system according to Irigaray. She writes: "In opposition to Beauvoir, for whom women are designated as the Other, Irigaray argues that both the subject and the Other are masculine mainstays of a closed phallogocentric signifying economy that achieves its totalizing goal through the exclusion of the feminine altogether" (Butler 2008, 13). If the Other in Beauvoir's sense is the production of the relative other for Irigaray, the Other in the radical sense, the outside of the phallocentric system must refer to the feminine unconscious. In *Gender Trouble*, Butler does not see the feminine radical alterity, which is not present in the phallocentric order as a possibility of a different future; she takes it as a form of essentialism. However, this reading is revised in 1995, in an exchange with Drucilla Cornell, which led Butler to think of feminine alterity in Irigaray's sense as "inaugurating a future within language and within intelligibility" (Cheah, Grosz, Butler, and Cornell 1998, 21). Butler herself uses the same strategy of appealing to the unconsciousness for the possibility of subversion in *The Psychic Life of Power*.

Butler criticizes Irigaray for appealing to phallocentrism as a "primary condition of oppression," which she sees as an imperializing gesture (Butler 2008, 19). The masculine signifying economy that appropriates and suppresses the Other "is one tactic among many, deployed centrally but not exclusively in the service of expanding and rationalizing the masculinist domain" (Butler 2008, 19). If appeals to patriarchy and the phallocratic economy of signification are misguided attempts to totalize oppression, how can the accusation about the order of compulsory heterosexuality escape from falling into the same kind of error? After all, does not Butler, too, appeal to the same system of power? If the category of "women" is normative and exclusionary, the categories of heterosexuality and non-heterosexuality can be normative and exclusionary as well. Heterosexuality is not always produced in accordance with the linear causal model that aligns sex, gender, desire, and sexuality. The heterosexuality of trans people can be a heterosexuality that might not be intelligible, especially if their gender presentation is not an intelligible performance in a society. In the new discourse of trans activism, women do not want to be explicated as performing gender norms; they want to be recognized as original and natural born women, independently of genital organs, on the grounds of their inborn feeling. Gender by self-identification can reclaim a sex identity category such as "woman" by appropriating the language of the originality of sex, even though this original sex may be unapparent and incongruent with the sex that medical science and society assigns to infants at birth. But if this natural, real, and original sex is acceptable in the case of trans women, on what grounds we can object to cis women's identification as women, by reclaiming their nature and culture? Why do we need to make claims about the biological reality of sex at all? I would accept that regarding all bodies as constructed might risk obliterating how differently they are constructed and the more oppressive consequences of some forms of construction over the others. Listening to experiences and how people signify themselves is important, but the existentialists' worry about understanding one's own beliefs and experiences cannot be effaced.

I am not clear how Butler's theory of gender can accommodate a metaphysical language of the naturality of sex as argued for in transfeminism. In a recent interview she gave to George Yancy, published in the *New York Times* on July 10, 2019, Butler addresses femicide as a global problem and acknowledges that the feminist critique of patriarchy is still valuable.

> This is important because it is not just that murder is committed on the basis of gender; violence against women is one way of establishing the femininity of the victim. The violence seeks to secure the class of women as killable, dispensable; it is an attempt to define the very existence of women's lives as something decided by men, as a masculine prerogative. (Butler 2019)

Here Butler is not saying that men killed women because they are women; instead, she says "the act of femicide makes the victims feminine." Sex is a product of the performativity of the act, in this case murder. Both the performativity account and the intersectionalist approach fail to cope with the fact that the number of femicides is rising at such a high speed in some countries, including in my country, Turkey. Great caution is needed in transferring the intersectionalist feminism's arguments to talk about cis women's historical privilege in being women to these contexts. Women from all classes, ethnic backgrounds, and gender identities suffer and die from male violence. To me, given that I live in a country where femicide is so painfully common, the heated debate over biologically real womanhood instead of a critique of male violence sounds odd, to say the least. Men argue that they killed trans women because they are pretenders or deceivers, knowing in advance and learning from similar murder cases that this is the line that they should adopt to get penalty reduction. They also say they killed their wives because they have been cheated on or were prevented from seeing their children. Men can use these arguments and get away with them because the judicial system is patriarchal and systematically privileges men over women.

Irigaray is the philosopher who would not dispense with the female. Sexual difference theorists return to Irigaray because in her texts they see an acknowledgment of sexual difference in nature, in the sense of the real that precedes discourse. I think that Irigaray appeals to the real in the psychoanalytical sense, but she does not make it an object of the biological sciences. The real as an object of scientific discourse is construed by the phallocentric signifying economy of the patriarchal ideology. In order to overcome that situation a feminist critique of science must be made. In my interpretation, Irigaray can accommodate Foucault's and Butler's point about the juridical function of the scientific discourses. The important question is whether or not this is where all research on sexual difference should come to an end. Irigaray argues that this is a realm that can and should be explored and cultivated. The claim that sex as a natural biological reality is an important category that we cannot dispense with and that is different from gender rests on the idea that feminist culture and politics depend on it. But isn't that a return to the old sex and gender distinction that feminists have problematized? This is not how I read Irigaray. For me, because her female morphologies function as sources of the new imaginary and the symbolic, she is concerned with resistance to phallocentric assimilation rather than with scientific biologism.

Butler raises the question of sex to law in Irigaray: "Indeed, it is often unclear within Irigaray's text whether sexuality is culturally constructed, or whether it is only culturally constructed within the terms of the phallus. In other words, is specifically feminine pleasure 'outside' of culture as its pre-history or as its utopian future?" (Butler 2008, 41). In psychoanalysis, sexual enjoyment depends on a relation to law. Hence, Irigaray would argue that sexuality is normative and culturally constructed. However, her point is that female sexual enjoyment cannot be understood if it is construed in phallic terms, even when it is represented as a relation to the Other (God) (as in the case of Saint Theresa) without finding the cause of desire in the phallus as a sign of the sexual organ. Irigaray's position is in fact not so unclear. She refers to the absence of a symbolic law for female sexual enjoyment, which means sexuality is a relation to a formative law. At times Irigaray speaks as if such a law existed in the prehistoric past, or is one that we can create in a culture of sexual difference. Admittedly, this is a fictional dimension of her text. A fictional acknowledgment of law implies the recognition that there is no sexuality outside the law. But this is different than the acknowledgment of a different discourse/power regime. Here the law seems to give a frame for, legitimate, and reduce systemic violence to sexes, so that their natural possibilities could unfold.

PERFORMATIVITY, REALITY, AND AGENCY

Gender Trouble starts with a critique of the metaphysics of subject as substance and defends the Foucauldian view that the subject is produced by the juridical systems of power. Foucault in *The History of Sexuality* considers sexuality as a domain of power. Butler interprets the claim that there is no sexuality before and after the law in the sense that there is no access to a sexuality that is in some sense "outside," "before," or "after" power. Here "the law" is not understood as a principle of will to obey, a command, or an injunction; it means hegemonic power. This is at the background of the general claim that the hegemonic prohibitions on sex produce the subject. Butler applies the same argument to explain what it means for a body to be gendered. In her theory, the assertion that there is a natural sex is conceived as a postulate of the performativity of power that genders bodies.

How does power function to gender bodies? In *Bodies That Matter* performativity is considered as "that power of discourse to produce effects through reiteration" (Butler 1993, 20). As Pheng Cheah remarks: "Butler's theory of gender performativity is intended as an improvement on social constructionism. While she accepts the premise that gender or sex are socially constructed, she urges us to understand construction as involving the materialization of the determinate type of bodies through the repetition of gender norms" (Cheah 1996, 11). Construction does not consist of attributing a new meaning to a preexisting material entity. Butler gives a new philosophical form to the argument she borrows from Foucault, by making the notion of "performativity" play a pivotal role. Power has double functions: It "encompasses both the juridical (prohibitive and regulatory) and the productive (inadvertently generative) functions" (Butler 2008, 40). And it does more than what it pretends to do due to the differential relations of its two functions: the prescriptive categories in their regulatory function can be *performative* in the sense of capable of generating subjects. In this approach, even though the law/power pretends only to regulate preexisting bodies, it performatively produces the gendered subject as a corporeal being.

Certainly, this is an ontological argument about bodies, about how they come into being as effects of gendering power. The living matter becomes, or is constituted as, a body when it materializes according to hegemonic power, which is the site of the pre-existing norms. In this philosophical framework, power functions as the organizing element, as the form that logically precedes matter, but there is also a sense in which normative regimes can be effective due to the performance of the bodies, which repeat and re-iterate their norms. The circularity here is ontologically irreducible.

According to Butler, the subject is, above all, a gendered body and an effect of performativity. This is the ontological framework Butler's critique of the feminist subjectivity and politics of representation proceed from. Indeed, her criticism is a special application of the theory of gender as performativity to the subject of feminism. Feminism normatively brings into being the subject (under the category of women) which it subsequently claims to represent. The implication is that the feminist discourse does not represent subjects that are already there; it only represents what it has produced in the first place. If this is really the case, feminism cannot emancipate an already existing oppressed subject; it is an exercise of power that brings a certain category of subject into being and makes it intelligible. And, in so doing, it excludes the bodies that do not fit in this category and are relegated to the realm of unintelligibility. The realm of the unintelligible is equivalent to the realm of the excluded, in which queer bodies are located. The term "queer" would be ontologized as well—an ontology that does not operate with the identity categories and acknowledges the fluidity of becoming in which the body materializes itself. Rejecting the conception of sexual difference as a biological determination, refusing the categorization of individuals under a sex category on the basis of the possession of a set of physical, psychical, and anatomical properties, and disallowing the correlation between sexual orientation and gender—Butler's view paves the way for a new understanding of the self. Self is now conceived as beyond sexual identity categories—in its fluidity. If all materialization is contingent and changeable, then there is room for saying that the self itself is ontologically queer.

The theory of gender as social construction implies that sexual difference is a discursive product like race and class. Social construction through discourse/power regimes does not simply classify bodies under certain categories; these categories presence bodies, make them appear by forcing them to materialize under their modalities that lead to the formation of groups and finally, hierarchical relations between groups are established. Hence some bodies are subordinated to others. A discourse/power regime drives the bodies to behave in certain ways, play certain roles, and think, feel, and speak in a manner that complies with certain norms. According to the prevailing standards of intelligibility in specific contexts, bodies appear or to hide in appearing, act or not dare to act, and be visible or disappear in their visibility. According to Hilde Lindemann, gender builds and perpetuates hierarchical relations of power, and that it subordinates groups to others. She writes:

> Gender, then, is about power. But it's not about the power of just one group over another. Gender always interacts with other social markers—such as race, class, level of education, sexual orientation, age, religion, physical and mental health, and ethnicity—to distribute power unevenly among women positioned differently in the various social orders, and it does the same to men. (Lindemann 2011, 141)

Sally Haslanger, who gave an account of race and gender in terms of social construction, makes a distinction between the intersectionality of experience and intersectionality of structural oppression. If I understand her correctly, she suggests we start from the intersectional experience of the oppressed to go to the experience to the intersecting structures of oppression. She rejects that we can give *a priori* theoretical accounts to questions such as: "How does social categorizations work and interact?" and "How does power work, more precisely the multiple axis of power interact to create structures of oppression?" (Haslanger 2014, 116).

Even though experiences can be illuminating, both the social constructivists like Lindemann and Haslanger and Butler are making general theoretical claims, which can be tested in concrete contexts of oppression. Gender concerns the normativity at work in the appearing of a material body in the world. If Butler's general thesis of the performativity of gender is cast in terms of Lacan's threefold distinction between the symbolic, the imaginary, and the real, it can be heard as a thesis about the productivity of the symbolic. Butler does not recognize the imaginary as a domain that can escape from the domination of the symbolic. Her thesis implies that the body is symbolic and imaginary, before it materializes as real in the social sense. The real as the impersonal and heterogeneous milieu in which there is not yet a distinction between I and the other has no recognizable place in this ontological framework. The body comes into being due to discourse/power regimes, which are historically manifest in different institutions and practices, and such regimes can be marked by the specific configurations of the symbolic and imaginary elements. In this theory, it does not make sense to speak of the biological sex as given and the lived experience of the body as an opening to the impersonal real. Sex ias a product of discourse/power regimes means that these regimes sexualize the body; they constitute bodies as sexed beings. The distinction between sex and gender collapses because if the access to the real is only via the imaginary and the symbolic; neither sex nor gender can be in the real prior to the symbolic and the imaginary. Indeed, the symbolic and imaginary processes construct the real in the social sense as divided into the two sexes. But what if the intersectionality of the experience contests that? Well, should we respond that it makes no sense to speak of sexual difference as real in nature, independently of construction? In *Gender Trouble*, Butler is critical of the distinction made between sex as biological and gender as cultural, because sex is as discursively constructed as gender, and the categorization and social designation themselves are expressions of power (Butler 2008, 10). *Gender Trouble* effectively fights the assumption that sexual difference precedes gendering and thus repudiates the paradigm of "sexual difference." I do not see how a Butlerian theoretical account can be combined with naturalist realism, even if this naturalism finds a way to assert itself via the intersectionality of experience.

A certain role is reserved to the acting body in the execution of its materialization. Indeed, this space in which the body can play with gender norms serves to subvert the essentialism of the symbolic. In Lacan, the body does not have a role in its taking a position in the symbolic system. In Foucault, the body seems to be a passive being determined by discourses. However, in Butler, the body comes back as capable of behaving, adopting, repeating, appropriating, and ex-appropriating a certain style of appearing by the performance of gender norms. Hence the body has the capacity to adopt habits as it encounters cultural norms and is gendered through the acts of assumption and transgression (subversion).

What is performativity, and how does it produce a body? Aren't bodies real before they undergo performativity? I think in the Butlerian framework a capacity of performance, of acting in accordance with norms, should be affirmed as real—as not produced. Is Butler opposing only the binary construction of sex by the biological science, or to all the naturalist accounts of sex that in principle enlarge the spectrum of sexual difference beyond the biological scientific construction of male and female? I think queer theory, in Butler's style, refuses the category of the real even if the real is conceived beyond the fundamental division the biological science conventionally makes into male and female bodies. The body materializes in virtue of its capacity to pick up habits; by reiterating the prevailing norms and improvising in accordance with them, Butler's frame does not need to refer nature as a legitimating source of authenticity. Queer theory makes the general ontological claim that all bodies are produced by power discourse regimes. It is in that sense that Butler's thought is for me a radicalization of Beauvoir: it does not make sense to speak of being born as woman or man (heterosexual or non-heterosexual, cis or trans). The question if we should ban all talk about natural reality is therefore legitimate. One may object that Butler's account should not be pushed too far and that it should acknowledge the categories of natural male and natural female and the medical science that rests on them—even to help non-gender-conforming people conform to the gender they feel like belonging. Wasn't Butler's fundamental target the heteronormative power that disregarded the lived experience of the body? Even though she also stressed the productivity of norms whose ideality is embedded in the double differential functions of power?

There is a sense in which norms transcend performance even though they depend on the performativity of power to maintain their ideality and validity. There is an irreducible circularity in the relation between performativity and performance. There is performativity only through performances, which reiterate norms in a certain worldly context, even though performance can be what it is due to the performativity of power/law. This concerns the problem of the nature of norms; the ontological status of normativity in Butler's account. Butler's own way of thinking about normativity is inspired by the Foucauldian and Lacanian approaches. There are various types of norms. Gender norms regulate symbolic exchange and communication, both linguistically and through corporeal gestures; they are the terms that mediate the encounters between bodies. They give rules about how bodies should interact and where they should stand in relation to each other. And more importantly, they set some bodies as intelligible and capable of meaningful speech and exclude other bodies from the position of subjectivity and agency. For Butler, the norms that indicate the place of the speaking subject in Lacan's symbolic system are just as historical, cultural, and constructed by power relations as the norms relating to sexuality of which Foucault has spoken. Butler's significant contribution to this framework is her theory of performance, in which norms are conceived as rules of behavior that could be assumed or subverted by the bodies, which regulate and produce them. In "Performative Acts and Gender Constitution," Butler writes that "Gender reality is performative which means, quite simply, that it is real only in the extent that it is performed" (Butler 1988, 527). On these grounds, Silvia Stoller concludes that "that gender is a performative act means that it comes into existence in the very moment of its performance. . . . Given that gender is real only in the extent that it is performed, Butler's theory of gender can be characterized as a theory of gender in *statu nascendi*—a theory of gender in the state of coming into existence" (Stoller 2010, 99). I think that this should not amount to the denial of the precedence of the elements of the symbolic to the real. But the becoming real of gender necessitates more than there being gender positions/norms in the symbolic system.

The third concept that we need to scrutinize to improve our understanding of Butler's ontology is "agency." Let me begin with the existentialist objection to her theory. Butler's theses have astonished and shaken feminisms that relied on existentialist ontologies. Existentialist feminism asserts that existence can be re-organized by choice often made in a situation, and often under historically sedimented conditions of facticity. To subscribe to the view that existence is produced by juridical systems of power destroys subjectivity and agency and condemns beings to inauthenticity. If being has no possibility of assuming its own produced existence and make something else out of it, there is no room for emancipation from oppression.

Butler rejects the modernist view that subjectivity is given on the grounds that we are human beings. This is an idea based on the modern philosophy of subjectivity and the humanism that stems from it. For Foucault the prisoner becomes the model for thinking the constitution of the subject. In *Discipline and Punish*, Foucault holds that power is not exercised from the outside to regulate the prisoner. The prisoner does not pre-exist as an individual who is then subordinated to the regulations of the institution. The prisoner becomes a prisoner as discourse confers an "identity" on him as prisoner. In Butler's words:

Subjection is, literally, the *making* of a subject, the principle of regulation according to which a subject is formulated or produced. Such subjection is a kind of power that not only unilaterally *acts on* a given individual as a form of domination, but also *activates* or forms the subject. Hence, subjection is neither simply the domination of a subject nor its production, but designates a certain kind of restriction *in* production, a restriction without which the production of the subject cannot take place, a restriction through which that production takes place. Although Foucault occasionally tries to argue that historically *juridical* power—power acting on, subordinating, pregiven subjects—precedes productive power, the capacity of power to *form* subjects, with the prisoner it is clear that the subject produced and the subject regulated or subordinated are one, and that compulsory production is its own form of regulation. (Butler 1997b, 84)

This is an ontological thesis about subjectivity. It implies that people are not, ontologically speaking, free individuals who can shape the world by their words and acts. Discourse/power regimes that corporate in institutions *form* the individuals by institutional regulations that impose ways of acting and being on them. Henceforth, they destroy individuals' spontaneous and creative initiative. In a system in which spontaneous action is punished and submissive behavior rewarded, individuals tend to preserve the status quo, instead of adopting innovative attitudes. Institutions make sure that the individual recognizes and respects hierarchies, if he or she expects to acquire a position of power as a speaking subject in the future. In other words, one must be subjected to power to become a subject. The process of subjectivation—which only produces the subject that is a means of power, consists of practices of subjection, and compliance with the conditions imposed by the institutions.

To count as a speaking subject and to be granted the authority to execute the institutional program, one must belong to the system or the regime in question, be shaped by it and speak its language. As a consequence, when a "person" attains a position of power, she has very little, almost nothing, to say coming from her own personal resources or experience. She has no feeling, personal memory, experience, and judgment of her own. She is so transformed by the system that she can no longer give her own experience of the world any weight to create new concepts to change the system's reality. In short, in the process of becoming a subject, the individual has internalized the system. It follows that there is no existentialist subject as a person capable of changing the world in accordance with her own values. The person has no possibility of transforming the system because she has very little resources to recognize who she is or to adopt authentic projects. The process of subjection/subjectivation leads people to make concessions that make them forget themselves. People who are allowed to speak are those who do what is expected of them; subjects are mere instruments of power with no agency of their own. As they keep performing the actions that discourse/ power requires of them, power will not be simply external to them; it will materialize their bodies, shape the way they feel, think, and speak. If this were the whole story, individual subjects could not change anything, and all change would be reducible to the self-transformation of the system. The problem is that this makes the philosophical statuses of Foucault's and Butler's discourses unaccountable. Either individuals can have agency on the basis of their different relation to the system or Foucault's and Butler's theories would be merely descriptive accounts with no philosophical ground.

Butler responds to this problem when she argues that the law also produces the opposite of what it intends to produce. This is how it is possible to subvert discourse/power regimes by performing the gender roles that we assume differently. Although Butler is critical of the existentialist subject, she does not want to lose agency in the structuralist vein of thinking. In her early readings of Beauvoir, she holds that agency is important. In *Bodies That Matter* (Butler 1993), she distances herself from the structuralist conceptions that, in Stoetzler's words "replace the subject 'Human' by another pre-existing subject, be that 'Culture,' 'Discourse,' or 'Power'" (Stoetzler 2010, 360). Nonetheless, if agency is not given, it must be a possibility in the performativity of power.

How is the room for agency created? Butler returns to Louis Althusser to answer this question. According to Althusser, "the category of the subject is constitutive of all ideology, but we also immediately add that the category of the subject is constitutive of every ideology only insofar as every ideology has the function (which defines it) of 'constituting' concrete subjects (such as you and me)" (Althusser 2014, 188). In *Excitable Speech*, Althusser's notion of "interpellation" is made pertinent to the social construction of the bodies and helps to the philosophical exhibition of the possibility of resistance. Interpellation does not address to someone who preexists the call but brings someone into social existence. "Language sustains the body not by bringing it into being or feeding it in a literal way; rather, it is by being interpellated within the terms of language that a certain social existence of the body first becomes possible" (Butler 1997a, 5). Due to the events of naming and calling, a body may appear in its corporeality either as recognizable or an abject entity. Hence interpellation inaugurates a body in social reality.

> It seeks to introduce a reality rather than report on an existing one; it accomplishes this introduction through a citation of existing convention. Interpellation is an act of speech whose "content" is neither true nor false: it does not have description as its primary task. Its purpose is to indicate and establish a subject in subjection, to produce its social contours in space and time. Its reiterative operation has the effect of sedimenting its "positionality" over time. (Butler 1997a, 33)

Why does the interpellation make the subject return toward the appeal, given that one does not know if she is the one addressed? And as Butler asks, "how, if at all, does linguistic agency emerge from this scene of enabling vulnerability?" (Butler 1997a, 2). This return, which is inscribed in the law, is anterior to the formation of the subject, which "means an opening, a permeability or vulnerability precedes all critical comprehension of the law" (Ong-Van-Cung 2011, 156). There is also, in the moment of interpellation, a reflexive return to the self, in which the subject can attain the awareness that his conscience is produced as bad faith, that norms that have been internalized undermine one's existence, hence the possibility of agency. In her essay, "Critique et subjectivation: Foucault et Butler sur le sujet," Kim San Ong-Van-Kun ties this discussion with Nietzsche's *Genealogy of Morals* and Foucault's politics of truth (Ong-Van-Cung 2011). The interpellated subject turns to the interpellator and to herself and realizes that a possibility of agency lies in the assumption of the name she is conferred upon in the interpellation. Butler writes: "a critical perspective on the kinds of language that govern the regulation and constitution of subjects becomes all the more imperative once we realize how inevitable is our dependency on the ways we are addressed in order to exercise any agency at all" (Butler 1997a, 27).

Butler supplements this moment in the *experience* undergone, of interpellation, with a psychological account of the possibility of resistance.

> Thus the psyche, which includes the unconscious, is very different from the subject: the psyche is precisely what exceeds the imprisoning effects of the discursive demand to inhabit a coherent identity, to become a coherent subject. The psyche is what resists the regularization that Foucault ascribes to normalizing discourses. Those discourses are said to imprison the body in *the soul*, to animate and contain the body within that ideal frame, and to that extent reduce the notion of the psyche to the operations of an externally framing and normalizing idea. (Butler 1997b, 86)

Take the designation of the "homosexual" as an example. Prior to that designation there is only the behavior of sodomy; the designation itself makes the homosexual become present as a member of a type or genre. The same thing holds for all gendering. A soon as a behavior is designated as "female behavior," masculinity too appears as a category, which refers to a set of behavior represented as opposed to "female behavior." A child is not "girl" because he or she plays with dolls or "boy" because he or she plays with cars. Anybody can play with dolls and cars. The problem is to separate the female behavior from the male behavior, and to represent femininity as the opposite of masculinity. This is not just naming an existing token by subsuming it under a universal real category; naming comes with prescription, a compulsion to adopt a certain style of behavior. Now, Butler argues that a domain of masculinity opens as a forbidden realm for the bodies that come into being by being designated as female and a domain of femininity is hinted as forbidden land for the bodies that materialize as male (Butler 2008, 22). She also acknowledges that as prohibitions function to regulate and constitute gendered beings, they create an unconscious realm in which other possibilities are renounced. The prohibition of homosexuality creates an outside constitutive of heterosexual desire and can give rise to a homosexual desire. It is noteworthy that Bataille, too, argued that the intensification and the eroticization of the desire at the face of prohibition, belongs to the inner movement of desire. Impossibility, obstacle, and aporia do not only trigger desire; they keep it alive. In Butler, too, negativity plays a major role in the dialectic of desire. I do not think that she condemns the psyche to melancholia; the psyche can be subversive because the unconsciousness has a reserve of virtualities. This, it seems to me, is a recognition of the imaginary as subversive of the symbolic. Psyche, which is different from the subject, has the possibility to resist gendering performativity, by the playing performance of gender norms.

In the course of our ordinary lives, while some of us encounter gender categories, norms, and structures very anxiously because our bodies do not appear as intelligible under their law, others enjoy heterosexual privilege and do not think they suffer pressure. According to Butler, heterosexuality depends on the renunciation of the homosexual desire and hence keeps melancholia in reserve. Is this true for non-heterosexual and trans people? Do they suffer from melancholia because they renounce to the compulsory gender roles? It seems to me that there is a sovereign enjoyment in the contestation of the existing norms, even if a certain style of performance leads to suffering due to exclusion by the society at large. Even though the process of constituting an identity and the creation of ipseity involve sexuality; sexuality as a fixed and coded determination is not an essential part of selfhood. As well known, queer theory contests an essentialist model of identity; it invites us to rethink the becoming sexed of a human being as a dynamic process that depends on the encounters with the others in a world in which gender regulates. In this sense, queer is a philosophical description of a social ontology. Refusing to talk about the natural forces, it is interested in the productive regulation of the social forces. Everybody encounters gender norms and wrestles with them, more or less painfully; some people experience less trouble than others, who suffer much more because their performance is gender non-conforming behavior. We all negotiate with gender norms, although some of us take more risk than others and pay higher prices.

To conclude, in Butler's ontology of gender, because gender identities are the effects of discourse/power regimes, they are not real independently of discourse and power. Although this may sound wrong to realists, most people will agree with the argument that our sexual identities are part of the reality constituted by discourses besides material processes. I tried to show that, according to Butler, that gender and sex are not real in the sense of

natural does not mean that they do not exist. Butler attempts to explain their
very being. Her point is that their reality is constituted by power discursively,
in symbolic and imaginary ways. In the next section, I shall turn now to the
naturalist ontologies of sex to lay out their objections to Butler's ontology.

BUTLER'S NATURALIST CRITIQUES

Are theories of sexual difference irreconcilable with queer theory? What can,
if anything at all, a rethinking of sexual difference contribute to queer theory? In this section, I take up Claire Colebrook and Elizabeth Grosz in order to
lay the ground for a naturalist approach to queer. In the attempt to compare
the Butlerian queer with the queer theories that are enrooted in Deleuze's
philosophy, I shall focus only on Grosz and Colebrook by reducing the
variety of naturalist queer theories in this expanding domain of research.
Both Butler and Grosz pursue the same ends because they object to the
normative ideology that imposes sex as divided into two and makes heteronormativity compulsory.

Broadly understood, the term "queer" implies the rejection of the claims
that sexual identity is determined by the choice of sex partner and that sexuality is a function or an attribute of a substance that remains the same through
space and time. Butler puts her notion of "gender" at the center of her
critique of heteronormativity while she dismisses the notion of sexual difference as unnecessary, irrelevant, and even harmful. As queer theory developed as a critique of heteronormativity, it also paved the way for a philosophical reflection on normativity.

For the Deleuzian feminists such as Grosz and Colebrook, queer theory
should take its departure from the natural reality of sexual difference. They
do not see sexual determination as a biological *determination* and reject
essentialism. Deleuze and Guattari's works, especially *Capitalism and
Schizophrenia*, have been the main source of inspiration for the Deleuzian
feminism and queer theory. In the first volume of this work, *Anti-Oedipus*,
Deleuze and Guattari object to the thesis that there cannot be an autonomous
expression of desire independently of its encounter with social norms (including the gender norms, with which Butler is specifically concerned). Although Deleuze and Guattari's criticism is primarily directed at the psychoanalytic thesis in its Freudian and Lacanian forms, it also applies to Butler's
queer theory. Butler, too, even though she combines it with the Foucauldian
notion of power, subscribes to the psychoanalytical view that desire is discursive and thus a symbolic construction, which cannot be without a relation to
law. This is why her queer theory too would be within the range of theories
targeted by Deleuze and Guattari.

According to Deleuze and Guattari, desire cannot be captured in the Oedipal structures that consolidate the family, that feed capitalism and sustain the state institution. Desire can have flows and configurations that subvert and undermine the capitalist organization of life. "Desire constantly couples continuous flows and partial objects that are by nature fragmentary and fragmented. Desire causes the current to flow, itself flows in turn, and breaks the flows" (Deleuze and Guattari 1983, 9). Deleuze and Guattari set themselves the task of describing not how law unifies bodies, but how bodies, coming from the chaos of life, continue to diverge, disperse, and differentiate: "their real object is the absolution of fragmented universes, in which the law never unites anything in a single Whole, but on the contrary measures and maps out the divergences, the dispersions, the exploding into fragments of something that is innocent precisely because its source is madness" (Deleuze and Guattari 1983, 43). The model of the desire that escapes regulation and does not fulfill a function that serves power's ends is referred to as "the body without organs." "The body without organs is produced as a whole, but in its own particular place within the process of production, alongside the parts that it neither unifies nor totalizes" (Deleuze and Guattari 1983, 43). Grosz in *Volatile Bodies* formulates Deleuze and Guattari's conception of the body as follows: "In this sense, their understanding of the body and subjectivity as excessive to hierarchical control implies that the body, as the realm of affectivity, is the site or sites of multiple struggles, ambiguously positioned in the reproductions of social habits, requirements, and regulations, and in all sort of production of unexpected and unpredictable linkages" (Grosz 1994, 181).

In *A Thousand Plateus*, the second volume of *Capitalism and Schizophrenia*, desire is conceived as positivity rather than negativity. This new notion of desire grounded on a vitalist conception of nature, and concepts such as "becoming woman" and "becoming minority" made this text the center of attention of the feminist theorists of sexual difference as well. Here, I shall not make an exegesis of Deleuze and Guattari to show how what they say can be relevant for feminism and queer theory of sexual difference. I shall mainly focus on Grosz's and Colebrook's queer theories to compare them with Butler's in order to make the point that although these thinkers have similar ethical and political ends, they operate with different ontologies. The ontological reflection I carry out here reveals that the plurality of queer theories results from a plurality of the ontological planes. Indeed, the debate over the queer theory cannot be separated from philosophical debates over ontology.

In *Volatile Bodies*, Grosz writes, speaking of Irigaray, that "The distinction between the 'real' biological body and the body as object of representation is a fundamental presumption. For her there is no question of superseding the body or biological functions; the task is to give them different meanings and values" (Grosz 1994, 17). Grosz rejects that "biology or sex is a fixed category" (Grosz 1994, 17). That being said, in contrast to Butler who denies the accessibility of the real independently of social constructions, Grosz is after the real. She does not think that biological differences are socially constructed. Similarly, she disagrees with the idea that bodies are constructed by intersecting ways of oppression (race, class, sex). In thinking sexual difference, she finds it more appropriate to begin with natural differences rather than the social forces. My body becomes present because its natural properties are perceived. I appear to others in such and such a form because I possess certain physical and psychical properties.

In her essay "The Nature of Sexual Difference: Irigaray and Darwin," Grosz claims that sexual difference is more fundamental and important than other differences. This is to say that sexual difference is irreducible: it is not just a difference such as race and class, it is the basis and the engine of the coming into being, the apparition of all other differences (Grosz 2012). She reinterprets Darwin's theory of evolution in the horizon of Irigaray's insistence on the priority of the question of sexual difference. According to Darwin, sexual difference is a product of evolution. Natural selection (that only those species with organs that enable them to adopt to changing environmental conditions survive, whereas other species that lack such organs perish) and sexual selection (individuals who have sexually attractive features have an easier time mating to perpetuate their kind) are the two principles of the evolution that intertwine but which must be considered separately. Sometimes the principle of sexual selection may work against the principle of natural selection. An animal in nature may have eye-catching features that make it attractive to sexual partners, but also catch the attention of predators. Sexual selection may give an animal features that make it harder to hide in nature and protect itself from predators' attacks. The processes of sexual selection and natural selection have worked together to produce sexual difference, thanks to which life differentiated, diversified, and enriched itself (Grosz 2012, 87). Grosz emphasizes that sexual selection cannot be reduced to natural selection because it operates according to its own logic. The individual that is most sexually attractive may not be the one fittest for survival with respect to natural selection. In the human world, too, similar paradoxes can be spotted. Some women try to become a size zero because the fashion industry makes them think that this is how they can become most attractive, but the starvation that they have to go through to get that body form can have devastating effects on their health.

Grosz claims that the division into two sexes that dominates our culture is a consequence of biological contingencies that have become cultural necessities (Grosz 2012, 73). If sex as divided into two is the transformation of a natural contingency into a cultural necessity, it follows that life could have been otherwise. If there is no necessity in nature for the sexes to be limited by two, why does culture absolutize or fetishize a contingency? The feminist answer to that question emphasizes the distribution of power in human societies. Keeping the sexual difference limited by two helps to justify the un-equal distribution between the sexes and guarantees the rights and privileges of men over women and other living and non-living beings. In Grosz's ac-count there are forces in nature, but power is social and cultural. She is aware that referring to the configurations of the natural forces cannot be used to explain the existing power relations in the social and political realm without running the risk of justifying oppression. If this risk is to be avoided, natural-ist accounts have to be complemented with a feminist critical analysis of power. Naturalism without a criticism of power is naïve because it only recommends replacing a system of power with a naturalist culture without worrying about how power works by subordinating some differences to oth-ers. Moreover, it is unclear how naturalism can prevent that. It seems to assume that if people knew more about nature, the conditions of oppression would disappear. It ignores the systematic nature of gender oppression and that it remains in being because it serves whatever the ends power has in view.

Grosz refers to nature to undo the cultural norms that obstruct the realiza-tion of the virtualities that are in some sense already in being. This paves the way for proliferating natural differences to attain cultural expressions. The assumption is that once the natural differences which keep proliferating are allowed for cultural expressions, power hierarchies in the cultural realm will change. This idea seems immature to me, because it neglects the fact that power struggle is about maintaining privileges and that it often seeks its justification in a fetishized nature. The problem is not the overcoming of a cultural limitation by learning to think of nature differently, it is about chang-ing the power structures through political action. Grosz thinks that expanding the sexual spectrum and allowing for a plurality of expressions will be suffi-cient to emancipate humanity. In this formulation she attributes to differ-ences a democratic, pluralistic way of coexisting, which seems like the intro-duction of a liberal ideal to the social existence of natural differences. Such a plurality of differences can give rise to new relations of power if we do not uphold non-natural ethical values and norms, which serve to regulate the relations between differences.

Butler abolishes the duality between sex and gender by looking at sex as a major supposition that lays the fundamental ontological ground of gendering. This means that without making the assumption of sex as given, gender mechanisms cannot operate as they have been. The idea that sex is determin-able by the inspection of the anatomical features of the body is now an outdated idea. For example, one can have male genitalia and not really be male. Not all XX people have primary and secondary sexual characteristics that are associated with the female sex. People can change sex or can identify with another gender without medical operation. Knowing whether a person is male or female without attending to the person's declaration is now seen as "gender policing." Legal acts of gender recognition that are reinforced in some parts of the Western world are based on the conviction that science should not pretend to normatively determine sex; instead, it should listen to people's experiences in order to criticize its own normative assumptions. Gender becomes a matter of "subjectivation." There is indeed a war over gender—instead of critical thinking, strategies of public shaming prevail. I think new norms can be invented in and through the deconstruction of the existing power discourse regimes. To overcome the practices of exclusion by making all subjects, independently of how they self-identify, subjects of rights is a great idea—the only worry here is not to cause harm to other oppressed groups. The category of sex may be important in fighting the discrimination against women, and it can be a ground for their struggles against oppression. When the interests of two oppressed groups are pitted against one another dialogue, rather than a violent politics of shaming, can solve the problem. Sex-selective abortion in India and China is happening because fetuses were sexed in ultrasonography as female. Women's reproductive rights are their sexed rights. Given that biological sex as definable characteristics of the human species has become an axis of oppression, how can we fight that oppression if we get rid of the category of sex as a construction and structure it differently by means of self-identification? Even if we deny the reality of the category of sex, isn't it important to take into consideration women's lived experiences of it? I personally think that a new ontology of sex inspired by Simone de Beauvoir's ontology can provide solutions to problems we have at present.

In contrast to Butler, Grosz's way of expanding the sexual spectrum is to rethink nature in a vitalist manner, as perpetually in evolution. Biologists deny that there is a spectrum of sex in nature. According to Grosz, the indefinite differentiation that stems from sexual difference effectuates not so much at imaginary and symbolic orders but belongs to the real. Butler's theory negates the possibility of the real independently of the symbolic and the imaginary. In contrast, Grosz is after laying out the arguments for discussing difference as a concept of naturalist ontology, rather than of social ontology. The real in Grosz's framework, that is, nature itself, precedes the social order. She rejects biological determinism or essentialism: given that nature continues its evolution incessantly, it remains in perpetual change, which does not permit fixed essences. The division into two sexes is an outcome of evolution, the actualization of a contingent possibility. Moreover, in nature sexual difference cannot be limited; sexual differentiation continues its evolutionary course. Thus, we cannot know how many sexes there are now or will be in the future.

Grosz's queer theory is vitalist; it takes its departure from life as given even though life inheres in itself not only that which is actual but also various virtual possibilities. In her project to derive queerness from life, she brings together insights and strategies from Darwin and Deleuze. The concept of life precedes the concept of person; it inheres in itself a plurality that cannot be effectively controlled by the person or by the social and cultural world. Butler refused to take the natural real as a starting point because she wanted to avoid a naturalist determinism. According to Deleuze and his feminist followers, neither nature nor culture are determinative. Butler's queer philosophy assumes that nature is a static being, which is transformed by culture. I am not sure if this reading of Butler is fair. Perhaps, rather than her commitment to a static conception of nature, it is her disbelief that nature can be spoken of independently of the imaginary and the symbolic that leads Butler to refuse to build her queer theory on sexual difference. This is where the most telling disagreement between Butler and naturalists can be found.

Grosz's materialist queer theory rests on Spinoza's monist ontology and Deleuze's empiricist conception of immanence, which seeks transcendence within immanence, and sharply opposes philosophies of transcendence that leave immanence behind. Thus, Grosz distances herself from the approaches that emphasize the constitutive role of discourse, naming, and hold the primacy of sense. For her, there is a real to go back to, and Deleuzian Darwinism enables us to speak of the real independently of images and symbols. This is where Grosz's theory has a hypothetical allure, because it is unclear how she would access phenomena independently of the scientific or philosophical discourses we make. Is this a return to Locke's naïve realism? And how to reconcile the talk about concepts as unlocking virtualities and the possibility to the real without significations?

Can Claire Colebrook, who is also a Deleuzian naturalist queer theorist like Grosz, be of help to us at this point? She argues that we need a new concept of nature, which in its unceasing change proliferates differences (Colebrook 2000, 77). She is also critical of the accounts based on representation and social construction. In "From Radical Representations to Corporeal Becomings: The Feminist Philosophies of Lloyd, Grosz, and Gatens," Colebrook discusses the disagreements between Australian feminists and Butler's queer philosophy, which is founded on the notion of gender. Colebrook offers a vitalist construction and a materialist conception of body in relation to images and concepts. Being consists of becomings, and all things undergoing the influence of nature find themselves in a flux of becoming. This is obviously a contestation of the platonic philosophy, which opposes being and becoming. According to Deleuze, images do not adequately or inadequately copy an original being; the unending process of the becoming of images is life, and the function of thought is not to remember but to create. The body is not a sign among other signs in thought; it is the place of thinking (Colebrook 2000, 82), for it sets the representation in movement. According to this model, there is not a knowing subject over and against nature; the images and concepts we use to understand nature are part of natural evolution and they serve to release its virtualities.

According to Colebrook, the difference between Grosz and Butler can be explained with reference to concepts of gender and sexual self-expression. Butler argues that sex is a presumption that is postulated and accepted as an axiom and that gender expresses and elaborates that in the cultural world. In Colebrook's reading, Grosz contests that by arguing that sex is an expression that takes its departure from itself, it originates from itself; it is, so to speak, an expression of an auto-genesis. While Butler describes sex as always already interpreted by gender, Grosz speaks of the sexual body as a becoming that sets itself in motion, as self-moving and self-expressing. In Grosz's understanding, the sexual body possesses the attributes of God of classical theology, except that it is always changing, always in becoming. Grosz's notion of the body does not limit the representations in its becoming; on the contrary, it sets in motion its becoming representation. In other words, it gives rise to its own imaginary and symbolic. This conception of the body opens the way for us to question the radical separation Butler sees between the ground or origin and signification (Colebrook 2000, 84). We cannot speak as if there can be a silent, inert, static nature outside of its becoming; indeed, the process of becoming inheres the events of signification as well.

What is an event of signification? Deleuzian feminism and queer theory begins with the processes of corporeal becomings in nature and culture, whereas Butler goes from the performativity of the symbolic processes to the bodies. Rejecting the classical phenomenological tradition that postulates an ego that lives experiences, Butler holds that the subject is constructed by power. Deleuze accepts neither a phenomenological approach that presupposes a transcendental ego that constitutes its own experiences, nor Butler's account of subjectivity as socially constructed. He affirms becoming, as the expression of a dynamic substance. An affirmation that gives rise to identity, for example, can be considered as an event of signification. Our sexed being belongs to our body's becoming. A being is hypostasized from within the process of becoming because a moment is now affirmed. Because identity consists of affirmation, it is neither static nor transparent to ourselves. And it sets itself as the same so long as it reaffirms itself. In Colebrook's account, a sexed being derives itself from corporeal becoming, and sexual identity is an interpretation and affirmation of that becoming (Colebrook 2000, 88). The body that does not have an essence in itself can set itself as presenting an essence due to processes in which thought and speech partake in and prolong the body's self-realization. This is to say that the body makes itself sensible and meaningful for itself and become an intelligible body (Colebrook 2000, 86). It follows that gender is independent of sex and people are different due to the differentiations of their bodies. Women and men can have different experiences, feelings, and moral reasoning processes as they undergo different corporeal becomings. The body is always dynamically related to the totality of pluralities. Therefore, on the basis of a positive understanding of becoming, Colebrook elaborates materialization as capable of generating significations.

As Colebrook sees it, the difference between these ontological positions concerns their conceptions of difference, origin, and direction: Deleuzian feminism's challenge is to explain how the natural gives rise to the cultural and symbolic production. For Butler, to make room for a wider spectrum of gender differences we need language and symbolic places, whereas Grosz argues that sexual differences exist and will continue to be even without symbolic representations. In Grosz's view, speech or signification does not bring anything into being; the "signified" (that which is spoken of, characterized as such and such) can become knowable due to that act of speaking and signifying, even though it exists, it is real before being the object of such acts (Colebrook 2000, 84). In Grosz's framework, the body is already in a natural process of becoming; it reaches one of its possible expressions by including symbolic representations to its being. However, we have to note that this sharp contrast is only a depiction of Grosz's early thought. In her recent work, she works the relation between the real and the irreal in a different manner.

Colebrook uses a different model to meet the challenge to derive the normative from the natural. In "Queer Vitalism," an essay that dates from 2010, she undertakes solving the problem of normativity. The idea that affirmation leads to identity which gives rise to norms seems to be circular because identity presupposes normativity. Colebrook defines vitalism "as the imperative of grounding, defending or deriving principles and systems from life *as it really is*" (Colebrook 2010, 77). This is to say that what ought to be the case will be derived from what is the case.

If life as it really is does not refer to life in a transcendent realm of Platonic ideas as grounded in The Good, but refers to sensible natural life, the question comes to mind: What if the real is bad, what if it inheres some violent oppressive state of affairs? What if life is lived under some maleficent forces that exercise physical, psychological, and economical domination? If nature gives rise to violence, how can naturalist realism avoid justifying violent treatment of the oppressed and refuse to ground unequal moral and political treatment in natural difference? Such a naturalism might operate with the logic of sexism and racism. Colebrook is aware of the problem and, in order to solve, it she makes a distinction between "life as it really is" and "actual life." The difference between "active vitalism" and "passive vitalism" sheds more light on the two different senses of the notion of "real life." By "real," Colebrook does not mean actual. Active vitalism starts with the actual life, therefore, from bodies organized in accordance with heterosexual humanity and family norms. The alternative way of thinking about the real is, by following Deleuze and Guattari, to align it with virtualities, that is with "a pre-individual plane of forces that does not act by a process of decision and self-maintenance but through chance encounters" (Colebrook 2010, 77). Virtualities are potentials that can realize in contingent (chance) encounters. Indeed, Colebrook distinguishes between two different ontological planes: the real life, in the sense of actual life, consists of bodies and their organizations in accordance with the capitalist economy of desire. This is also the layer at which the body is organized according to the heterosexual family norms and is imagined as the corporeal ground of a spiritual and moral person who is attributed the capacity for deliberate action. Underneath that stratum lays the impersonal layer of a multiplicity of forces. The domain of the organized bodies does not give us access to the real as it embeds virtualities. Virtualities belong to the forces of composition that differ from those of man and productive organism. Colebrook argues that passive vitalism is *queer*. She believes that it is possible to find a queer vitalism in Deleuze, because, like Leibniz, he refuses to find a unity over the expressive multiplicity of perspectives (Colebrook 2010, 79). "Every body in this world is possible as an individual because it gives some form and specificity in time and space to a potential that always threatens to destabilize or de-actualize its being" (Colebrook 2010, 80). Colebrook appeals to Leibniz's *monad* to elaborate an internalist model of individuation. The body does not individuate materially in its relation to the externally regulating laws of the social realm. In the monad there are perceptions that are apperceived but also an unapperceived, unconscious realm of perceptions. This should be conceived as a realm of virtuality, which become real in accordance with the unfolding of the monad. Our experience of encountering other beings in the world is reducible to the unfolding of the monad's perceptions and affections. And the materialization of the body is also made possible by it. Colebrook thinks this is a better model to conceive the queer: queer materialization resembles the unfolding of the monad, a continuous passage of the virtual to the actual, a process that does not permit rigidity. Hence Colebrook uses Leibnizian monadology as a model to understand queerness, as the openness of sexual identity to transformation:

> My body is a soul or monad because it is capable of perceiving and being affected in an absolutely singular manner: no other body has the same unfolding of time and space, the same perceptions and affections as mine. And within this body are a thousand other souls: a heart that will beat according to all the hormonal, nutritional, climactic and nervous perceptions it endures (and so on with every organ, and so on with every organ's cells, and so on with every microbiological event). Far from a body being individuated through subjection to norms, a body is absolutely individuated above and beyond (or before) any of the generalising norms that the laziness of common sense applies. This vitality is therefore essentially queer. The task of thinking is not to see bodies

in their general recognisable form, as this or that ongoing and unified entity, but to approach the world as the unfolding of events. (Colebrook 2010, 83)

If active vitalism is a *macro analysis* at the level of bodies, which are historical and political, passive vitalism is a *micro analysis* because it focalizes on the infinitely small vital potentials of which bodies are composed. Our bodies are composed of monads (thousand souls) as in Leibniz's metaphysical framework. I doubt that this metaphor fulfills well the role it is supposed to play. What Leibniz means by the constitution of the material body by the monads is controversial. How can material beings be composed of immaterial beings? If for "monads" we have to substitute "forces," what does it mean to call forces "souls"? Are we talking about psycho-physical forces? Do bodies materialize thanks to the affections and perceptions of the souls? I do not know what we gain by throwing ourselves in this metaphysical language, which is obscure. How to borrow the monad model without committing to the onto-theological claims that Leibniz makes by introducing the term? God created the monads and he knows all about their experiences because he chose the best possible world in which their perceptions are compossible. If in monadology there are no external relations, and all relations are internal, in what respect can we talk about "encounters"? Do encounters take place within the monad; are they always already inscribed in its concept? It is difficult to borrow some notions from a metaphysical system without pulling the whole metaphysical web of related concepts. And what guarantees that the perceptions that unfold from within the monad would not be organized in accordance with the norms that pertain to the heterosexual family of the patriarchal capitalist system?

Colebrook is heading toward an ethics and politics that dispense with the notion of the "person." Deleuze and Guattari reject moral subjectivity based on the deliberative model, which presumes that we are capable of weighing reasons before we make moral decisions. There are competing forces that underlie "decisions" and the reason why we acted in such and such a way can be explained as an effect of minute difference of forces. The absence of the person in this ontology brings with it the collapse of the politics of representation (of women's issues, gay rights, minority values) and thus the struggle for recognition no longer makes sense. The aim of politics is *mobilization* (Colebrook 2010, 86) of the forces. Butler and the naturalists share the anti-humanist perspective; they are both against the ontologies that assume free subjects who are capable of creating autonomous lives as persons by acting in accordance with values. Butler shows why this freedom is difficult to have by pointing to how the subjects are effects of power. On the Deleuzian side, the debate over freedom is more complicated because we are an intersection of the impersonal forces and it does not make sense to speak of free choice.

The only thing we can do is to attain the awareness of the forces of which we are effects.

Butler believes in the unlimited multiplicity of gender performances and Grosz believes in the unlimited diversity of sexual differences—they both seek a politics to expand cultural representation. They ontologically disagree about how diversity should be understood. Should it be conceived as having a biological ground in nature or is it linguistically, symbolically produced by power? For Grosz, sexual difference is real and not culturally constructed. More accurately, that which is corporeally lived is as much given as invented difference (Grosz 2012, 73). To speak of the creation and invention of the body implies the entrance of nature into culture and the cultural transformation of the body. If that is the case, the right way of understanding sexual difference requires at once a pondering on how nature presents diversity and how some of that diversity retreats and disappears in nature.

In her recent writings, Grosz argued, following Irigaray, that corporeal biological difference is a source for spiritualization. Her new strategy rejects the setting of opposition between nature and culture. Culture is a complex expression of nature, but in the actual culture only some of these expressions are prevalent. For the natural multiplicity to attain culture we need new imaginary and symbolic interventions. In *The Incorporeal: Ontology, Ethics and the Limits of Materialism* (Grosz, 2017a), she holds that the articulation of identity requires incorporeal frameworks (space, time, the cosmos, ideality, God). What she designates as "onto-ethics" is not merely a new philosophical description of the being of beings (which are in constant change) but speaks of what might become and what ought to happen (the domain of normativity). In Grosz's late work the realm of normativity does not directly derive from the corporeal but is spiritual creation. Her position goes beyond a naturalist position in meta-ethics that reduces values to natural properties. Irigaray had stressed throughout her work that in Western civilization the symbolic frameworks reflected a unique type of subject, which is the male subject. Grosz argues that we cannot understand the material world if we neglect the incorporeal conditions of materialization. In "Irigaray, the Untimely, and the Constitution of an Onto-Ethics," she recognizes the irreducibility of the duality between the nature and law, nature and spirituality, even though she emphasizes that nature precedes the spiritual realm (Grosz 2017b). She places Irigaray among the philosophers who aimed at restoring the continuities of the real, "the return of respect to not only the materiality of things, including living things, but also to their incorporeal conditions, to the framing conditions under which space, time, and sense or representability give possible order to the world of things" (Grosz 2017b, 19). This approach attempts to overcome the great problem of materialist feminism, which is reductionism. One way to solve the problem is to efface the opposition between nature and culture and talk about the sexed body as a "materialsemiological assemblage." In materialist feminisms that are inspired by Irigaray, female biology as ova producer is considered to be an indispensable natural category. The plurality of the sexual differences should open up from the binary. This is a refusal to efface the female in the name of plurality of the sexes; the strategy is to affirm it and acknowledge that women's political struggles depend on that affirmation. In this framework, "gender identity" can be conceived as an expression, in contrast to, for example, Beauvoir's feminism that would look at it as a complex effect of historical material reality. In Grosz, the lived experience of the corporeal is articulated through the incorporeal conditions that are cultural inventions; in Colebrook, the internalist model individuates and individualizes sexual difference in such a way that no room is left for feminist critique that makes use of terms such as "patriarchy," "masculinity," "gender," "male domination," etc.

Grosz's onto-ethics takes the material and the immaterial forces as the ontological forces of the real world. Her concept of the "real" has at first shifted the focus from the symbolic structures to the material forces of nature; though, with the appeal to the immaterial, reality takes on a new sense: it is now seen as something that can also be fashioned. It is now redefined as the continuity or the bond between the material and the immaterial forces. In her onto-ethics the immaterial has a major role to play for the materialization of the body, which is always in becoming in its worldly reality. A metaphysics of subjectivity and politics of recognition are rejected. However, the creativity of the incorporeal is deemed necessary to open the space for the bodies to materialize in their diversity with the right to define, know, and order reality. This is the ontological proposal to undo the regime that benefits only one sex, the call for a new order of cultural and ethical regulations that allows for the plurality of the sexes, without effacing the biological female. Surely, Grosz is highlighting the ontological significance of social and cultural framing and, in so doing, makes possible the way for an ethical coexisting of the nature's dynamic forces. She stipulates that existence of "real forces, real actions, real histories, and geographies, forms, and directions of sense that makes individuals possible and constitute their conditions of existence and flourishing" (Grosz 2017b, 9) and borrows Simondon's distinction between the pre-individual and the individual to argue that the pre-individual forces can be the conditions for the existence and flourishing of the individual (Grosz and Hill 2017, 13).

I think both Butler and Grosz are pursuing a Hegelian problem: Hegel comprehends reality as the dialectical unfolding and concretization of the idea in nature and spiritual world. There is an ontological continuity between nature and the spiritual human world. We cannot understand spiritual reality just by considering individuals' acts. Butler rejects a naturalist standpoint that beings with the effectivity of the natural real forces. The thesis that the performativity of power materializes bodies is quite stronger than the recognition that there are incorporeal frameworks of materialization for bodies that are already real in the natural sense. Butler refuses to see reality as an unfolding of an idea in the Hegelian sense, a concretization of a symbolic thesis; she sees our corporeal reality, existential reality, as a production of power. In Butler's *Gender Trouble*, the problem is not just the opposition between the symbolic and the real, language and nature, gender and sex. It results from the fact that the second term arises as a logical consequence of the operation of the first term and reduces to being a postulate of it.

Butler believes, like Grosz, that difference and dynamism is the engine of change, but she rejects the claim that sexual difference is a fundamental difference. It is worth noting that her criticism of sexual difference is not similar to Catherine A. MacKinnon's critique: given that difference is a relation, if X is different from Y, Y is different from X. It is unclear what difference can establish in view of the unequal distribution of power. Difference does not tell us anything about why men have more power over women. Why then talk about sexual difference instead of social and political inequality? The sexual difference view risks falling in the trap of patriarchy and can reinforce the patriarchal prejudices. Butler's reasons for opposing the sexual difference thesis are different than MacKinnon's reasons. Butler rejects the sexual difference thesis on ontological grounds: the reflection must shift its focus from sexual difference to gender because corporeal materializations depend on the performativity of the normative representations that pertain to discourse/power regimes. *Bodies That Matter: On the Discursive Limits of Sex* (Butler 1993) is a restatement of that position. If this is the case, we have no philosophical ground to know anything about sexual difference that is not constructed. In "From Radical Representations to Corporeal Becomings: The Feminist Philosophy of Llyod, Grosz, and Gatens," Colebrook rightly remarks that even though Butler rejects that the difference between sex and gender is a necessary distinction that we should keep, she in fact intensifies a duality (Colebrook 2000, 78). However, even if Butler's account implies a duality between sexual difference and gender, there are no grounds to speak of the former; it remains unspeakable. Colebrook accuses Butler of being too occupied with the duality between matter and representation for this is an opposition as typical as male/female, nature/culture in Western thought. I agree that we have no means to speak of matter without representation. And how to understand representation without pitting it against matter? To figure that out, we can look at how Colebrook describes a particular form of empiricism, which Deleuze called "radical empiricism," which she also refers to as a "superior empiricism," and a "transcendental empiricism" in her book on Deleuze: "The principle of immanence demands that we do not see experience as the experience of some being or some ultimate subject. Rather, there is a flow or multiplicity of experiences from which any being or idea is effected" (Colebrook 2000, 87). Not only beings and ideas, but norms, too, come out of the flow of experience. At times, Colebrook sounds as if she argues against normativity and does not like to think about how norms regulate incorporation. She is critical of Butler's account because in the gender approach the bodies materialize in their encounter of the law, norms, and prior ideals. Colebrook takes queerness as a problem of individuation. Bodies are individuated because of the potential differences that infinitely exceed and divide bodies. It is not in relation to law but due to this monadological constitution that bodies are individuated. Colebrook's naturalist materialism fails to make sense of the operations of the gendering power on bodies; in contrast to her, Grosz has a way to explain that. From Butler's perspective, it is unclear how the natural forces can counter power that organizes bodies. In Grosz, however, it is possible to claim that changing the immaterial conditions of materialization can help to transform the exercise of power. I think that naturalist feminisms can enlarge our conception of nature beyond teleology, essentialism, and sexual determinism, but they are doomed to fail insofar as they cannot account for normativity. Grosz's version of naturalist feminism that comes to value the role of the immaterial and the incorporeal holds that values and norms are human spiritual creations, which give us frames of materialization. Beauvoir's materialist existentialism concentrated on the interaction between the forces of production and reproduction. Grosz's version of naturalism enables us to see that the forces of sexual difference go beyond their roles in reproduction and create new cultures.

Indeed, the old feminist debate over sex and gender is far from being outdated and still haunts our present gender politics. These terms have such a long history in which several attempts have been made to redefine them. With all the complexity of that history, these terms are still central to alternative queer ontologies. Butler's queer ontology denaturalized sexual difference by working out a new concept of gender. In contrast, the naturalist ontologies of sex of Grosz and Colebrook embraced the term sexual difference and aimed at the "renaturalization" of differences. The naturalist endeavor to redefine "the real" beyond the opposition between nature and culture opens to a plurality of sexual differences and fights compulsory heterosexuality. Butler's queer theory began with a dismantling of the category of "woman" as the subject of feminism, and concentrated, following Foucault, on the way power produces subjects. This is an ontology of power that focuses on how power is diffused in discourse and practice, effectuates submission and exclusion, materializes bodies, and creates hierarchies among them by rendering some intelligible and others unintelligible.

These alternative queer ontologies lead to different sexual politics. As I read her, Butler offers a peaceful and transformative strategy to overcome exclusion; her theory makes people think from the other side of a binary understanding of gender, and does not foreclose itself to philosophical questioning. In her ontological framework, "gender" functions as the key concept for an anti-essentialist account of sexuation. Although she acknowledges that the specific configuration of power relations must be approached in their specific context, there are still universal explanatory concepts and structures. As soon as these are forsaken, gender as a major critical concept will be lost and we would be left with a politics of bodily becomings and their monadic experiences. The assemblages that they form can be mobilized to carry out an affective politics of shame, anger, and hate, and engage in politics of war. This war may not be fought against patriarchy, male violence, and power embedded in sexist and racist institutions, but target the closest allies, such as feminists and queer theorists. If the self-affirmation of vulnerable subjects comes with an unquestionable moral justification of their right to verbally injure, attack, label, silence, and exclude other theoretical and political voices and concerns from the public space, the feminist field would no longer embrace multiplicity. Nobody should be forced to agree with an ontological view about which one has reasons to doubt. And we need to question the harm caused by the violent politics of shame carried out by activists all over the world. Is it morally right to violently target radical, socialist, materialist feminists, and queer theorists in non-Western parts of the world, in contexts where patriarchy is still very strong, femicide is a serious problem, the state power bans pride parades and feminist marches with police force, and the historical gains of the women's movement are constantly under patriarchal attack? How does that fit with intersectionalism? How can the arguments of intersectionalist black feminism apply in contexts such as my country, Turkey, where ethnic difference has become politicized due to state oppression, where the government openly withdraws its support for gender equality in universities, and where women's studies risk being closed down?

From my point of view, an ontology that takes into account the lived experience of the body, that signifies within the framework created by the immaterial forces of materialization, and that recognizes the importance of the feminist critique of patriarchy, restitution of the male domination by the institutionalized power, is preferable to the alternative ontologies of sex. In a world in which men kill women every day, we should not dispense with the feminist critique of patriarchy. Race is not a scientific category; the "reality" of race is the reality of the lived experiences of racism, which are historically constituted. The reality of sex, too, is created by the history of sexism, but if women suffer violence because they are gendered on grounds of their female biology, they should be able to defend themselves with sexed rights. Identity being among the multiple effects of power, identity politics cannot be a good strategy to fight power. If resistance is the subversion of power and the destabilization of its function and effect, it should not be based on sameness, control, unification, and be an instrument of power's reign over bodies. For Hegelians, subjectivity depends on recognition, and this is also where Butler started in her first work. The politics of recognition is identity politics. However, according to Butler, the construction of subjectivity through being recognized as an identity on the grounds of difference leads to melancholia because the question of self exceeds the category of identity. Ontologically speaking, identity remains always wanting, deficient, and transitory. However, in certain situations, the assumption of an identity can help the subject to transform itself into a resisting subject. There may be situations in which identity politics is the only inevitable way to fight the domination that aims to dissolve the agency of the oppressed, to stand up against the forces that relegate people to passivity and apathy.

Colebrook problematizes the view that the politics of resistance depends on recognition by suggesting that the assemblage and articulation of becomings can organize a becoming minority. The goal of politics is not the reconciliation of a minority through its recognition by the majority (Colebrook 2010, 86). On this view, the existence and effectivity of plurality does not rest on its being recognized or accepted by the majority, it comes from its multiple becomings. Granting that there are multiple becomings, the question what makes them good and not harmful remains to be answered. If the good reduces to the liveliness of the forces, there would be no good reason for wanting them to trump over the other forces that have other concrete problems on their agendas. If the call for equalization implies cancelling and replacing persons and groups who have access to the means of symbolic production, how different this is than the ruling power's strategies based on resentment which enjoys the civil murder of their opponents? We have seen how the resentment caused by the secular repression of the religious style of life can backlash as injustice and persecution of the secular style of life. The symbolic realm has its own dialectic and does not simply evolve by the clash of the emotive forces. Naturalism must theorize and re-evaluate justice and equality before it can assert that multiple becomings bring emancipation. In the sixth chapter, I shall talk about how a politics of subjectivation can contribute to the ontological debate over sex, without which politics of assemblage risks turning into a politics of war and persecution. However, before I do that, I shall follow the second trajectory of my elaboration of ontology of sex and devote my fifth chapter to Jean-Luc Nancy's ontology of sex and erotic relationship.

REFERENCES

Althusser, Louis. 2014. *Ideology and the Ideological State Apparatuses*. Translated by G. M. Goshgarian. London: Verso.
Bettcher, Talia Mae. 2014. "Trapped in the Wrong Theory: Rethinking Trans Oppression and Resistance." *Signs: Journal of Women in Culture and Society* 39, no. 2: 383–406.
Butler, Judith. 1988. "Performative Acts and Gender Constitution: An Essay in Phenomenology and Feminist Theory." *Theatre Journal* 40, no. 4: 519–31.

———. 1992. "Gendering the Body: Beauvoir's Philosophical Contribution." In *Women, Knowledge and Reality: Explorations in Feminist Philosophy*, edited by Ann Garry and Marilyn Pearsall. London and New York: Routledge. First published 1989.

———. 1993. *Bodies That Matter: On the Discursive Limits of Sex*. London and New York: Routledge.

———. 1994. "Variations on Sex and Gender: Beauvoir, Wittig and Foucault." In *Feminism as Critique: Essays on the Politics of Gender in Late Capitalist Societies*, edited by Seyla Benhabib and Drucilla Cornell, 128–42. Cambridge: Polity Press.

———. 1997a. *Excitable Speech: A Politics of the Performative*. New York: Routledge.

———. 1997b. *The Psychic Life of Power, Theories in Subjection*. Stanford, CA: Stanford University Press.

———. 1998. "Sex and Gender in Simone de Beauvoir's *Second Sex*." In *Simone de Beauvoir: A Critical Reader*, edited by Elizabeth Fallaize, 29–42. New York: Routledge. Originally published in *Yale French Studies* 72 (1986).

———. 2008. *Gender Trouble: Feminism and the Subversion of Identity*. London and New York: Routledge.

———. 2019. https://www.nytimes.com/2019/07/10/opinion/judith-butler-gender.html.

Cheah, Pheng. 1996. "Mattering (Review Essay of *Bodies That Matter* and Elizabeth Grosz's *Volatile Bodies*)." *Diacritics* 26, no. 1: 116–18. http://muse.jhu.edu/demo/diacritics/26.1er_butler.html.

Cheah, Pheng, Elizabeth Grosz, and Judith Butler. 1998. "Irigaray and the Political Future of Sexual Difference." *Diacritics* 28, no. 1 (Spring): 19–42.

Colebrook, Claire. 2000. "From Radical Representations to Corporeal Becomings: The Feminist Philosophy of Llyod, Grosz, and Gatens." *Hypatia* 15, no. 2 (Spring): 76–93.

———. 2002. *Gilles Deleuze*. New York: Routledge.

———. 2010. "Queer Vitalism." *New Formations* 1 (March): 77–92.

Deleuze, Gilles, and Félix Guattari. 1983. *Anti-Oedipus: Capitalism and Schizophrenia*. Translated by Robert Hurley, Mark Seem and Helen R. Lane. Minneapolis: University of Minnesota Press.

———. 1987. *A Thousand Plateaus: Capitalism and Schizophrenia*. Translated by Brian Massumi. Minnesota: University of Minnesota Press.

Foucault, Michel. 1977. *Discipline and Punish: The Birth of Prison*. Trans. Alan Sheridan. New York: Vintage Books.

———. 1980. *The History of Sexuality: An Introduction*. Vol 1. Translated by Robert Hurley. New York: Vintage Books.

Grosz, Elizabeth. 1994. *Volatile Bodies*. Bloomington and Indianapolis: Indiana University Press.

———. 2012. "The Nature of Sexual Difference: Irigaray and Darwin." *Angelaki* 17, no 2 (July): 69–93.

———. 2017a. *The Incorporeal: Ontology, Ethics and the Limits of Materialism*. New York: Columbia University Press.

———. 2017b. "Irigaray, the Untimely, and the Constitution of an Onto-Ethics." *Australian Feminist Law* 43, no. 1.

Grosz, Elizabeth, and Rebecca Hill. 2017. "Onto-Ethics and Difference: An Interview with Elizabeth Grosz." *Australian Feminist Law Journal* 43, no. 1: 5–14.

Haslanger, Sally. 2014. "Race, Intersectionality, and Method: A Reply to Critiques." *Philosophical Studies* 171: 109–19.

Heinämaa, Sara. 1997. "What Is a Woman? Butler and de Beauvoir on the Foundations of Sexual Difference." *Hypatia* 12, no. 1 (Winter).

Kontturi, Katve Kaisa, and Milla Tiainen. 2007. "Feminism, Art, Deleuze, and Darwin: An Interview with Elizabeth Grosz." *Nora Nordic Journal of Women's Studies* 15, no. 4 (November): 246–56.

Lildemann, Hilda. 2011. "What Is Feminist Ethics." In *The Ethical Life: Fundamental Readings in Ethics and Moral Problems*, edited by Russ Schafer-Landau. Oxford: Oxford University Press.

Ong-Van-Cung, Kim Sang. 2011. "Critique et subjectivation. Foucault et Butler sur le sujet." *Actuel Marx* 1, no. 49: 148–61.

Sandford, Stella.1999. "Contingent Ontologies, Sex, Gender and 'Woman' in Simone de Beauvoir and Judith Butler." *Radical Philosophy* 97: 18–29.

Stoetzler, Marcel. 2005. "Subject Trouble: Judith Butler and Dialectics." *Philosophy Social Criticism* 31: 343–68.

Stoller, Silvia. 2010. "Expressivity and Performativity: Merleau-Ponty and Butler." *Continental Philosophical Review* 43, no. 1 (April): 97–110.

Chapter Five

Jean-Luc Nancy

An Ontology of Sex

Jean-Luc Nancy's reflection on sex (*le sexe*) is an ontological inquiry that concerns sex as force and act and elaborates the Being of sex as giving rise to the multiple possibilities of body's embodiment through sexuality, in sexual relations. This is a philosophical discourse that resists subscribing to the well-known distinction between sex and gender—a distinction that has come under critique from within feminism, even though it still determines the horizon of feminist debates. The controversy between those who embrace the concept of gender as a key concept and the feminists who prefer to focus on sexual difference continues to be a major schism in feminism and queer theory. Before the appropriation of the term "genre" to translate gender, which is, in fact, recent, French language did not distinguish between sex as biologically determined and gender as culturally acquired. *Le sexe* in French meant both genitalia and gender traits: it was Simone de Beauvoir who, in *The Second Sex*, reinvented this concept by showing that biological sex, even though it is natural and real, cannot be an essence or a cause that determines existence. Her notion of the "body as a situation" served to ontologically redefine sex as a matter of existential, historical situation. Women were made into who/what they were by being in the situation of the second sex. This perspective paved the way for a reflection on *le sexe* to take a direction toward gender. Today, social constructionism continues to have a respectable place in social sciences insofar as it is still useful in undermining the naturalist metaphysical strategies of legitimating sexual inequality and the oppression that accompanies it.

Nancy's reflection on *le sexe* as it unfolds in the second volume of the *Corpus* (Nancy 2013) and *Sexistence* (Nancy 2017a) is very different from the feminist reflections we are so far acquainted with. Nancy does not engage with the history and problems of feminist philosophy. No doubt, his work would have been more interesting if he took feminist thinkers into account. I think that his not doing this is a problem; however, I also believe that his lack of engagement should not stop us from asking how his contribution to the ontology of sex might be relevant to feminist philosophy.

The most significant concept of Nancy's ontology of sex is "sexistence." To exist means for Nancy to be outside of one's self; the neologism "sexistence" alludes to the push from within to the outside by sex, which makes sexistence an effect of sex (Nancy 2017a, 29). The notion bears in itself the question whether sex is detachable from existence, and Nancy affirms the inseparability of the former from the latter. Nancy returns to the question whether sex can merely be considered as a purely ontic matter without ontological significance. In the task to create an ontology of sex, he takes his inspiration from diverse philosophical sources. Throughout this chapter, I shall point to the ways in which Nancy's ontology of sex relates to the ideas coming from Plato, Martin Heidegger, Jacques Lacan, Georges Bataille, Michel Foucault, and Jacques Derrida. Although all of these figures are Nancy's philosophical interlocutors, in this chapter I cannot pay to all of them the attention they deserve. In my exposition, Bataille, Heidegger, and Foucault play lesser roles than Derrida and Lacan. The only reason for that is my wish to pursue an explication of Nancy's thought in relation to Derrida and Lacan. I would accept that working on his implicit and explicit references to other philosophers can shed as much light to Nancy's ontological approach than an investigation of his relation to Derrida and Lacan.

In the first section, I give a brief account of Nancy's reading of the question of sex in history of philosophy before he proceeds to elaborate his own concept of sex. The second section focuses on Derrida's discussion of sexual difference to show in what respects Nancy's account differs from it. Finally, my third section turns to Nancy's convergence and divergence from Lacan. I argue that Nancy follows Derrida's ontological approach to sex, though he conceives the ontological problem differently: he substitutes for sex as dissemination sex as relationality, which paves the way for a notion of the erotic relation as care. I also show that Nancy's discussion of signification of desire in the erotic relationship enables him to reject Lacan's notorious claim that there is no sexual relation.

PROVIDING A PHILOSOPHICAL BACKGROUND TO NANCY'S NEW CONCEPT OF SEX

What moments of the philosophy of history have inspired Nancy in *Sexistence* in the creation of his new concept of sex? In *Sexistence* Nancy asserts that we do not actually have a concept of sex. Even if we have a concept, it does not have a unity; it consists of bits and pieces, fragmented meanings, and experiences (Nancy 2017a). This statement sounds rather unfair given the contribution that thinkers such as Michel Foucault and Claude Lévi-Strauss, among others, have made to the concept of sex. Foucault associated sexuality with biopower and Lévi-Strauss with the political and social organization of societies. Indeed, sexuality is an immense apparatus that serves to establish a social order with norms, representations, taboos, and religious rituals. Foucault shows that in the modern era, too, we are not exempt from the production of society via the reformation of the sexual relations and the revision of sexual practices. Political power invests on sexuality as it manages life. Symbols and myths about sexuality are still prevalent in societies. Nancy does not object to what Foucault and Lévi-Strauss have said about sex; however, he thinks that sex in the ontological sense requires a different analysis. It requires a suspension of the sociological and the political to attain a purely philosophical level. This is an analysis of what sex is, independently of how the performativity of power shapes bodies, and bodies as the effects of discourse/power regimes. Nancy does not believe that the ontological question reduces to the question of historical and social power. Foucault's analysis provides for important criticism in the effort to comprehend the relation between sex and power, but this is not sufficient to form a philosophical concept of sex.

There seems to be a tension between Foucault's occupation with the relation between power and sexuality and his demand that philosophy becomes a regime of living. Can there be sexual life beyond power, if power is diffused even at the micro levels? In contrast to Foucault, Nancy is not interested in carrying out an analysis of power. I believe he can be read as sympathetic to the Foucault of *The Use of Pleasures*, who recommends a life lived not by observing an ethics of principles or commands but in self-problematization in the style of ancient virtue ethics. In virtue ethics, self-control, mastery over pleasures, was not separated from the soul's relation to truth in the metaphysical sense. Foucault sees self-problematization as an integral part of the relation to truth (Foucault 1985, 5 and 23). For Nancy, such a hermeneutics of the self belongs to the reflection on relations and, more significantly, on the sexual relation considered in its neutrality.

Nancy sets himself the task of considering sexuality and along with it "being sexed" as questions of being. This reflects in the way Nancy frames his investigation: he is neither interested in sexual difference nor in different sexualities; he wants to raise the question of the sex itself. Rather than looking at sex as organ or function, he approaches sex as it takes place in time and space as relation, as waiting or expectation, enjoyment or deception (Nancy 2017a, 13). *Comme une poussée s'exerce, comme une excitation s'excite*. In fact, this pulsion is nothing else than to exist—this thrust outside of oneself in its character of upsurge and multiplicity. This is an origin that cannot be assigned to anything else than to its opening and push (Nancy 2017a, 39). These expressions serve to introduce the act of sex to manifest itself without a subject. We do not have sex; sex is not something that we possess; our being is sex or is sexed, as sex sexists (Nancy 2017a, 13). The act of sex is thrust or propulsion into existence, which Nancy conceives as a meeting place of different energies. Although sexual energy is not our sole energy, it is one of the most energetical among our existential resources. Although we cannot attribute sexual energy to existence, as if all existence is or must be sexual, once that energy is in existence it is also the most exceeding.

In *Sexistence*, Nancy highlights the remarkable moments of the history of philosophical reflection on sex from ancients to moderns. Philosophy was not foreign to sexuality since its early beginnings. We cannot oppose sexuality to philosophy, presuming that the former has to do with affects and affective intensities, whereas the latter is occupied with concepts. In Plato, philosophy cannot be indifferent to an affect such as love insofar as it provides the energy to attain the idea. Ancient Greek philosophy did not see sexuality as an activity that merely serves the purposes of the reproduction of the species nor reduce love to a sensual play of the bodily pleasures. Plato conceived love as related with knowledge and truth. In *Symposium*, the primary object of love is the form of Beauty. As Diotima puts it, those men are capable of loving wisdom discover that the beauty in all beautiful bodies is the same by undergoing an experience of loving that begins with loving the beautiful body of the beloved. Loving a single body makes them apperceive that there are other bodies like it, and at the third step, they can relate to the whole group of beautiful bodies. This succession precedes the apprehension to love beautiful souls and make possible the desire's ascendance to the beauty in the souls, which is identical with the good (*Symposium*, 210 b–e). In *Phaedrus*, Plato assigns a role to the erotic desire in the intellectual quest for the beings themselves (forms). Beauty is the only higher reality that manifests itself in the sensible where it unleashes the most avid appetites besides the highest aspirations. The intellect is presented as such a higher object of sexual enjoyment, that, if the faculty of right judgment and the capacity to distinguish truth from falsity could be incarnated in a human being, it might trigger an erotic frenzy (*Phaedrus*, 250d; Nancy 2017a, 30). According to Nancy, philosophy in Plato's text caught an energy that would have been expended on sexuality, and by making transcendent the erotic desire that transfuses corporeal existence, appropriated a *phronesis* (a practical cognition that enables right action) to transform it into theoretical knowing.

The history of Eros is interwoven with the history of divinity. In Plato, Eros is referred to as a God. Even though Eros is clandestine, Ancient Greek culture represents him as a God that has an active and effective presence in the world. The divorce of Western culture with polytheism was also a break from love as something livable in the world. Afterward, God becomes the primary object of love. Carnal love and divine love are opposed, though this opposition hides a common ontological ground. In *Erotism*, Bataille puts his finger on the resemblance between eroticism and religious mysticism. He points to the presence of sexual energy in religious transcendence, even though the revealed religions have firmly rejected that sexuality can inhere in itself something divine, sacred, and infinite. In monotheistic religions in which God's transcendence predominated, the meaning of divine presence has changed. The mountains that were the abode of Gods could no longer be referred to as sacred places; they were now perceived as immense natural objects.

Nancy remarks that our civilization is still restless and anxious about sexuality. This is probably because monotheistic religions, which project sense to the beyond of the sensible world, are still anxious about the remaining traces of divinity in love and sexuality. It is important that Eros in Plato is the only figure of God that acts to bring about a transformation: Eros brings into being, drives beings into presence, and the reason for this push is not to enable nature to reproduce itself as the same without any surplus value. Moreover, Eros touches all the other Gods. He diversifies nature and transforms the human world. In monotheisms, the problems of truth and knowledge are sharply separated from the topics of Eros and desire. This leads to the forgetting of the association between Eros and philosophy. The language of sexual relation signifies differently than a language that makes an objective state of affairs manifest, either by ostension or description.

Saint Augustine is a special case because, in his writings, in the relation of desire to truth thought excels without leaving sensibility or affectivity behind. As thought tries to ascend to the truth in the sense of God's presence, affectivity intensifies. However, as God's truth glows, God himself eludes the approach of the subject who wants to enter into an intimate relation with him. The problem is not concerned with the representation of God as exterior to me. He is exterior precisely because He is more interior than my own interiority. Saint Augustine writes in *Confessions*: "I searched for you outside myself, while all along you were within me. You were in me, but I was not in You" (Augustine 1993, 117 translation modified).[1] "Being admonished to return to myself, O Lord, I entered into my own depths, with You as guide, and I was able to do it because You were my helper" (Augustine 1993, 192 translation modified).[2] God is even more interior than our own interiority, which is supposed to be closest and most present to us. But this new frame that directs love to truth in the sense of God, makes the bodily love sin, depreciates its value and deprives it of its truth, presents it as an obstacle on the way of salvation. Hence, Augustine marks the withdrawal of sexuality from philosophy; he closes the possibility of an ontological reflection of sex beyond a condemnation of sex, which makes it a phenomenon of falling in the worldly existence.

What about modernity? Nancy observes that in contemporary philosophy sexuality returns to philosophy. Freud plays a significant role in this return because he understands philosophy and art as activities that are made possible by the sublimation of erotic energy. Nancy speaks of Freud's grounding of human activity in libidinal energy by relating it to a prominent thesis of Kant's philosophy.

Kant says in the *Critique of Pure Reason* (A: 1781/B: 1787), Transcendental Dialectic Chapter III, in the fourth section, "*Being* is obviously not a real predicate" (A: 598/B: 627). At issue is *being* in general, and not just *existence* in particular. Thus, the claim has broader significance than the standard interpretation attributes to it. It is not just intended to refute the ontological proof of God's existence, and it becomes a turning point in Reason's self-understanding. For Nancy, this claim Kant made in the *Critique of Pure Reason*, opened a new era in which Reason itself was lead to consider itself as *Trieb* (impulse, thrust, tension, desire), which tends toward an "unconditional" that reveals itself in Reason's own thrust. This understanding of being assumes several names: in Schopenhauer and Nietzcshe it is designated as "will" and in Freud as "pulsion" (Nancy 2017a, 31). Nineteenth-century French literature echoes this philosophical terminology in speaking of sex. For example, when Flaubert in *Madame Bovary* speaks of sexuality with reference to the forces that we feel operate on us (Flaubert 1965). Sartre in *Idiot of the Family* quotes the sentence "I believe that you are suffering from an illusion, and a big one, as always when one effects an action, whatever it may be" (Sartre 1987, 426). Flaubert shows how predispositions, delusive ideas, ideas that are not acted on are as real as actions. Nancy agrees with him in that we feel the sexual forces, which are inside and outside. According to Nancy, the forces of Eros are the forces of the origin, which provide for the possibility of life and death. This origin does not have an origin because it is always lesser and greater than itself. This is the desire for the unconditional, which mingles all with nothing.

Mythologies attest to this *Trieb* as a force that stimulates God, and thus represent it as the origin that makes the world begin to be. Why do Gods exist? There is a desire that brings them in being, wants them to be. But the reference to desire does not constitute a good answer to a philosophical or metaphysical question. According to Nancy, the only philosopher that could find an answer to such a question is Spinoza: he manages to give an answer to it by identifying God with nature; God is the *Trieb* for being to be.

We are creatures of desire. Desire gives every one of us shape, intensity, and color. Desire always comes back to its origin, it re-originates itself; in other words, its creation continues. In the Koran, God repeats that He could destroy and re-create, hence reconstruct the world as he wishes. This is analogous to a sexual being that has its origin, that is, desire present in it, which renders it capable of destroying and recreating its life. In the creativity of the sexual being, origin repeats itself. In short, Eros has the power to destroy and rebuild our world anew, more than once, and sometimes by repeating itself.

For Nancy, the experience of sexuality resembles the experience of reason that seeks truth. The experience of sexuality, too, aims to reach in enjoyment a bright, radiant being. In Plato's allegory of the cave, the journey to the outside world reaches its peak with the gaze directed to the sun, which is a metaphor for the idea of the Good. In a sense even the intelligible is sensible, sensible at the highest degree. Glowing light and brilliance are not the objects of optics but of form. This sensibility toward glowing, sparking, flashing, radiating beings is at work in sexuality, desire, and pleasure. Derrida in *Glas*, which is a text that dates from 1974, underlines the fact that Jean Genet designates the homosexual act as a rubbing and shining. *Lux*, radiance, flooding of light, excessiveness, debauchery, lust, fluidity, bad desire . . . these are the metaphors for both knowledge and enjoyment. There is enjoyment in the knowledge of being and truth in sexual relation.

The philosophical claim that "there is truth in sexual relationship" asks for scrutiny. What kind of truth is that? Is it a metaphysical truth, a truth about a psychological state, or a political truth? Foucault in *The History of Sexuality* speaks of the injunction to talk about sexuality, the incitation to display and uncover sexual lives. Discourses that circulate everywhere do not in fact reveal anything. Levinas in an unfinished novel about Eros, confessed that our own intimacy is never obscene; love is obscene only if it is that of others (Levinas 2009). I think Nancy here is directed to an existential notion of truth, truth not in the sense of being in a silent genuine dialogue with one's self, but the truth that manifests itself in the communication with the other. Communication that is not simply grounded on empathy but in letting the other's signification enter in you. This is the truth of Sexistence.

Bataille, who is one of Nancy's interlocutors, in his reflection on sex, speaks of eroticism as "inner experience." Inner experience is a limit in signifying; it reveals a sense that is impossible to say or to express without excess. Definitely, Nancy's philosophy of sex calls for a comparison with Bataille's discourse on sexuality. Unlike Bataille, Nancy does not consider sexuality in relation to taboos and sexual prohibitions and does not define eroticism in terms of the transgression of prohibitions. Bataille's account of sexuality is informed by Claude Lévi-Strauss's structuralist anthropology. Anthropology explains that primitive people perceive sexual energy in its immediacy as dangerous. Taboos are instituted at times and places they felt the threat of violence. Bataille argues that religions specify the limits in which sexual acts prohibited by the taboos can be performed by the transgression of the prohibitions. Indeed, the sacred world could only open up by the regulations that introduced the boundaries in which transgressions are acceptable. The same act that appears to be a perversion or a crime can become perfectly legitimate if the sacred law determines the limits in which the case for the exception is made. In the secular world in which God's existence makes little or no effect on the private and the public sphere, the sacred reduces to superstition and fantasy. From a religious standpoint, the disappearance of the sacred brings about a really dangerous situation. In *Brothers Karamazov*, Dostoyevski said, "If God does not exist everything is permitted" (Dostoyevski 1880). That statement grounds moral values in religious values and does not trust any secular normative morality based on a form of moral reasoning. But at the end of the day, even if God exists, we need to make our own moral decisions. The meaning of God's words is not immediately present to us. God's revelation has to go through the human mind, unfold in its concepts, which signify something insofar as they are constituted historically. Whether God can be separated from that history is a philosophical problem precisely for that reason. Hegel laid out this problem. Nancy argues that the modern secular worldview, which evacuated God from the human world, has released an immense energy, and that is what made sexuality a topic of intense interest and curiosity. Indeed, he sees Bataille's and Lacan's reflections on sexuality as provoked by this historical situation. The problem for Nancy is that in the secular world we do not know how to think of sexuality.

DERRIDA ON SEXUAL DIFFERENCE

Nancy's reflection on sex is interesting because he attempts to conceptualize sex and sexuality in a new manner, by rejecting both the naturalism of the biological, scientific discourses and the social constructivism of the social sciences. He begins by retreating from such discourses to a phenomenological starting point. According to him, sex is neither physiological, nor psychological, nor sociological, even though these elements feature in the phenomenon of sex. Like Derrida, in his interpretation of Heidegger's marking of sexual difference in "Geschlecht I" (Derrida 1983), Nancy approaches sex and sexuality as ontological questions. This is why it is worthwhile to discuss Nancy's work in *Corpus* and *Sexistence* by putting it in a dialogue with Derrida's essay. Both Nancy and Derrida are Heideggerians who commit to neutralization in their philosophical accounts of sex. Although I juxtaposed Nancy's ontology of sex with Derrida's in "Geschlecht I," Nancy does not refer to this text. When he raises the question what sex means in Derrida, he prefers to interpret *Glas*. Nancy's reading of sex in Derrida in "Jouis Anniversaire" (Nancy 2017b) gives us a very illuminating analysis of sexual difference and erotic experience in Derrida.

Derrida in "Geschlecht I" considers necessary to discuss what it means for *Dasein* to be sexed, by beginning from the neutralization Heidegger has made in his existential analytic. Neutralization is the reduction of all knowledge transmitted to us about sexual difference and sexuality by the natural and human sciences such as biology, sociology, anthropology, and psychology. Evidently, this is radically opposed to Simone de Beauvoir's interdisciplinary strategy in *The Second Sex*. The naturalist queerness that I have discussed in chapter 4 would not survive this reduction either because it draws a lot from the sciences of life. Nor would the queerness in Butler's philosophy, because it is based on a problematization of naturalism by relying on the Foucauldian archaeology into discourse/power regimes. In order to carry out a more originary philosophical reflection on sex, it is necessary to neutralize both sex (natural sexual difference) and gender. Derrida argues that *Being and Time*'s notion of being-in-the-world, the basic state of *Dasein*, is the correct starting point for us to attain the appropriate level for an ontological reflection on sex. The problem with this approach that inscribes sexual difference in the framework of ontological difference is that it tells us very little about sexual desire, erotic experience, and sexual relationship. An account that neglects such components of sexistence would be incomplete. Nancy's philosophy of sex as it unfolds in *Corpus* and *Sexistence* can be interpreted, at least to a certain extent, as a further elaboration of the Heideggerian Derridean line of reflection, to supplement for its deficiencies.

Indeed, neither Heidegger nor Derrida spoke of desire and sexual relationship, even though they were not silent about sex and sexual difference. Derrida was not a thinker of desire. He has never explicitly raised the question of sexual desire as, for example, Freud and Lacan have. In *Of Grammatology*, the metaphysical desire (or nostalgia) for presence, unity, order, control, closure, and which restrict the play of signifiers is pivotal. Derrida identifies "logocentrism and the metaphysics of presence as the exigent, powerful, systematic, and irrepressible desire for such a [transcendental] signified" (Derrida 1997, 49)

But isn't there a difference between the metaphysical desire of presence and sexual desire? Is sexual desire a desire for immediate presence and access to life without *différance*? That would be what Lacan calls *demand* in distinction from desire. It seems to me that Derrida's text intimates that he agrees with some of Lacan's ideas about sexual desire. For instance, Lacan's claim that desire is organized by a veiled signifier may be transformed in Derrida into the formula that sexual desire is structured by *différance*. In reading Rousseau, he stresses the delay, the spacing, the supplementarity of significations between desire and pleasure (Derrida 1997, 351), which may be referring to Lacan's distinction between enjoyment and satisfaction of desire. As he writes in a footnote about Anteia's desire in Homer's *Iliad*: "Within an infinite chain of representations, desire carries death via the detour of writing" (Derrida 1997, 349, footnote 1).

Deconstruction in the early work enumerates binary oppositions such as truth and illusion, real and simulation, subject and object, presence and absence, speech and writing, sun and moon, nature and culture, and man and woman. For Derrida, the pair of opposites reduce differences. Logocentrism is at the same time phallocentrism. Arguably, early deconstruction inheres a deconstructive evaluation of the male and female positions in the symbolic system. In phallogocentrism, Derrida argued, "woman" is represented as lacking and "man" as a whole, which is contradictorily, in need of supplementation. The logic of supplement was for Derrida the contradictory logic of phallogocentrism. "Woman" was like *pharmakon*, the outside within the inside of the system to be deconstructed. Like Lacan, Derrida marked woman's position as a site of an enjoyment that the system cannot contain and account for. Rather than associating feminine *jouissance* with a relation to the Other, he considered it as a play or masquerade. As Ellen K. Feder and Emily Zarkin remark in "Flirting with Truth," women know that although the patriarchal culture is built on man's fear of castration, women know that castration has not taken place and that men do not possess the phallus. This knowledge is the power of dissimulation that gives rise to masquerade, which plays the game of seduction according to the rules of patriarchy, while, at the same time, mocks man (Feder and Zarkin 1997, 35–36). He saw himself and Nietzsche as also occupying this position in writing. In *Spurs* it is possible to read Derrida as doing a transsexual philosophy because of the abundance of the symbols of sexual multiplicity and performance in writing.

Spurs is an attempt to disclocate the category of woman and to shed suspicion on the demand for gender equality. Derrida follows Nietzsche in taking a distance to feminisms of equality that are based on woman's desire to be in the same moral and political position as man. His polemic against equality feminism opposed woman's struggle for equality to femininity as masquerade. Arguably, in *Spurs*, Derrida offered a Lacanian reading of Nietzsche, when he associated truth with the masquerade conceived as the play of concealment and unconcealment in the Heideggerian sense. Not the truth as adequation, but the truth as such, in the phenomenological sense is woman. We may wonder what, if anything, that contributes to women's emancipation. Of course, Derrida does not claim to know the truth of woman; if woman is truth, she has no truth (Derrida 1981, 53). Presuming that "woman as truth" functions as a metaphor that destabilizes the phallogocentrism, would it pave the way for thinking of feminine sexual difference beyond duality? Derrida's insistence on thinking sex beyond the opposition male (man)/female (woman) does not follow from his dissatisfaction with his early deconstructivist position in which sexual difference had no sense beyond metaphysical oppositions. The wish to overcome this initial position and to make room for feminine sexual difference beyond phallogocentrism might have provoked him to make a defense of Nietzsche. However, this deconstruction re-inscribes phallocentrism because *Spurs* rehearses patriarchal privilege (Feder and Zarkin 1997, 24) inasmuch as it subverts it.

In "Geschlecht I," Derrida can be heard as responding implicitly to the difference feminism. Indeed, he can be objecting, without naming her, to Irigaray's claim that Heidegger has forgotten the question of sexual difference. Derrida argues that sexual difference is inscribed in the existential analytic, which is a necessary condition for thinking the meaning of Being. In the introductory note Derrida says that "Geschlecht" means "sex, race, family, generation, lienage, species, genre/genus" (Derrida 1983, 65). Differences that situate us in facticity intersect with each other. In contemporary feminism, the term "intersectionality" refers to the way gender works through and by means of other differences. Why not take the polysemy in "Geschlecht" as a sign for the intersectional, interweaving differences? There is no reason why "Geschlecht" should not be thought as embedding an intersectional logic in its capacity to refer to all these differences at once. But Derrida does not entertain the idea that this swarm of senses in a single term can give way to an intersectionalist approach. This is not the project he pursues.

In "Geschlecht I," Derrida considers sexual difference in an interpretation of the *there* (*Da*) as dispersion, dissembling, and dissemination. This is the big thesis of his meticulous reading of few passages in *Being and Time*. He claims that Heidegger's method of neutralization amounts to an ontological positivity that liberates *Dasein* from the binary division of sex into male and female. This sounds like a revolutionary step because the modern scientific and psychoanalytical approaches operated within a paradigm determined by the binary model of sexual difference.

> At first the concept of neutrality seems quite general. It is a matter of reducing or subtracting every anthropological, ethical or metaphysical predetermination by means of that neutralization, so as to keep nothing but a relation to itself, bare relation, to the Being of its being; that is a minimal relation to itself as relation to Being, that the being which we are, as questioning, holds with itself and its own proper essence. (Derrida 1983, 69)

The "neutralization" aims to get rid of all the corporeal attributes and determinations (hormones, chromosomes, primary and secondary sexual characteristics, etc.) to have a relation to the Being of its being. This relation is at the heart of an authentic relation to one's self (ipseity) which is not reducible to identity. It is possible to speculate that Derrida, by stressing upon the necessity of neutralization, sets himself on the same page as contemporary queer theory. As I understand it, neutralization suspends both the natural and

social determinations and gives rise to a conception of sex in the dynamic
relation of the being to the Being of its being, a relation that swarms with
possibilities and virtualities. An experience that demands resolutions, appro-
priations and ex-appropriations, involves transformations and conversions,
and is like a process that implies coming face-to-face with one's self, not
once but in a recurrent manner. Remarkably, this neutralization does not
make *Dasein* an asexual being; on the contrary, it reveals an originary sexuality, which is full of positivity, which Heidegger also calls "power."

> Then, from that sexuality, more originary than the dyad, one may try to think
> to the bottom a "positivity" and a "power" that Heidegger is careful not to call
> sexual, fearing undoubtedly to reintroduce the binary logic that anthropology
> and metaphysics always assign to the concept of sexuality. Here indeed it is a
> matter of the positive and powerful source of every possible "sexuality." (Der-
> rida 1983, 72)

Sexuality beyond a division into male and female is not an undifferentiated
unity. As thrown being, *Dasein*'s being is dispersed in the world. Thrownness implies an assignment to a body (*Leiblichkeit*), which in its dispersal
into factical possibilities, seems to possess a disseminating unity. The pivotal
point of Derrida's reading is the claim that *Dasein* in general hides, shelters
in itself the internal possibility of a factual dispersion or dissemination (*fak-
tische Zerstreuung*) in its own body (*Leiblichkeit*) and thereby in sexuality
(*und damit in die Geschlechtlichkeit*). Every proper body is sexed and there
is no *Dasein* without its own body. The dispersing multiplicity in the body
plays against what is my own in the body in the sense of object that I possess.
In this framework, which is not very easy to grasp, the corporeal unity does
not precede dissemination; unity and dissemination are co-originary. Arguably, this is not an organic unity; unity comes about because the body gathers
itself by assuming a position, a stance, a style of being.

Making use of the concepts of Heidegger's ontology, Derrida speaks of
the sexuality in the "original" sense, as a disseminal unity. Feminist readers
of Derrida have evaluated this original sex understood as a disseminating
unity as a post-neutral masculinization of *Dasein* because the ontological
metaphor seemed to them to be a resignification of an ontic biological event,
the ejaculation of the sperms by the male sex organ. Why is *Dasein*'s dispersal into possibilities conceived in the metaphoric of ejaculation? Maxine
Sheets-Johnstone makes the following remark in *Roots of Power: Animate
Form and Gendered Bodies*:

> Thanks to an irreducible, ever-voluble Organ, Derrida can productively read
> off multiplicity from an original Oneness, the factual existence of individuals
> from an Ur disseminality [. . .] the "internal possibility" of Dasein is cast from
> a decisively-if always veiled-male bodily mold, thus strongly suggesting that

females "are mere egg repositories waiting for something to happen." (Johnstone 2016, 113)

From a feminist point of view, one may ask: Can this be true of all sex? Why to think the ontological notion of dispersal as sexual? Is this because the male sexuality understands itself in terms of the ejaculation of sperms that disperse in the world? Is there a necessity for taking up the ontological issues by the metaphoric of male morphology and sexuality? Why should dispersion be the metaphor of originary sexuality? Does Derrida fall within the phallocentric economy of signification in this argument? He makes a morphological, biological metaphor play a central role in the argument he offers to lift sexual difference from the ontic to the ontological plane, and in so doing, he resexuates *Dasein* as male. At the ontological level, the ontic neutralization undergoes a reversal, and creates the effect of masculinizing all *Dasein,* thereby effacing all other sexual difference.

Derrida claimed that by making a neutralization Heidegger undertook an ontological investigation of ipseity—which is to be sought in the relation of the being (that can ask the question of Being) to its own Being. According to Derrida the original disseminating unity precedes the binary division of the sexes. Although Heidegger neutralizes *Dasein*, takes out sex from the structure of its Being, and refuses to associate the binary sexual difference with ipseity—which must be sought in the relation of *Dasein* to its own Being— he does not exclude the possibility that ipseity could be difficult to dissociate from sexuality that ontologically precedes duality. Derrida notes that if such an original sexuality belongs to the ontological constitution of ipseity, then sexual difference may not even be a question. In other words, it becomes dubitable that it can properly be called a question. If there is a *Geschlecht* that precedes the division then it must be inscribed in the structure of the question of Being. This suggests that instead of envisioning a question of sexual difference that precedes the ontological difference, we should think sexual difference as belonging to the structure of the question of Being.

How is *Dasein*'s corporeality related to such an ipseity, which is more primary than all identity? Derrida emphasizes that *Dasein* is thrown into the world as assigned to a body.

> Every proper body of one's own [corps proper] is sexed, and there is no Dasein without its own body. But the chaining together proposed by Heidegger seems quite clear: the dispersing multiplicity is not primarily due to the sexuality of one's own body; it is its own body itself, the flesh, the Leiblichkeit, that draws Dasein originally into the dispersion and in due course [par suite] into sexual difference. This "in due course" (damit) insists through a few lines' interval, as if Dasein were supposed to have or be a priori (as its "interior possibility") a body found to be sexual, and affected by sexual division. (Derrida 1983, 75)

We must not imagine a worldly space, given in advance, in which *Dasein* would be thrown. *Dasein*'s spatiality—original spatiality, which is the ground of objective space—rests on *Dasein*'s thrownness. Thrownness implies dissemination, dispersion, disassembling, division, etc. Such terms refer to an original dispersion in *Dasein*'s body (*ursprüngliche Streuung*), which Derrida also associates with *auto-affection*. "Auto affection" designates a movement of repetition that differentiates—an economy of signification that—despite all the metaphysical desire to reduce alterity, cannot dispense with alterity. Indeed, in this framework the body should be understood in terms of the movement of *différance:* Sexual difference comes down to perpetual difference, division, dispersion, and dissemination, in the movement of *différance*, which is both the condition of possibility and impossibility of the symbolic system; the very movement that gives rise to it, and which brings about its deconstruction. This is how Derrida comes up with a notion of sexual difference that is not limited by two. Although sex as coextensive with the "there" is innumerably divisible, the imaginary anatomy of Derrida's philosophical language gives rise to the effect of the ontological masculinization. From a Irigarian point of view, it is possible to see here a contradiction between the text that Derrida ended up writing and his original intentions: in his desire to overcome the binary, he risks falling into phallocentrism because he does not think it is necessary to reckon with female sexual difference outside of the binary.

NANCY'S RELATION TO DERRIDA

I think that the first important difference between Nancy and Derrida lies in Nancy's lack of interest in what Lacan and Derrida had to say about "woman." Primarily, this is because Nancy knows that there is no such thing as "woman" as such, and that to gather women under a category is a problem. Secondly, Nancy does not want to start with sexual difference as divided by two. Thirdly, Nancy prefers to occupy a neutral position in writing about the sex. This can be problematized from a feminist point of view because, historically speaking, sex is attributed to women whereas men have identified with humanity in the neutral sense. Although he does not engage with feminism, Nancy has no problem acknowledging that women's demand of moral and political equality is legitimate. He does not interpret the demand of equality as women's desire for masculinity or their failure to see that the masquerading position could be politically more attractive. Unlike Lacan, he does not presume he knows something about women that they do not know.

Jane Gallop, in her essay "'Women' in *Spurs* and Nineties Feminism," argues that Derrida, when he first read this paper in 1972, was addressing 1970s feminism. "*Spurs* shares some presuppositions with the specific femi-

nism with which it is contemporary. *Spurs* belongs to the era of 'woman'"
(Gallop 1997, 7). This is why for contemporary feminist readers may feel
that Derrida writes from a position of mastery when he comments on woman's position without having to lend an ear to women's experiences. It is hard
to make *Spurs* relevant to Nancy's reading of sex. Even the analogy between
woman and truth in *Spurs* is in no way akin to Nancy's reflection on the
relation of sex to truth. Nancy's position is more commensurable with Derrida's in *Geschlecht I*, inasmuch as he retains from Derrida's account the
necessity for neutrality and the refusal to divide sex by two. In Nancy,
neutrality can be reconciled with the moral and political equality claims that
feminists make. Indeed, understanding sexual difference in an ontological
manner can be accompanied by a commitment to moral and political equality.

The second important difference I see between Derrida and Nancy concerns the scope of neutrality. In Derrida neutrality leaves out from his ontology of sex all discourse about nature. Not only all information that comes
from scientific research on sex, but also all philosophy of nature is precluded
from mixing with the ontological account. In contrast to Derrida, who remains loyal to Heidegger in that sense, Nancy allows himself to speak of
nature as *force*, as in the tradition of German idealism. The forces of bur-
geoning and growth imply difference, and sexuality operates in nature as a
motor of difference. An amoeba divides and the division gives rise to two
individuals. Etymologically, the term "sex" comes from the Latin *sexus* (gender, gender traits, male and female genitals), which is of uncertain etymolo-
gy, and is also connected with *secō, secāre* ("divide, cut"), with the idea of
division of the species. Generations succeed previous generations; they come
after their ancestors and accompany them for a while. Sex is the difference of
nature from itself, the nourishing nature of the other. It makes nature escape
from itself and renders its self-coincidence impossible.

How is this natural force of sex connected with the act of sex? Nancy
speaks as if nature gives rise to the spiritual human world by exceeding itself.
Because it becomes other than itself there is both continuity and discontinuity, and that saves Nancy's reflection on sex from being reducible to ontological naturalism. He talks about sex as both force and act—but what distinguishes act from force? Although humans feel the forces of sex, in human
life sexuality is act. Acts belong to the realm of signification, in which drives
also operate. Both drives and acts are organized by significations. In the
realm of signification sexuality is conceived as act that gives rise to sexual
relation. The idea that the act of sex opens the space of in-between indispensable for the sexual relation is laid out in an appeal to Heidegger's ontological
difference. Just like in Nancy's reading of Heidegger Being is differentiation—a movement that differentiates Being from existents, the existents from
each other, and existents in themselves—sex is the act that differentiates

itself from all sexed beings (existents), all existents as sexed beings from each other, and in themselves. However, this is a very abstract formula if we do not philosophize about the sexual relation to explain what Nancy means by that. Henceforth, Nancy's reflection takes the direction toward an ontology of sexual relation.

Thirdly, Nancy differs from Derrida in his philosophical orientation toward the notion of desire. Derrida regards desire as a metaphysical concept and in his philosophical approach, the lived experience of desire should be seen as an effect of *différance*. He may have grounds to subscribe to the view that the sexual relation is only possible as impossible, but to establish that one needs to know more about what he understands by sexual relation. And we have insufficient resources for more speculation. In contrast to Derrida's silence about sexual desire, Nancy considers the experience of desire to be an indispensable notion, and locates the impossibility in the difference between the satisfaction of desire and enjoyment. Both Derrida and Nancy start with neutrality in order to get rid of the phallocentricism that lurks in the assessment of masculine and feminine positions in the symbolic system. Derrida attempts to avoid it by going back to the *Da* (there) of *Dasein* in Heidegger's existential analytic. Nancy prefers to go in another direction and focuses on Being-with rather than the *Da* (there) of *Dasein*, which enables him to speak of the sexual difference as it manifests itself in the erotic relation with the other. Derrida lacks the relational ontology Nancy embraces.

Nancy philosophizes about questions that did not come to Derrida's attention insofar as he focused only on the constitution of the "there." It is in the existential of the "there" that Derrida found dispersion and dissemination, in short, all the terminology he thought was required to talk about sex. Nancy does not want to go in that direction. He starts with a different existential in his elaboration of subjectivity as a desiring subject. This new starting point leads him to consider the body as body of relation (relation-body). In "The 'There Is' of Sexual Relation," he starts with "distinction," as a specific modality of being separate. Relation is based on distinction not only because we single each other: the other distinguishes me and me the other. At issue, is not merely the distinguishing of one another, but also the distinguishing one's self:

> distinguishing a self, distinguishing it from the other, distinguishing it by the other, distinguishing it by distinguishing the other, distinguishing oneself with the other, that is, with and from the other. Everything that remains indistinct is accounted for by this *with*, this *co-* of the *community* or of *copulation*. (Nancy 2013, 10)

Hence, a space of in between opens up in the relation where Nancy locates desire and sexual differentiation. Arguably, this betweenness of the relationship is a space of transitions—transitions of sex, as well as gender, desire, and sexual orientation.

> Sex is not just its own difference but also, each time, the properly infinite process of its own differentiation. I am each time a certain degree of composition and differentiation between man and woman, homosexual man and heterosexual man, homosexual woman and heterosexual woman and according to the various combinations that open up to each other as well as close themselves off from each other, that touch and penetrate each other. (Nancy 2013, 10)

The passage above interprets differentiation as giving rise to sexual difference, and asserts that fluidity is always at work in a sexual relationship. In *Touching—On Jean-Luc Nancy*, Derrida remarks the difficulty of this deduction in Nancy's *Corpus*. This is the "'deduction of sexual difference as the reference of one flesh to another' in accordance with sexuality, and more specifically the 'a' or 'the' sexual difference" (Derrida 2005, 241). Here I will not go into the argument about touching and self-touching, which Derrida takes up to problematize what he calls "deduction," even though the ultimate difference between Derrida and Nancy can be formulated in terms of touching. I will focus on the greater picture: Nancy sees the sexual relationship as a site in which one finds the possibility of intimacy that becomes infinite. In Derrida, insofar as sex is concerned, the relation is not at issue; more precisely, it is as if there is no relation. The subject of sexual desire is only a solitary disseminating body, not a body of relation. In distinction from Derrida, Nancy is a thinker of relation. Lacan, too, was a thinker of sexual relation, though he only addressed the possibility/impossibility of the heterosexual relation. In Lacan's framework, sexual difference, as it is marked by the symbolic system, did not derive from the relation, but partook in the explanation of its impossibility. By contesting Lacan, Nancy paves the way for thinking sexual difference from within the sexual relationship: we no longer speak of a systemic difference or a difference as an attribute of an isolated subject. Sexual difference brings itself forth within the movement of differentiation, which belongs to potentially and actually existing sexual relationships. In Nancy's view, our sexed being enters into a process of becoming because of its relationality.

How are the movement of difference that differentiates existents and the erotic or sexual relation tied up with each other? Nancy wants to avoid both a comprehension of being as unity (one) and totality (whole) and of the relation as a unity with the other, the constitution of unity by the duality. Evidently, there is a metaphysical problem here, the problem of one and many. How to count the existent of a sexual relation? Is there only one? Are there two? Or more? If the relation is also conditioned by distance and separation, two do not make one. Plato had thought of desire as the soul's retrieval of its other for a reunification with it. The androgynous myth of Aristophanes in Plato's *Symposium* lays out the problem: even if there were an originary division, this division must not be conceived as the division of one. If one did not exist before the division, what was divided in the first place? That question has no answer. We can only acknowledge that there is more than one at the origin or in the principle. If this is the case, there has never been one. Sex teaches us the lesson that one does not exist; there is no such thing as one. If one is inseparable, there should not be two either; if this is the case, a relation is not one plus one, the unity of two.

Derrida argues that woman is understood as lack in the history metaphysics in contrast to the whole, which man is supposed to be. In *Of Grammatology* he writes: "Man allows himself to be announced to himself after the fact of supplementarity, which is thus not an attribute-accidental or essential of man. For on the other hand, supplementarity, which is nothing, neither a presence nor an absence, is neither a substance nor an essence of man" (Derrida 1997, 244). This is at the heart of the heterosexual relation between man and woman as metaphysics described it, and which Derrida aimed at deconstructing. For Nancy, "being whole" in the sense of "being entire" cannot be a presumption because no one is a whole in the first place. There is no whole because being cannot constitute itself as whole. Just as two does not make one, a relation is not about the supplementation of a term that is considered to be already one or whole, by the other term that is considered as "not-whole" in the sense of lacking. Thus, sexual relation is not a relation between one and one. Not being one each, they do not make two either, as if by way of addition. The relation should not be conceived as a medium in which something is communicated from one to the other. Bataille had already rejected that notion of communication and envisaged a communication in which self is infused by the other, and hence the blurring of the boundaries of the self. For Nancy, the sexual relation is capable of supporting itself, self-sustaining, and self-communicative. Such a sexuality does not aim at reproduction; no essence or end can be assigned to it. Nancy disagrees with the view that sexuality aims at pleasure. Sexuality gives pleasure, creates offspring; these are the surprises and gifts of sexuality. Just like Bataille, he sees sexual relation as the sharing of an intimacy in immanence, which allows for transcendence in the shared experience of proximity. In this transcendence a pure and immanent nature eludes itself and self-differentiates. In other words, the difference in sexuality is the difference of nature from itself. In sexuality nature is always at the verge of bursting beyond itself. This explains why sexuality has to do with the impossibility of identity.

In his elaboration of the sexual relation, stoic philosophers inspire Nancy. Kant spoke of relation as a category and derived three categories of relation from the table of judgments. These categories apply only to the empirical world of objects; they are not helpful in speaking of sexual relations in which the self (*ipseity*) is at stake. In Nancy's ontological framework, relations sexuate bodies and bodies become sexed in relations. Stoics reflected on the relation in terms of space, time, void, and *lekton* (that which is said). Nancy focuses on the *lekton* to reflect on the differing and deferring of bodies in betweenness of the relation. The *lekton* refers to the relation as a space of signification, and that is where language comes in. I think Nancy would agree with Lacan that sexual difference has very much to do with language, but Nancy does not agree with his idea that language, in which desiring subjects appear, make their sexual relation impossible.

In my reading, Nancy gives an answer to the question of what makes a singular sexed being possible. Being sexual—which, in psychoanalysis, has to do with drives and libidinal energy rather than the natural instincts—does not have to be normatively limited by sex as divided by two; difference is impossible to limit or to enumerate in the movement of becoming in which erotic relationship is situated. In Derrida, the unlimited is based on the movement of *différance* that implies the differing and deferring of signifiers. In Nancy, the question of sense and signification is inseparable from the possibility of the erotic relation, but that does not prevent it from becoming a site of profound, infinite intimacy.

In "Jouis Anniversaire," Nancy returns to *Glas* to address sex in Derrida's text. As it is well known, *Glas* is a double text; one column speaks of G. W. F. Hegel and the other of Jean Genet. In these columns Derrida presents various scenes at once and makes them speak to one another. Familial, genetic, evangelical, tragic scenes are juxtaposed with obscene scenes of sex and violent scenes of crime and robbery. The juxtaposition sets all these scenes in relation with one another inviting the reader to realize the impossibility of separating the noble from the vulgar, the fall from elevation, and authenticity from inauthenticity. Derrida does not establish a simple opposition between Hegel as the philosopher of the patriarchal metaphysical tradition, in which sex is conceived as divided by two, versus Genet as the writer of sex disseminating itself beyond the binary, as the seeds of a flower are dispersed in the natural world. Nancy argues that Derrida sees the hermaphroditic origin of sexual differentiation in Hegel's dialectic. If hermaphroditism is at work at the heart of the Hegelian dialectic, neither the opposition nor the distinction between the sexes can be originary (Derrida 1974, 129, and Nancy 2017b). So there is no simple opposition between Hegel as a thinker of patriarchy who comments on the importance of the family in which women are subordinated to the male head of the household, for the sake of the continuation and well-being of the state and Genet as a thinker of sex without reproduction, as pure expenditure, and dissemination. For Derrida, Genet is also a thinker of interiority. In his commentary of Genet, desire does not return to the same; it loses itself in its destination, becomes incapable of reflecting on itself. Sex exposes an interiority that flows, ejaculates, spits out. In the sexual sphere *différance* no longer multiplies differences but glues together the exteriorized elements that are out there. Derrida thinks of sex as dissemination but neither in the restricted economy of the family scene nor in the clandestine general economy of the sexual dispersion, there is relation in which self relates to itself in a relation of shared intimacy. From a feminist point of view, one may observe that sex as division in the originary sense is caught up in a duality between the binary sexual difference, which aims at the sexual reproduction in the family and the promiscuous sexual dispersion outside of the social organization of the family. In the logic of patriarchy these two different sexual economies complement each other—to create the male privilege of having sexual experiences without responsibility and without breaching the family contract. Genet's style of enjoyment subverts the double life of hypocrisy and thereby opens a space for a different interiority.

Being caught up between love as caring attachment and desire as the relation to the unknown other culminates in fragmentation. This is a modality of ipseity that cannot be shared in a relation of desire, and which evades infinite intimacy. Instead of self-relation, one is caught up in the tension of sexual experiences that are cut off from each other, that do not speak to one another. Nancy's response to Derrida consists in arguing that an originary self-relation or ipseity is not found in sexual dispersion; it is a gift of the sexual relationship. Without that possibility, the desire is a fire that appears in flames, flashes, and sparks but becomes dead in cinders as it consumes and destroys the gift. This can perhaps be described as sexual enjoyment without adoration and truth. Derrida does not regard sexuality as an act that leads to sexual relation—which is a site for sexual differentiation and truth of ipseity that reveals itself in the being-with as shared intimacy.

To conclude, both Derrida and Nancy prefer to give an ontological account of sexuality as a movement of differentiation and speak from a ground of neutrality that leads to diversification. In contrast to Derrida's dispersion and dissemination Nancy goes back to the *there is* of the relation as the in-between of separation, distinction, communication, and sharing of intimacy. This ontological reflection on sex helps us go beyond a heteronormative conception of sex, without committing to naturalism. The problem with naturalism is its incapacity to think the *Da* of the relation. Derrida claimed that identity is an effect of the movement of *différance*; Nancy, on the other hand, thinks *ipseity* as a function of the shared intimacy. Nonetheless, if in the sexual relation sense is a product of signification, and signification is made possible by *différance*, Nancy would accept that the experience of sense can never be an experience of full presence without alterity and absence. This is perhaps why there is enjoyment in its impossibility. I shall turn to the question of the impossibility of enjoyment in the next section.

NANCY BETWEEN LACAN AND BATAILLE: ENJOYMENT

Lacan is definitely an important interlocutor to whom Nancy responds in his ontological reflection on sex. We can recall that Lacou-Labarthe's and Nancy's early work on Lacan, *The Title of the Letter*, was praised by Lacan himself in 1973: *Encore: The Seminar of Jacques Lacan: On Feminine Sexuality, the Limits of Love and Knowledge* (Book XX), where Lacan speaks of woman's enjoyment in relation to God. Lacan acknowledges Jean-Luc Nancy and Philip Lacou-Labarthe's book as the best book written on him so far. Lacan enjoys and recommends the book to his students, even though he rejects the last ten pages where the authors take a critical approach. In *Corpus II*, approximately forty years later after the publication of *The Seminar XX*, Nancy finally responds to Lacan. Although he complicates Lacan's thesis that there is no sexual relation by carrying out the task of thinking the *there is* of the sexual relation, he also underscores the importance of Lacan's thesis that sexuation is of a speaking being. For Lacan, sexuation takes place in the symbolic system. In contrast, Nancy thinks of sex as acting, forming, and creating. This is why he prefers to talk about the act of sex rather than the sexual act. For him, the act of sex sexuates the individual, shatters the one in itself to form an ipseity, so that the between opens to make possible a sexual relation. Indeed, the act of sex can also create groups. Nancy designates the act of sex as an act of signification in which intimacy is shared. In Lacan, on the other hand, this is precisely an illusion because the signification cannot escape from alienation. It alienates in the Other, and subverts the relationship between me and my partner. In our attempt to share intimacy, we lose ourselves in the Other. Lacan argues that there can be a sexed being because the symbolic system sexuates—a system that one can enter only as castrated. The symbolic system has laws, norms, and positions. This echoes Bataille who thought that sexuality is enjoyable only in relation to laws, prohibitions, and restrictions that are already in place in human society. Lacan makes the point that no matter how great our sexual energy is; we start out as subjects of desire who had to cope with absence by undergoing division in our interiority. In other words, if the lack had not been felt, there would have been no need for signifiers that would split and constitute the subject of desire. According to Nancy, Lacan's statement that "there is no sexual relation" is tied up with the impossibility of enjoyment (*jouissance*). In fact, these two statements mean the same. Their truth cannot be empirically tested; for such statements should be seen as conclusions that derive from a structure. For this reason, they can be qualified as *transcendental* or, perhaps, *quasi-transcendental*. The critiques that objected to such structures on the grounds that they contradicted reality, because they are supposed to deny the lived experience of heterosexual sex, have misunderstood their epistemological status. Nancy stresses that these statements that Lacan endorsed, do not at all concern the existing sexual relations; they are about the being of sexual relations; in other words, they are about those truths that make concrete relations what they are. This amounts to saying that not only sexual difference but also sexual relation should be conceived within a framework that invokes Heidegger's ontological difference. According to Nancy, sex is an act that differentiates, proliferates sexual difference in space and time. Sex here behaves like Being in relation to entities, which are sexuated beings and sexual relations. Sexuated beings and sexual relations come in existence thanks to the act of sex. But if on this account sexual relation is possible—the claim of the impossibility of *jouissance* must undergo a new interpretation. Nancy will turn to the notion of desire to explain that.

Let us take up the issue of the specificity of the human sexual relation as a relation. When a couple mates there is no explanation for that; it has no return to us, we do not possess a measure or proportion to judge a sexual relation. Someone can have a sexual relation with someone, but if we set aside all that is said about it from the points of view of the disciplines such as medicine, sociology, psychology, law, and religion, we do not know how to philosophically speak of it. The sexual relation is not a substance, it does not have an essence that actualizes and accomplishes itself. In Kant, "relation" names one of the four groups under which judgments and categories are categorized. In this group there are three types of judgment in virtue of which we can speak of the relation between substance and its properties, causal relations, and reciprocal interaction. This logic of relations enables us to speak of the relations between things, but it is not useful when we need to talk about love, because in love, dynamic and active possibilities and personal narratives are involved (Nancy 2013, 6). Sexual relation in the ontological sense must take its departure from desire.

Insofar as narratives are concerned, the first thing that imports in a narrative of sexual relation is the declaration of desire. There is no sexual relation without a declaration of desire. Desire must be expressed to the other, so that the other may acknowledge it, before she accepts or refuses a sexual relation. When Nancy speaks of *sex*, he does not have the biological notion of sex in mind, nor is he willing to use the notion of gender as this implies some position determined by power and accords to the individual a social status. Sex is for him what makes possible a sexual way of being in relation to the other. But in that way of being, sex is as much hidden, concealed, masked, as displayed and exhibited. The demand for recognition may only be implicit. In Nancy's view, sex is fully in the declaration and it is not declared once for all times, the effort to declare sex is infinite. One can never know where the declaration begins. I must first declare my desire to myself before I declare it to the other. Clearly, declaration opens sexual relation to the problem of sense and language.

But how can desire be ontologically described? The desiring soul is neither a strainer, not a leaky jar that empties itself as it is filled, as in Plato's *Gorgias*, nor can it create a plenitude in itself that does not inhere absence. Desire is not an absence in my being that is filled by the presence of the other. In a relation of desire with the other, my desire overflows itself, becomes infinite and makes me enter into a process of differentiation and transformation. To the ontological plane of desire belongs the body as a body of relation; a being that is corporeally inscribed in a dynamic web of sense. In other words, the body at issue is not just a body among others; its intercorporeity makes it what it is. This relates to both Nancy's notion of *being singular plural* and to his notion of *exposition*. As Husserl first recognized, and Merleau-Ponty further elaborated, the phenomenological investigation of the possibility of the sense of the world should begin with the body's experience of the world. And at this level, given the operative intentionality and the system of experience it creates, it makes more sense to speak of *intercorporeity*, rather than to presume the separateness of the body. This is why Merleau-Ponty in *The Visible and the Invisible* prefers to use the notion of *flesh* rather than the body. In Nancy, the body is exposed to other bodies, and this makes it a medium in which the sense that lays in intercorporeity can be investigated. In this ontological approach the body is conceived as a "singular plural being." It is in this concept that we find the ontological move that radically transforms our understanding of sex, sexual difference, and erotic experience.

According to Freud, in the pre-Oedipal phase, all the organs of the body can be attributed erotic value or sense. Nancy rethinks the body in its intercorporeality; as auto-affective body—which is always already hetero-affective because intercorporeal—as a locus of sense. This is to say that the body can turn to its own corporeal sense and give rise to new significations by refusing to surrender to sedimented or ready-made significations. Here Nancy returns to Merleau-Ponty's reflection on touching hands to consider affectivity as the corporeal production of sense. In French the word *sens* has threefold meaning: the organs of sensation, meaning, and direction. However, the body in/on/through which sensible meaning circulates is chaotic; there are various senses in it that can turn into pleasure and pain and resurface and take different shapes in various significations.

The upshot of Nancy's thought on sex is that by being in a relation of desire, the body becomes a body of relation, which means it incorporates together with the other's body. In the incorporation with the other there is an affective exchange of sense. This is to understand one another in flesh; a nonconceptual understanding. Such an understanding involves words, but now words do not just mean due to a linguistic operation of signifiers, they became signs of desire. Nancy takes up the question of trouble in sexuality by underscoring the thesis that the body's relation to exteriority is not organized by the signified. The signification of words cannot be well-understood by taking as essential that which is said in them or by reducing them to their reference; for, in so doing, we forget that they declare desire, that they signify the desire's movement forward, its *élan*, or its retreat. This is why language of desire is open to vagueness, ambiguity, indefiniteness, equivocity, and multiplicity of meaning. This language becomes accessible as the addressee apprehends the sense offered and prepares a response. Indeed, the indefiniteness, the indecision between various possibilities of determining a signification can be so enjoyable that one may not want to rush to achieve clarity. Everything may not be said immediately and with so much clarity because precision in language makes us face bluntly with some aspects of reality, which we may not know how to cope, and which may result in the retreat of desire. Complete openness may decrease and even close off possibilities. In other words, there may be a tension or disparity between the flow of corporeal sense and linguistic communication.

For Nancy, there are "trouble" and "anguish" because there is language; it is due to language that the third participates in the relation with a "thou." There is a flow, but the relationship cannot escape from taking a form in accordance with the language of the third. The discursive relation of *signification* is an extension of the corporeal making of sense and signifies within the flow of corporeal sense, though it also leads to trouble, anguish, interruption, and loss in the relationship. The third brings in objectivity, neutrality, exteriority, and imposes strategies of action in accordance with social norms and values. The question arises if the perspective of the third might not also redeem? For example, in a violent relationship of immediacy where exteriority is absorbed and distorted, the language of the third can be useful for self-defense.

According to Nancy, desire does not come to an end with satisfaction, because there is no meaning in satisfaction. Freud speaks of sexuality as tension and release of tension. This is perhaps because he takes male sexuality as a model. Enjoyment does not have to be understood by means of this model. Let us take our first love, our first encounter: there, enjoyment may not be an actual indulging in the sexual act, a practice of sexuality. In the case of enjoyment, there is no absolute difference between the actual and potential. Enjoyment should not be confounded with the satisfaction of desire. In Lacan too, enjoyment does not have to do with the sexual act itself; it is not lovemaking. In enjoyment there is a meaning, a value that is wholly foreign to sexuality. Enjoyment is something that occurs in me. Repetition and lack of measure belong to enjoyment. Aristotle asks the question: Why do people spend an effort to repeat a sexual relationship? Why do they always recommence the sexual relation with their partner, whereas animals do not build a bond and break apart after mating? Why is there enjoyment in repetition? Rather than desire's satisfaction of itself by consuming the object of desire, what is at issue in enjoyment is the way desire reaches its object, its manner of getting at it. Enjoyment concerns the scenario of reaching the object despite the impossibilities, aporias, and obstacles of desire.

If repetition is the first feature of enjoyment, the lack of measure is its second feature. Nancy follows Bataille in endorsing that human sexuality lacks measure. Bataille remarks that, because we are human, we are acquainted with the violence of eroticism that leads us to despair. He makes manifest the instability, impossibility of stabilizing or fixing our sexual being, which is always in difference, tension, expectation, frenzy, ecstasy, and enthusiasm. Nancy associates Bataille's way of talking about sex with reference to the image of the overflowing with milk of the feeding breasts. This is an image about maternity, which directly alludes to the oral drive. Communication, desire of life, and joy of life: Bataille thinks of life as a kind of excessive joy that does not exclude pain. Immediate, unreflective sense is found in "expulsion, "discharge"—terms that are metaphors for enjoyment. In other texts, Nancy points to the presence of the anus in Bataille's texts, suggesting that the destructiveness of the anal drive is tied with the rejection of the morality of the profane world in capitalist culture.

According to Nancy, the condition for enjoyment is not the presence or the absence of sexual practice, satisfactoriness, or inadequacy of love, but there being some *glimmering*. No doubt, a distinction can be made between a real glimmer, brilliance, flood of light and a fake light. Fake light can stem from self-deception, and sometimes one can deceive oneself because one enjoys to desire. One can also pretend to desire because one intends to manipulate the other to control and subdue her freedom for some non-erotic ends. Perhaps our greatest sameness or equality lies in the fact that we all have sexual excitement, sexual desire, and sexual enjoyment. There can be conditions that render sexuality impossible, or impossible to live, and turn it into something we do not know what to make of. Even when pleasure is really impossible, there is enjoyment. In contrast to pleasure, enjoyment cannot be attributed to an insulated, isolated subject; it is always a symbolic and imaginary relation with the other.

Nancy locates enjoyment in the relation of desire to sense and signification, that is, to language. Following Bataille, he sees a moment of sovereignty in enjoyment. This moment belongs to the signifying language, which is productive of sense. What is the relation of sense and signification? In fact, according to Nancy, sense does not belong to the order of signification; it cannot be signified. It is force, impulse. This is what sex is, a push, a thrust, an impulsion, an origin that has the power to bring us forth from nothing. In contrast, signification depends on an enchainment of signifiers. Signification does not merely express in language a sense that already exists in the world or in the sexual relation. Nancy argues that sense appears at the limit of signification. This is precisely the event of signification, the manifestation of

sense through signification, which Bataille sought to describe in his literature. Nancy thinks that Bataille's writings attest to this important problem of
modern literature. Moreover, he believes that the deconstruction seeks to
inhabit that limit as well. This is why, according to Derrida, deconstruction is
about enjoyment. Deconstruction aimed at showing that the conditions of the
possibility of that which is deconstructed are in fact the conditions of its
impossibility. This is the very structure of enjoyment. The possibility of
enjoyment depends on its impossibility.

On the one hand, compulsion to repeat, which Freud associated with
death drive; on the other hand, the possibility of growth, excess, and expansion. These two threads are interwoven in enjoyment. Freud says that people
who are asking for the meaning of life are a little ill. He takes a pessimist
view about human psyche because so many experiences culminate in unhappiness in the course of human life. This is how people live. But why do they
live like that? Why don't they commit suicide if they are unhappy? It is the
death drive (*Trieb*) that tends to repeat the structures that entrap and suffocate a life. Strangely, the death drive does not kill but keeps us alive. It is
precisely the repetition of "the mistakes" that prevent someone from changing her situation that the person continues to live, remains in life. There is
enjoyment in our troubles, something that keeps us continue to live an unhappy life. *Trieb* means here that I am not the one who sets my life in movement;
it moves me. We philosophize, give birth to children, and make love. . . .
Why have I burdened my life by giving birth to my children? Why do I keep
a sex partner in my life? Why am I taking care of so many animals? Why
have I assumed so much responsibility? Should these activities be attributed
to a subject? Is making love an activity that could be attributed to a party at
all? Life is an impersonal force, which resurface in the enjoyment that turns
into trouble and despair.

An alternative way of explaining the impossibility of enjoyment is to
appeal to the high probability of trouble and loss that enjoyment implies. For
Bataille the risk of loss went hand in hand with growth and expansion.
Moreover, in Bataille there is a consciousness that associates loss and the
experience of the summit. Awareness of loss belongs to sovereignty. There is
no beyond of sovereignty, which means there is nothing else after the summit. What Bataille calls sovereignty is that of which there is no experience,
that which can never become an object of experience, the experience of sense
that does not lend itself to phenomenological description. This is the "absolute" for Bataille. By "absolute" he does not mean a unity, entirety, or wholeness; the absolute is the climax. The absolute separates itself from everything
else; it ab-solves itself. There is something absolute in the erotic experience
as an experience of sovereignty, because the enjoyment is separated and
detached from everything else. The zenith of desire is not the satisfaction of
desire, it is found in enjoyment that opens a way for thinking. Bataille asso-

ciates the absolute with selfhood as not-knowing rather than as an object of knowing. Moreover, this selfhood is recognized as a space for communication in which the I and the other are not separable. Nancy rethinks enjoyment as the sharing of an interior depth with exteriority, embodiment in relation, and sharing one-self with the other in relation. Nonetheless, taking both Lacan and Bataille into account, he recognizes in it a negativity that cannot be eliminated, which appears as impossibility, unrest, and trouble.

Let me note that Nancy also refers to Lacan's description of woman as not-all (*pas-toute*), he recognizes that Lacan is not making the point that women are not-whole or that they lack something. He is only interested in the separation of the woman from her own sex (other women) due to women's position of being the phallus in the symbolic system. A differentiation that desire makes at the ontic register. It concerns the relation to one's own sex (gender as a universal). Lacan specifies it as a condition of being desired as a woman. As such the claim is postulated as an *axiom* (Nancy 2013, 8). Lacan associates her not being all with the existence of an enjoyment specific to woman. Does a woman have excessive sexual enjoyment because she believes she is irreplaceable for a particular man? In what way *not being like all other women* would give rise to excessive enjoyment? It could be that her separation from other women is interpreted as a sign that she is not pursued for mere sexual satisfaction and that he enjoys the relationship. But if her enjoyment depended on his enjoyment, it would still be phallic. Isn't her excessive enjoyment independent of how she is desired by the other? Why she should not be capable of affirming her sexual pleasure independently of his satisfaction and enjoyment? It could be that she enjoys excessively only by exempting herself from the relation to him. In order to make room for that possibility Lacan construes the non-phallic enjoyment as a relation to the Other, by arguing that it cannot be represented in the symbolic system in which she is positioned as woman. Here, we have an *impossible* at hand that is possible, and is perhaps actually lived by some women. Thus, Lacan is making a statement about the possibility of feminine enjoyment. In Nancy, however, this does not deserve a specific treatment. There is enjoyment of the relationship to the other, and the impossibilities that have to do with repetition, trouble, excess, and loss. Women's case does not seem to ask for any specific explanation. And the commitment to neutrality prevents Nancy from saying anything else about that.

Let me conclude my reflection on Nancy's relation to Lacan by raising some questions: Nancy understands sexual relation as the sharing of intimacy of desiring beings. He emphasizes that the specificity of human sexuality lies in the difference between the satisfaction of desire and sexual enjoyment. This makes the focus shift to the relation as the site of desire, sense, and signification. In enjoyment there is repetition and exceeding—a sexual relation to the other construed as making sense on the grounds of signification.

Yet that does not exclude the possibility that only the satisfaction of sexual desire can be sought. Indeed, some men explicitly say they do not want sexual relationship, but that they only want sex. Although some women can behave in the same way, more women seek to invest in the possibility of sexual relationship when they engage in the sexual act. How does the insistence on having sex without engaging in a caring relation to the other (and by refusing to share life and responsibility with a sex partner) fit with the distinction between enjoyment and satisfaction? Should we say that people who prefer to live in this way refuse enjoyment for the sake of satisfaction? Is this a denial of relationship or the absence of recognition of it? Is it not a refusal of enjoyment but a form of enjoyment? Is the sexual exploitation of the female bodies by refusing relationship a manifestation of misogyny? Or, is it just a manifestation of sex as dissemination in Derrida's sense? I believe these questions invite us to return to the major difference between Derrida and Nancy: for Nancy, relation is conceived as an integral part of sex; in contrast, for Derrida, sex does not necessarily open a space for relationship in the sexual encounter. For Derrida, sexual encounter with the other is only a site of dissemination of my being. Although Derrida's discussion of sex does not lead to a care ethics of Eros, in Nancy, I believe, there is room for that.

My next chapter, which is on subjectivation as a sexuated being, involves a discussion of Paul Ricoeur's texts on justice and political rights. There, I shall further pursue some of the questions that have been already raised in this chapter. In this chapter, a relational ontology of sex has been propounded, and sexual difference has been addressed as a problem of ipseity, a matter of being singular-plural. In the next chapter, I shall further elaborate relationality by claiming that sexual subjectivation cannot be separated from the question of what it means to be speaking subjectivity, agency, narrating subjectivity, ethical and political subjectivity. Even though Nancy avoids using the language of subjectivity and Ricoeur attempts to offer a new phenomenological philosophy of subjectivity, it is my contention that Ricoeur is a valuable philosophical resource to return to, for feminists and gender theorists to resist the morally unacceptable proposals to affirm the political strategies of depersonalization and dehumanization.

REFERENCES

Augustine, Saint. 1993. *Confessions*. Books I–XIII. Translated by F. J. Sheed. Indianapolis and Cambridge: Hackett Publishing Company, Inc.
Bataille, Georges. 1978. *L'Expérience Intérieure*. Paris: Editions Tel Gallimard.
Derrida, Jacques. 1974. *Glas*. Paris: Éditions Galilée.
———. 1981. *Spurs: Nietzsche's Styles*. Translated by Barbara Harlow. Chicago: University of Chicago Press.
———. 1983. "Geschlecht: Sexual Difference, Ontological Difference." *Research in Phenomenology* XIII: 65–83.

———. 1986. *Glas*. Translated by John. P. Leavey Jr. and Richard Rand. Lincoln: University of Nebraska Press.

———. 1997. *Of Grammatology*. Translated by Gayatri Spivak. Baltimore, MD: Johns Hopkins University Press.

———. 2005. *On Touching—Jean Luc Nancy*. Translated by Christine Irizarry. Stanford, CA: Stanford University Press.

Feder, Ellen K. and Emily Zarkin. 1997. "Flirting with the Truth: Derrida's Discourse with 'Woman' and Wenches." In *Derrida and Feminism: Recasting the Question of Woman*, edited by Ellen K. Feder, Mary C. Rawlinson, and Emily Zarkin, 21–52. New York and London: Routledge.

Flaubert, Gustav. 1965. *Madame Bovary*. Translated by Paul de Man. New York: W.W. Norton.

Foucault, Michel. 1985. *The History of Sexuality: The Use of Pleasure*. Vol. 2. Translated by Robert Hurley. New York: Vintage Books.

Gallop, Jane. 1997. "'Women' in *Spurs* and Nineties Feminism." In *Derrida and Feminism: Recasting the Question of Woman*, edited by Ellen K. Feder, Mary C. Rawlinson, and Emily Zarkin, 7–20. New York and London: Routledge.

Kant, Immanuel. 1998. *Critique of Pure Reason*. Translated and edited by Paul Guyer and Allen W. Wood. Cambridge: Cambridge University Press.

Lacan, Jacques. 1999. *Encore: The Seminar of Jacques Lacan: On Feminine Sexuality, the Limits of Love and Knowledge, 1972–1973*. Book 20. Edited by Jacques-Alain Miller. Translated with notes by Bruce Fink. New York and London: W.W. Norton & Company. Originally published as *Le Séminaire, Livre XX, Encore* (Paris: Éditions du Seuil, 1975).

Levinas, Emmanuel. 2009. *Carnets de captivité et autres inédits. Œuvres*, Vol 1. Edited by Rodolphe Calin and Catherine Chalier. Paris: IMEC /Grasset.

Nancy, Jean-Luc. 2001. *L' "il y a" du rapport sexuel*. Paris: Éditions Galilée.

———. 2013. *Corpus II: Writings on Sexuality*. New York: Fordham University Press.

———. 2017a. *Sexistence*. Accompagné d'un Frontispice de Miquel Barceló. Paris: Éditions Galilée.

———. 2017b. "Jouis Anniversaire," *L'Entretien no. 03: Jacques Derrida*, edited by Laure Adler and Alain Veinstein. Paris: Seuil/Éditions du sous-sol. English translation in *Philosophy, Language, and the Political: Post-Structuralism in Perspective*. Translated by C. Cordova, edited by Franson Manjali and Marc Crépon. Delhi: Aakar Books.

Nancy, Jean-Luc and Lacou-Labarthe, Philippe. 1992. *The Title of the Letter: A Reading of Lacan*. Translated by Franöois Raffoul and David Pettigrew. Albany: State University of New York Press.

Plato, 1984. "The Symposium." *The Dialogues of Plato*. Translated by Reginald E. Allen. New Haven, CT: Yale University Press.

———. *Gorgias*. Translated by Robin Waterfield. Clarendon: Oxford University Press.

———. *Phaedrus*. Translated by Robin Waterfield. Clarendon: Oxford University Press.

Sartre, Jean-Paul. 1987. *The Family Idiot: Gustave Flaubert 1821–1857*. Translated by Carol Cosman. Chicago: The University of Chicago Press.

Sheets-Johnstone, Maxine. 2016. "The Roots of Power." *Google Books*. N.p., n.d. Web. Dec. 3, 2016.

NOTES

1. For behold Thou were within me, and I outside; and I sought Thee outside and in my unloveliness fell upon those lovely things that thou hast made.
2. Thou were within me and I was not with Thee.

Chapter Six

Subjects of Rights

From Vulnerability to Autonomy

This chapter goes back to some classical notions of modern philosophy and feminist theory such as "autonomy" and "subjectivity" to discuss how Ricoeur redefines them. I believe this is meaningful because we still continue to use these concepts in making policies about concrete life issues. We talk about listening to the experiences of the subjects to understand the specific form of oppression they undergo and ponder on what are the best ways to respect their autonomy. Our language forces us to theorize about these issues in a relational ontology that does not make problematic presumptions.

In "Autonomy and Vulnerability," an essay included in *Reflections on the Just* (Ricoeur 2007), Paul Ricoeur considers the ethical and political concept of autonomy (*autonomie*) in terms of vulnerability (*vulnérabilité*). In Kant's moral philosophy, the concept of autonomy follows from the second formulation of the categorical imperative. Persons deserve respect as ends-in-themselves because they can set themselves ends. They are free. Self-governing, receiving the law from one's self rather than from another, is a remarkable characteristic of the Enlightenment's ideal of humanity. For Kant, autonomy is not just solitary thinking that refuses to hear what others have to say, or the practice of rational speech in a solipsistic mode. Moreover, being free to choose ends independently of others does not make one autonomous, if some object in the world determines one's will. As it is well known, autonomy depends on the will's capacity for being determined by the moral law alone. An action motivated solely by the moral law indicates that the rational agent has the capacity to act without being determined by the worldly interests, institutions, and ideologies. Kant's notion of autonomy implies the rational being's capacity to transcend, in the ethical sense, the empirical subjectivity and the concerns for the world by which this subjectivity is determined. Despite his strong emphasis on the capacity for autonomy, Kant acknowledges vulnerability throughout his moral writings because the will is often determined by pathological desires, inclinations, besides the immaturity of the mind, that make it submit to authorities.

In *Being and Time*, Heidegger refrains from using the Kantian term "autonomy" because it belongs to the metaphysics of subjectivity. Given that "the ontological constitution of the self is not to be traced back either to an 'I'—substance or to a 'subject,' [. . .] the everyday fugitive way in which we keep on saying I must be understood in terms of *authentic* potentiality-for-Being" (Heidegger 2001, 322). In the existential analytic, the notion of authenticity (*Eigentlichkeit*) is associated with freedom. Authenticity requires separation from the "they" (*das Man*) and the recognition of one's own possibilities. Authenticity as a *condition* of freedom is thought without any reference to principles or law; it is explained in an existential analysis of the basic state of *Dasein*. Ricoeur follows Kant, in his insistence to speak of the autonomy of the person for ethical and political reasons; nonetheless, he does that in an Heideggerian ontology. He does not start with a monadic, individual subject; instead he commits himself to a relational ontology in which relations with the other and the third condition the constitution of subjectivity.

Ricoeur's discussion of autonomy is interesting for philosophies of gender and sexual difference that appeal to an ethics and politics of Eros. This is because even though we admit the view that we live in a world in which gender norms, laws, and discourse/power regimes materialize our bodies, it is also true that we make decisions about our bodies, we determine how we navigate our own process of materialization. We hermeneutically explore our own sexual orientation, discover and play with possibilities, and make sense of our desire. The existential situations in which we find ourselves can force us to assume certain styles of materialization over others. The gender performances of gender-nonconforming people can make manifest the compulsory norms of corporeal materialization as much as the extent of social conformity to stereotypical norms. If we are in a complex field of sexual difference, which I have been exploring throughout this book, different perspectives on gender still coexist and continue to engage with each other. The question about how bodies materialize should be kept open. For women who are oppressed as women, gender is a matter of norms that oblige them to materialize in certain ways because their bodies are assigned the female sex on the basis of their biological characteristics. But there are also people who desire to live by gender self-identification. Should the institutions and authorities or only persons themselves, who declare their intentions to change sex, determine how bodies are going to materialize? Should such decisions be left to a constellation of scientific, religious, and legal authorities? And what role should science play here? These are politically urgent questions, and many countries in the world wrestle with them. It is my contention that in order to solve these applied ethical issues of our age, we need to go back to the notion of subjectivity. Indeed, the burning debate over the interdisciplinary field of gender calls for a philosophical discussion of autonomy and speaking subjectivity, a corporeal subject who must be heard before "he" or "she" is made the object of the institutional discourses.

Considerations of the most recent trans issues make manifest why questions of subjectivity and autonomy are indispensable for sexual politics of emancipation. However, there is a major difficulty here. The person who is exposed to misogyny, homophobia, transphobia, or systematic gender discrimination is a vulnerable subject. The subjectivity of such a subject is constituted by the conditions of sexual oppression and the subject's resistance to it. Trans people want medical help and religious and legal recognition though they do not want science, law, and religion to predetermine their sexual difference/gender identity. I think that Ricoeur's discussion of autonomy and vulnerability may help us deal with these concrete existential issues because it offers a philosophy of autonomy for subjects that suffer the effects of symbolic structures and the violence of the institutional power over bodies. It would also acknowledge that it is questionable to frame the issue as an ethical and political problem of autonomous subjectivity without taking into consideration the medical market and the cultural industry that such a political discourse paves the way for and the risk of manipulation of people for economic profit.

If "Autonomy and Vulnerability" (Ricoeur 2007) is read side by side with "Who Is the Subject of Rights?" (Ricoeur 2000), Ricoeur's approach to autonomy looks more Aristotelean than Kantian because he grounds autonomy on an ontology or philosophical anthropology in which the concept of *capacity* plays a central role. This ontology articulates the conditions for the actualization of capacities by exploring being-in-the-world rather than making a recourse to abstract subjectivity in the form of practical reason. Ricoeur's discussion of autonomy is interesting also because it helps to redefine vulnerability. It enables us to supersede an understanding of vulnerability as a subjective emotional state or a psychological determination, and it paves the way for a new comprehension of vulnerability understood in terms of theories of oppression. Vulnerability results from a systematical disruption, hindering of the process of subjectivation at various levels of the constitution of subjectivity. However, Ricoeur himself does not develop that implication. For this reason, I will combine Ricoeur's ontology with feminist theories of oppression. This strategy enables me to explore the political implications of his theory of subjectivity for feminism and gender studies.

I think Ricoeur neglects the role gendering/becoming sexed plays in the process of subjectivation. One may argue that because his subject is implicitly male, he neglects the question how we become sexed or gendered bodies, and the question of vulnerability because of sexual discrimination, sexual oppression, phallocentrism, compulsory heterosexuality, homophobia, and transphobia. What happens if the sex assigned at birth does not match the gender type one identifies with? What about the significance of castration raised by the psychoanalytical accounts of subjectivity? Lacan, following Freud, would admit that the subject enters the symbolic system as vulnerable from the start, because it is faced by absence, loss, and deprivation. Recently, in a collection entitled *Feminist Explorations of Paul Ricoeur's Philosophy* (Halsema and Henriques 2016), some aspects of Ricoeur's philosophy have been underscored as relevant to feminist theory. What I am doing here can be considered as a contribution to this new area of feminist research. I strongly believe that Ricoeur's reading of subjectivity in terms of the problem of autonomy of a vulnerable subject deserves feminist attention because his approach can make significant contribution to the feminist analyses of sexual oppression.

Radical feminism has pointed to the vulnerability of women as gendered subjects and addressed the conditions of possibility of their becoming autonomous beings. This ideal of autonomy came under attack by the Foucauldian feminists because it presupposed that the subject is essentially free, ignoring that the individual, who looks like a monadic subject, could be constituted by power. In the structuralist paradigm, very little remains of the subject because subjectivity is understood as an effect of the structural laws and relations. Even if the subject manages to free herself from a particular form of submission, whether or not she would be liberated from power persists as a fundamental problem. In Foucauldian feminism, the notion of gender becomes even more encumbering. Subjects do not ontologically precede power relations; such relations produce them. Therefore, autonomy in the sense of liberation from power relations is considered an illusion. Ricoeur's thought can support the feminist theorizing about subjectivity over against the postmodern critiques of the classical feminist subject because it accommodates the claim that a subject of action comes into being from within a domain of power relations (the Foucauldian and postmodern critique of subjectivity) but still achieves subjectivity and autonomy in social relations.

According to Ricoeur, one becomes a subject of rights by expressing one's subjectivity at various levels or stages of subjectivity. Vulnerability results from the difficulties and obstacles power erects before the proper exercise of such capacities. An ethical or political subjectivity comes into being by going through the ontological processes productive of subjectivity in concrete social, historical, and political contexts. The universal declaration of human rights presupposes that a subject of rights is always already there in virtue of being born as human. Hannah Arendt shows in *Origins of Totalitarianism* that this is a presumption made in the eighteenth century. The question is whether subjects of rights can be constituted even if they are not there in social reality in virtue of being born as human. I argue that in Ricoeur there is a process of subjectivation. By "subjectivation," I refer to the process of constitution that creates a subject of rights. Vulnerability is present in a subject when it cannot satisfy the ontological conditions of subjectivation given the obstructions in the actualization of such capacities. The reasons people cannot fulfill the conditions for becoming a subject are often not personal at all; they have to do with the systematical, structural, and institutional oppression. Investigating Ricoeur's theory of subjectivation along with the feminist theories of oppression is helpful to rethink subjectivation in a context of sexual oppression.

SUBJECT OF RIGHTS

In "The Perplexities of the Rights of Man" in *Origins of Totalitarianism*, Hannah Arendt rejects the eighteenth-century view that takes human rights to be grounded in human nature. Instead of giving a metaphysical account of human rights, she prefers to offer a political reading by focusing on what happens to human rights when nation states weaken or no longer guarantee human rights to some groups of citizens (Arendt 1962, 292). It is worth noting that her strategy is a good example of what we may call a "phenomenology of crisis." She makes a brilliant application in the political realm, of the originally Heideggerian phenomenological insight that something is best seen (in its being) in a situation in which there is a failure in its proper functioning.

> Not only did the loss of national rights in all instances entail the loss of human rights, but the restoration of human rights, as the recent example of the State of Israel proves, has been achieved so far only through the restoration or the establishment of national rights. The conception of human rights based upon the assumed existence of a human being as such, broke down at the very moment when those who professed to believe in it were for the first time confronted with people who had indeed lost all other qualities and specific relationships—except that they were still human. (Arendt 1962, 299)

The apparition of a stateless people during World War II is sufficient evidence for refuting the eighteenth-century view that human beings have inalienable rights precisely because they are humans. Persons have the right to human rights if and only if a nation-state guarantees them such rights. When nation-states collapse or deprive a group of people from their citizenship rights, we suddenly begin to encounter groups of human beings to whom everything can be done with impunity. In the contemporary era, refugees who flee wars or immigrants who enter an affluent country in illegal ways as alien entities share this situation. When the sovereign suspends the reign of law, the destiny of those who have been declared "internal enemies" is quite the same. These people who are deprived of their social and economic rights, and thereby excluded from the public sphere and lost their liberty of traveling have indeed become *homo sacer*. Following Roberto Esposito, we can interpret the state of emergency as state's immunization (Esposito 2008, 45–77). When the state makes enemies of certain groups and strives to get back its health by condemning those who are alienated to civil death, tens and hundreds of thousands of stateless people emerge who are locked up within the borders of a state. For sure, this will poison society and hurt its historical being: the oppression that ensues from being less than citizen will be transmitted like a trauma from generation to generation. We can extend the question to those who are not directly targeted by the state oppression, and who seem to officially continue to enjoy their rights. How real can their subjectivity of rights be? Can they afford to freely use their rights? Women are the most telling example. Even in those places where they are entitled to human rights, they may not freely use their rights as citizens and human beings. Discrimination is the cause of that insufficiency. United Nations General Assembly has accepted in 1979 an international treatise (CEDAW) to end all discrimination against women so that they can transform themselves into actual subjects of rights.[1] The international and national support is indeed indispensable; however, is it sufficient?

The question concerning the constitution of the subject of rights is still fundamental. Even if the institutions overcome the practice of discrimination against certain groups, people do not automatically become able to use their rights. Ricoeur teaches us that in order to use one's rights one has to go through a process of subjectivation and thus fulfill certain ontological conditions of the constitution of one's self as a subject. My term "ontological conditions" should not be understood as those conditions that are given to us in virtue of being human; they are the conditions that should be created, brought into being through activity, effort, struggle, and performance.

Autonomy, rather than being a pure ontological possibility, is a possibility that can be realized in the social and historical power relations in which we are caught up as embodied beings. If the social and historical conditions are not favorable, a person can give up the effort and struggle to become a subject and even can believe in discourses that close off the possibility for subjectivation. For example, in some anti-secular places dominated by radical Islam, men force women to completely cover their bodies or to remain in the domestic sphere, or attack women in the public space. This violence can succeed only if it is supported by the theological discourses that function to legitimize and naturalize this oppression. Such discourses also try to persuade women to limit their process of subjectivation and discourage them from performing acts that cross the sexist boundaries.

Is vulnerability caused by the consciousness of finitude, which is traditionally attributed only to human beings, of being a living being with needs to satisfy, which nonhuman animals share with other animals? To attribute vulnerability to corporeal and finite living matter, independently of consciousness, discloses an unsatisfying naturalism. The naturalist approach to vulnerability fails philosophically because it misses the political and ethical dimension in which the question of fragility and vulnerability should be considered. Of course, we are living beings that have needs, but for a philosophical discussion on vulnerability in the political sense (political vulnerability), we need to spell out how autonomy and vulnerability are philosophically related in their very structure.

Ricoeur's essay "Who Is the Subject of Rights?" offers a phenomenological explication of subjectivity. This explication consists of the sequential stages or ways of subjectivation that culminate in ethico-political subjectivity, which provides the concrete ground for the legal subject, without which the subject of rights remains a formal, empty, and legal category. According to this phenomenological ontology, political subjectivity is the necessary condition of legal subjectivity, if the end of political subjectivity is to become an accomplished subject of rights, that is to say, a person who can fully use her rights. Ricoeur's approach assumes also that political subjectivity is conditioned by ethical subjectivity. Ethical subjectivity must be more or less constituted in order to attain political subjectivity. Remarkably, it does not reduce to conform with the moral standards of one's own culture or society.

I do not mean by "ethical subjectivity" a subject that makes morally right decisions. I assume that whether and why actions are right or wrong must remain open to discussion because actions can be evaluated differently from different normative perspectives. It is naïve to speak of political subjectivity without recognizing that ethical subjectivity plays a role in its constitution. Leftists who are suspicious of ethics as a bourgeois ideology, and associate ethics with liberalism, cannot thereby evade the ethical evaluation of political acts. Such discourses miss the connection between subjectivity and autonomy in the ethical sense with political subjectivity and autonomy. The ethical agent is the person who is morally worthy and deserves respect. What is the basis of a person's acknowledgment of the moral value attached to the self? Can a person respect one's self solely on the grounds of the recognition coming from others? This is an important question, if respect for the self is an essential constituent of ethical agency, a condition of its possibility. The relation between ethical integrity and ethical agency is certainly an intricate problem that deserves attention, and which we cannot discuss here. I shall content myself with making the following point: the phenomenological tradition sees a relation between the ethical and political subjectivity; it claims that politics presupposes ethics. Rather than giving a phenomenological interpretation of Aristotle, Ricoeur makes an Aristotelian interpretation of the phenomenological constitution of political subjectivity. This enables him to overcome some major ontological problems of the liberal modernist tradition of human rights.

Ricoeur's account of subjectivity rests on an analysis of human capacities. This is the famous capability approach that we find in Martha Nussbaum, for example. Capacities and faculties are certain potentialities, the actualizations of which culminate in the achievement of subjectivity. Aristotle's psychology is based on an understanding of being in terms of *dunamis* and *energeia* (potentiality and actuality). Ricoeur, in phenomenologically reviving this tradition, grounds autonomy on capacities, and accounts for the stages of the emergence of a subject by their realization. Capacity is like the power to become something by doing or acting. Ricoeur's conception of capacity can also be interpreted as possibility in the existential sense, because he does not speak of capacities on a psychological plane.

HUMAN CAPACITIES

Our capacity to speak is primary for Ricoeur. We can become speaking subjects because we can speak; we have the capacity to speak. We are not born as speaking subjects, so we cannot be considered as speaking subjects from the start. Infants begin to speak by applying the linguistic patterns that they pick up in determined contexts, to other similar contexts. That they repeat patterns is so striking that one may doubt the real existence of a speaking subject. It is always possible to ask the question who is really speaking. There is an "I" who speaks only if one can refer to oneself as the author of the expressions one makes use of in speaking. However, we rarely create words, and expressions; we belong to a system of language from which we borrow syntax and vocabulary, form and matter. Both linguistics and psychoanalysis are aware of the impersonal forces and structures at work in the act of speaking that make hard the attribution of speech to a subject as the author of his or her own words. Ricoeur takes this challenge seriously. As Lacan argues, in order to become a speaking subject, one must enter a symbolic system—a system that has structures, positions, rules, and norms. He acknowledges that as soon as someone starts speaking, the prevailing power regimes, normative structures, unconscious forces, and relations determine her saying (Ricoeur 2007, 76). But this "transcendental" condition does not imply the impossibility of the speaking subject. On the contrary, according to Ricoeur's new concept of subjectivity, the so-called speaking subject comes into being in the relations of the diverse forces, has a changeable position, seeks a way to express itself under different determinations. In short, speaking subject is a process of becoming, an emergence. At times it emerges and poses itself as a saying, and at other times it surrenders itself to that which is already said and submerges in it. The familiar distinction between *la parole parlante* and *la parole parlée*, the *saying* and the *said*, underlies Ricoeur's claim here. This distinction expresses the condition of the speaking subject.

At the second level of constitution at issue is the capacity to be the subject of one's acts. In case this potential is not realized, it is hard to consider the subject as the subject of rights and duties, because the subject does not own her acts. Law presupposes the ethical subject who has a free will and is conscious of right and wrong and just and unjust. This subject is capable of making choice of actions. Although this metaphysical presupposition is implicit, it becomes the ground for judgment when, for example, a culprit is on trial in the criminal court because of the crime he committed. What are the conditions for the attribution of an action to an actor? The reply to the question makes recourse to the notion of the will, which is the faculty of desire that pursues ends and demands that actions are to be chosen to achieve them. The faculty of the will makes the decision of the right course of action and decides about the form it will take. In this task, the will is assisted by the intuitive faculty of knowing values, and the faculty of judgment that sets forth the relevant features of the situation for moral evaluation. In the phenomenological tradition, Edmund Husserl distinguished between the axiological problem of valuing and the operations that pertain to the faculty of the will, by going against the Kantian moral tradition in which the will is spoken of as capable of being determined by desires, affections, and inclinations, besides reason. Both Kant and Spinoza have thought of the will as determinable. According to Kant, the subject is not free (autonomous), if an object in the world determines the will through a subjective desire, inclination, or passion. He thought that the will is autonomous on the condition that the moral law alone determines the faculty of desire (Kant 1964, 114).

I think Kant's concept of autonomy is a quest for transcendence because it transcends every singular factual situation in the world by choosing a rule of action that can pass the test of the categorical imperative. However, it makes more sense to ask what autonomy can be in being-in-the-world, in trying to act freely under impeding factical conditions. Spinoza, in order to make the point that freedom is not granted, writes in *Correspondance* that human beings may be aware of their own desires but not of the real causes of their actions.

> Further conceive, I beg, that a stone, while continuing in motion, should be capable of thinking and knowing, that it is endeavoring, as far as it can, to continue to move. Such a stone, being conscious merely of its own endeavor and not at all indifferent, would believe itself to be completely free, and would think that it continued in motion solely because of its own wish. This is that human freedom, which all boast that they possess, and which consists solely in the fact, that men are conscious of their own desire, but are ignorant of the causes whereby that desire has been determined. (Spinoza 1955, 390)

Spinoza argues that freedom is about understanding. Hegel takes up this point in *The Science of Logic* to make the claim that necessity is blind until it becomes conscious (Hegel 2010, 487). Marx, too, agrees with Spinoza and Hegel when he subscribes to the view that freedom is the consciousness of necessity. According to him, mental activities such as thinking, knowing, and willing are subject to class determinations. This tradition is very different from the Cartesian tradition that attributes infinity to the human will and takes it as absolutely free. The Cartesian tradition gave rise to the modern understanding of subjectivity, and the individual agency of the liberal political economy based on the mind and body dualism. Once we give up our commitment to dualism one comes to doubt that every act that a person performs belongs completely to her. And the will's capacity of transcending the physical and psychological determining factors becomes dubitable. We cannot attribute to the autonomous subject an infinite will, which could be independent of the influences of the forces the subject undergoes in the world.

The will is the faculty to desire, to adopt a policy of action, and to choose an action; but that power does not function independently of the faculty of thinking, understanding, and interpretation. We desire something because we think that it is good. This good can be a social purpose that transcends the individual and for the sake of which the individual may sacrifice herself. To believe that something is good and to desire it presupposes that the will and the faculty of thinking are disposed in certain ways. *Freedom and Nature*, the first volume of Ricoeur's philosophy of the will, which dates from 1950, presents Ricoeur's philosophy of action. For him, the problem of action has to do with intentionality, though the fundamental problem is the articulation of the bond between the voluntary and the involuntary. Ricoeur, inspired by Gabriel Marcel's concept of incarnation, conceives being-in-the-world as incarnated and questions what it means to be free in the world as an incarnated being. Our bodies are part of nature, but that nature is not merely mechanism without sense. As the horizon of our actions, it mysteriously abounds with senses and significations, and as such it is not fully comprehensible. Nature does not determine the subject in a situation, but it inheres significations that motivate actions. It follows that our habits and even our free acts arise from a background that involves the involuntary. In that sense, as Grégori Jean argues, nature of which our bodies are part is like *natura naturans* in Spinoza's thought (Jean 2018). Ricoeur regards nature in this sense not as an object of scientific explanation but of hermeneutics.

For Ricoeur, the involuntary and the voluntary are not sharply opposed in a dichotomy, even though they are reciprocal and reconcilable; there are involuntary dimensions in a voluntary act. Although the motives for a decision are the motives of that decision, hence taken on by the voluntary, they still set the voluntary act in touch with the involuntary. The reciprocity implies that

> need, emotion, habit etc., acquire their complete significance only in relation to a will which they solicit, dispose, and generally affect, and which in turn determines their significance, that is determines them by choice, moves them by its effort, and adopts them by its consent. The involuntary has no meaning of its own. Only the relation of the voluntary to the involuntary is intelligible. (Ricoeur 1966, 4–5)

The involuntary can take several forms. It can appear to me as a force of my character or of my incarnation, or it can come from nature.

> [T]he uneasiness felt by a few vulnerable natures—like Vigny or Rilke—who experience themselves as a charge they cannot sustain: something seems lost from the very beginning because something has been decided for me, before me, or worse, because something is found to be decided without having been decided by anyone. Though in his secrecy the freely choosing man is alone, in a proud and modest freedom, the invincible nature to which he is united isolates him in a heavier solitude because here freedom submits before it can do. (Ricoeur 1966, 448)

Moreover, Ricoeur recognizes in *The Symbolism of Evil*, which dates from 1967 (Ricoeur 1972), that symbolic forms can be part of the involuntary. In fact, he engages with the problem in *Freud and Philosophy: An Essay on Interpretation* (Ricoeur 1970), which derives from the lectures he gave at Yale University in the autumn of 1961. There Ricoeur writes:

> Let us do justice to Cassirer: he was the first to have posed the problem of the reconstruction of language. The symbolic form, prior to constituting an answer, delimits a question, namely, the question of the composition of the "mediating functions" within a single function, which Cassirer calls the *Symbolische*. "The symbolic" designates the common denominator of all the ways of objectivizing, of giving meaning to reality. (Ricoeur 1970, 10)

The problem goes beyond the constitution of the objectivity of objects. And is not simply about the structures of the subject's mind. Discourses can compete to determine our will; persuasion means that a discourse won the upper hand over the others and became dominant. Foucault goes beyond the problem concerning how discourse determines the mind for he conceives discourses as power regimes, which through their regulative functions also produce subjects. Discursive determinations are interwoven with institutional practices of power. A significant number of debates over Foucault's thought are concerned with the death of the subject for he claimed that discourse/power regimes do not only control but also produce the subject.

Lacan grounds the same idea in structuralism at the intersection of linguistics and psychoanalysis and claims that the speaking subject comes into being by taking a position in the symbolic order. One can neither be a subject of desire nor of speech prior to the entrance into the symbolic order. We may believe that we are speaking subjects, the authors of our own words, the creators of meaning, but in fact language, the unconscious may be speaking. What I call my desire can be kidnapped by the anonymous impersonal Other that inhabits language. This is why the questions such as "Is this really my desire?" and "Am I really the speaker, the signifier?" are not tautologies but open problems that are worth inquiry.

What place, if any, do autonomy and freedom have in this framework? Should we simply give up the value we attribute to these notions? To realize how our will is determined, the consciousness or the awareness of the forces under the yoke of which we make decisions can pave the way for seeing and assuming a possibility. Discourses fight other discourses, and forces clash with other forces; thinking involves engagement in a symbolic struggle in which one tries to take away the weapon at the opponent's usage. Can there be a genuine way of thinking that does not involve epistemic and conceptual violence? Epistemic violence is the only emancipatory violence, and it is the necessary condition for autonomy, because it can prevent the sacrifice of the other to one-sided determinations. We need to hear experiences, but we should also understand that there are symbolic structures, constructions, positions, relations. There are histories of oppression (economic, sexual, racial) that give rise to privileges and disadvantages that underlie these experiences. The speaking subject is not an empirical subject, with no unconscious, a subject who is completely present and in control of its lived experiences. To engage in politics by ontologically and epistemologically relying on the modern Cartesian subject, to take refuge in the sovereignty of that subject, for example, in the attempt to escape the sovereign state, is according to Jacques Derrida, to prefer one form of sovereignty to another (Derrida 2009, 67). Marx, too, refuses to see the will of a free subject as a primitive, irreducible concept, which one may appeal to, without further discussion. Even from Hegel's point of view, the Spirit—as a universal subject—determines the will of the individual and the effort to derive the Spirit from the individual spirits, amounts to personalism, which is a naïve form of idealism. In short, if various forces and influences always play on the will, freedom and choice arise from self-questioning in shaping the will, which keeps it open to the forces coming from diverse perspectives. We all have rubbles in our minds. Philosophical questioning and critical thinking can remove the rubble and clean the ground so that the will may be ready to give way to a new determination. The same can be said of an organization, a club, a religion, and a worldview. Reflection makes human beings aware of various determinations and gives them a chance to make choices. Hence, people who do not question themselves have no chance of making choice; unrecognized forces would carry them away. Critical and philosophical thinking interrupts a rigidly delimited rhetoric that organizes people to take an immediate action without questioning where that action leads.

It is possible to say that at the core of the capacity to act lies an agent as a power to act, though it is also true that the agent comes into being, in the full sense of the term, due to its activity. The agent is "a self" on the grounds that speech and action can be attributed to her. Indeed, if the agent cannot be spoken of as a self, it will be difficult to distinguish it from a being that is manipulated as if it were a thing. According to Ricoeur, the existence of a self requires a "narrative identity." What is at stake here is not an unchanging sameness; a narrated identity is organized temporally and accepts change; though its temporality is radically different than the continuity of a thing in linear time. From an ontological point of view, in case there is no speaking and acting subject, there is no narrating subject who can tell her own story. To write my story, I have to see myself as the author of my acts; I should be able to say, "I have acted in this way," "I have not done that," and so on. Everybody has a story or stories; should we then say that everybody is a speaking subject? No. Only a few of us can tell their story. Only a few of us can always tell their story everywhere and to everyone. For example, women could not tell their life stories and write their own histories. Oppressed people might have had difficulty in expressing themselves and making oppressors hear what they have to say. One must struggle to tell one's own story, and people are often determined by the stories other people recount in their place or have to cast their experiences in formulations that keep a hierarchy, which preserves the existing status quo in place. It takes a cognitive leap to realize that one has been repeating the narratives that others recount, which are often cast in the oppressors' language or make sense in accordance with the oppressors' norms. This is why sharing one's experiences with other people making sense of the similarities between different narratives, and questioning the attitudes that perpetuate oppression can be the first steps toward emancipation. The necessary condition of narrating is to be able to say, "I think," "according to me," even if the self might be a function or consequence of narrating. Moreover, the possibilities of change open up for the self through the transformation, modification, and the deconstruction of the narratives on which the self has so far depended.

For example, the answers to the question "who," can be given by pointing to a person's character traits. But in order to exhibit such character traits in the concrete, one needs anecdotes, lived experiences, and stories. If we do not have such concretizations, the attribution of properties to a person is unwarranted. Character is represented as identity in the sense of sameness—even if we accept in principle that someone's character can change—and the narratives of concrete experiences and events confirm that the character in question has indeed such and such traits. We appeal to character traits as explanatory, for we believe that they play a role in giving narratives their particular shape. This person makes a specific decision and acts in a certain way because she has such and such a character. We get ourselves in a circle here, one that we do not try to escape. According to Ricoeur, self-worth and self-respect depend on the narratives one tells oneself as well as to others. Ricoeur associates morality with duty and ethics with the good. Ethics is about good life whereas morality concerns obligations. One may do the right thing even if one has no narrative, but creating a good life by way of actions is not possible without ethical integrity. He holds that our lives are entangled with other people's lives. "Life stories are so intertwined with one another that the narrative anyone tells or hears of his own life becomes a segment of those other stories that are the narratives of others' lives" (Ricoeur 2000, 7). The other's narrative completes or confirms mine or leads me to question my own narrative, opening it for new interpretations. We can often witness that the same event can be lived differently by different people and figure other-wise in diverse stories. An experience is not more adequate to reality than another; there are various parties, interests, engagements, and goals in the light of which experience can make different sense to different people. Given the differences in how a state of affairs is lived, the totality of the meaning of a situation might seem like an intricacy formed by the recounting of what happened from various points of view. This fact, however, does not lead to a world in which there are no norms and principles that serve to evaluate a situation. In the ethical dimension the subject has to explain how she per-ceives and evaluates a situation and thus relates her action to her judgment as ground to consequence. Here concepts, feelings, and norms work in an inter-related manner.

For Ricoeur, subjectivity in the ethical sense is the ground of subjectivity in the legal and political sense. Why is the ethical subjectivity the necessary condition of the subject of rights and political subjectivity? If we cannot evaluate behavior as right or wrong and judge states of affairs as good or bad, we cannot be considered as a person worthy of respect, a subject to whom ethical and legal acts can be attributed. An adult person with no autonomy, in complete submission to the authority of another, is giving up moral agency even though he or she would still be morally responsible for his or her acts.

Subjectivity in the ethical sense is often measured by one's social stand-ing; by the honor other people can give to the person and take back from her. However, the honor that depends on others should not be confused with dignity. Private and public persons honor us because of our acts, and they may take it back on the basis of their decisions, likes, and dislikes. In contrast, no one can take our dignity from us. The only way to lose it is to make moral mistakes such as deceiving and coercing others. For example, if a state violates human rights, an initiative to organize to resist it cannot be designated as a struggle for dignity. Dignity is not something a state can touch. If someone was tortured, the person's dignity would not be automatically lost because he or she is tortured. But the aim of torture is to destroy the person as a human being, and if the person breaks down, human dignity could be jeopardized. If the individual suffering the torture makes a false testimony or betrays his comrades fighting for a good cause, then he or she would be harming his or her own moral dignity. As long as the person under torture does not morally collapse, the dignity of the tortured is not damaged. Only the torturer's dignity is harmed, because he is the one who acts in the morally wrong way, in violation of the human rights. In ethics, dignity rests on the intrinsic value a human being has, in virtue of being human. It is worth struggling for the recognition of this value by the state. For a state to care for human dignity is to respect human rights. By failing to do that, a state cannot take away our dignity, but it loses its liability and legitimacy as a state. If in the struggle to resist such a vicious state the individual chooses to sacrifice herself, refusing to comply with the conditions of defeat, that choice can be designated as an act exhibiting heroic courage that may be honored, rather than a defense of dignity. One may decide to die if one cannot win. However, the rationality of that decision is open to discussion. Dignity is a concept about ethical subjectivity and one that is interwoven with one's life story. A person's sense of self-worth, his or her self-respect, depends on that; this self-valuation is grounded on a person's ability to avoid moral wrongs and performing morally right acts as much as commitments to the promises one has made to one's self and to others.

RELATIONS WITH PERSONAL AND INSTITUTIONAL OTHERS

In order to genuinely occupy the positions of legal and political subjectivity, we must actively use our subjective capacities. Oppression does not destroy these subjective capacities but creates the conditions that make their use impossible. A person who is capable of being a subject of rights, to become such a subject, needs to have the conditions in which these capacities can be actively used. This is precisely where we can locate vulnerability. Capacities are actualized in relation to others. The other, for Ricoeur, is a person in interpersonal relations. Family relations and friendships are examples of personal relations. My partner in a love relationship is an other with whom I am in an interpersonal relationship. In order to be a subject, I need to actualize my capacities in my relationships with others. For example, I should be able to have an argument with my mother, explain to my friend why I preferred to do something, tell my lover my life story. It may happen that others make it difficult for me to be a speaking and acting subject who fashions and tells her own narrative. Others can impede or support me in the process of becoming an ethical and political agent instead of being someone whose behavior is automatically regulated by the norms that are already established in a cultural environment. My relations to others may also be shaped by my struggles with them because I refuse to give up my effort to be a subject. At the end, even to exercise one's capacities for subjectivity in a single interpersonal relationship can count as a significant achievement. The exercise of one's capacities for subjectivity must not dominate the other in an interpersonal relationship. In an ideal relationship, I actualize my subjectivity by letting the other have the space to do the same. However, the accomplishment of subjectivity in interpersonal relations is a necessary but not the sufficient condition for subjectivation, for subjective capacities should also be actualized in institutional relations. As long as the subject is too intimidated to speak to institutions, subjectivity remains enclosed in the private domain and cannot become fully actual.

Institutional relations are the relations with the third party. In other words, Ricoeur grounds institutions on the relations with the third. When we deal with institutions, we are expected to relate to others fairly, in accordance with fair institutional procedures and practices. A just institution disallows favoritism, that is, the prioritizing of interpersonal relations. Nepotism in institutional relations is an indication that everybody is not treated equally and fairly, and that institutions are not sufficiently strong and just. Institutional relations are public relations and, on this plane, even the persons who are in interpersonal relations should be treated by suspending their priority, in accordance with impersonal procedures, that is, as if they are third party. This means that I should not accept to see a friend first, when he or she is not the first in the line of people waiting to see me in a professional context. My relative has the same status as other people I encounter professionally. Institutional mediation contributes to the actualization of the subject's capacities thus paving the way for becoming a subject of rights. It is not enough to take up the word only in interpersonal relations; one must also speak to institutions, address them. This implies that I must try to speak to the third party, to defend an argument, to criticize, to take responsibility for an action as my own, as an agent. I must give reasons for my action, construct a narrative in which I appear as a subject in a situation. This makes me come into visibility as "the subject of a situation." Such a subject has its own evaluation of the situation and takes responsibility for it. An ethical way of relating to the situation is a *sine qua non* condition for being a legal and political subject. If we fail to satisfy these conditions in institutional relations, our rights remain purely formal, rights that are *de jure* there though they are abstract. And because we do not really use them, we can only be professedly subjects of rights.

The institutional third, at the linguistic level, is the criterion of comprehensibility, acceptability, the recognition of the rules that distinguish one natural language from others. It implies, at the same time, the promise of truth as embedded in the act of speaking, the presupposition that a speaker means what they say. This promise and that presupposition are there even when people engage in deception. And the very possibility of deception depends on them. These conditions are there as soon as we speak with an other—whether intimate or distant, familiar, and foreign. Ricoeur acknowledges that in interpersonal relations, the relation of discourse with the other is mediated by the institutional other. In a relation of intimacy some cultural and social rules of courtesy can be suspended, but that does not mean they are not primary as conditions of possibility of linguistic relations. Furthermore, the third is again already there insofar as the possibility of action is concerned, because all actions belong to a social order and its moral significance transcends the personal relations of the agent. For example, take male violence suffered by a woman, be it domestic violence. Here feminists do not simply judge an action located in the realm of interpersonal relations, they insist that male violence must be condemned as a social and political problem. There is here a universal phenomenon, which may figure differently in different cultural contexts. This is why, rather than personal attitudes, structures and systems that produce and perpetuate such attitudes should be problematized. Indeed, if we look at the plane of responsibility, where the attributions and assumption of responsibilities are at stake, responsibility is of intersubjective character. "The other is implicated here in multiple ways: as beneficiary, as witness, as judge, and, more fundamentally, as the one who, in counting on me, on my capacity to keep my word, calls me to responsibility, renders me responsible" (Ricoeur 2000, 7). "The other" is no longer "you," but "everyone," although the third is not designated as a single person, the third is not just the anonymous other insofar as responsibility expands to a group of oppressed and mistreated people. Why does Ricoeur think that responsibility is intersubjective? His claim that the ethico-juridical imputation implies the third is merely a logical point. Another reason could be that, even if the juridical system may fail to sufficiently acknowledge that, harm suffered at the interpersonal level, could also be a consequence of a social and institutional problem.

If the first condition of being a subject of rights is to be someone to whom actions can be attributed, hence, to earn respect as the author of one's actions, the second condition is to be a citizen, to have a place in the public sphere. Without the mediation of the interpersonal and institutional relations, the capacities from which the process of subjectivation takes its departure cannot be actualized. The relation to the state, too, is a relation to a set of institutions. Individuals, who have no institutional relations, they can neither become persons nor autonomous subjects in the full sense. Ricoeur writes in a way that echoes Aristotle: "Without institutional mediation, individuals are only the initial drafts of human persons. Their belonging to a political body is

necessary to their flourishing as human beings, and in this sense, this mediation cannot be revoked" (Ricoeur 2000, 10). Women in the countryside who
are not schooled at all, and who do not come into contact with the state
institutions, can be empowered by their local cultural tradition in certain
ways within certain limits determined by traditional gender norms, but have
only limited possibility to challenge patriarchy. Most states in the world do
nothing to empower women and on the contrary, implement policies that
weaken gender equality. This is certainly true for my own country, Turkey,
in 2019. Yet, women's self-awareness as citizens and their challenge to male
institutions make a difference.

Having situated the question of vulnerability in the problematic of subjectivation, it becomes clear that Ricoeur's theory of the constitution of the
subject enables us to relate vulnerability to institutional oppression. Let us
take again women in the Middle East as example. Women can be automatically citizens of a state because they are born within its borders or have
native parents. But they cannot really benefit from their citizenship insofar as
they cannot become speaking subjects, agents, ipseities, ethical subjects, and
subjects of rights. If women have these capacities why do they remain, for
the most part and most of the time, virtual? The reason for that lies in
women's miscarriage in actualizing these capacities in relations with personal and institutional others. The pressure that they undergo in the public
sphere plays an important role. Even in places where there is no explicit legal
ban, female presence in the public sphere needs social and political support.
When women are condemned to the private domestic sphere, the mediation
of their interpersonal relations with the third is strictly limited. This facilitates the exploitation of their labor of care for the lives and needs of the other
family members. Moreover, as Seyla Benhabib emphasizes, when women
are held responsible for the care for children and elderly these responsibilities
are represented as not belonging to liberal states (Benhabib 1992, 65).

Pamela Sue Anderson argues that Ricoeur admits that "the course of
recognition for the capable subject encounters existential difficulties of identity, alterity, differences, violence, inabilities undergone, failures of memory,
and endless conflict on the level of lived-through experiences" (Anderson
2016, 216). Ricoeur does not discuss how gender might partake in the subjectivation process, hindering and enabling the capacities of the living bodies
as psycho-physical beings. How does gender sexually differentiate bodies
and what has sexual difference to do with subjectivity? As Pamela Sue Anderson remarks, "descriptions of flesh, especially including the female
body's association with she who is abjected from her own subject position,
remain part of the ethical, social, and spiritual imaginary of Western cultures" (Anderson 2016, 216). In *Symbolism of Evil*, Ricoeur explores how
religious symbolism shapes thoughts and bodies and produce psychological
and political effects in people's lives. He realizes that symbols prepare the

ground for the development of the inner attitudes that make people embrace social and political structures, and sometimes to challenge them. He also notes that some of these symbols are feminine. Although Ricoeur does not reflect on the question of symbolism as part of historical gender oppression, feminist theologian Mary Daly draws from his work on symbolism in her feminist theory (Arel 2016). Indeed, the investigation of the various topics in Ricoeur's philosophy for feminist philosophical ends has just begun. My view is that Ricoeur's theory of subjectivity needs to be supplemented with a theory of oppression that explains how sexism, misogyny, and gender inequality undermine women's capacity to attain freedom in vulnerability. Women are vulnerable not only because they suffer historical inequalities as corporeal beings that have needs and desires, but as relational beings who care for others.

OPPRESSION

Autonomy is an attribute a subject of rights can possess. The ordinary understanding contrasts it with fragility and vulnerability so that, autonomy implies the absence of fragility and vulnerability and vice versa. However, Ricoeur speaks of a "paradox" or "antinomy" here. Antinomies are contraries that resist being refuted. Hence, we should either keep or eliminate both. The same human being can be fragile and autonomous from different points of view. "The autonomy in question is that of a fragile, vulnerable being" (Ricoeur 2007, 73). One can be autonomous because one starts out as a vulnerable being having the capacities for autonomy; and vulnerable because one is capable of autonomy. Fragility, loss of confidence, precariousness, and dependence characterize the reverse of autonomy, insofar as they are interpreted as the miscarriages of subjectivation. As Ricoeur recognizes, it is often unconvincing to put the failure to become an autonomous subject on personal account by forgetting the conditions of oppression under which a person lives her life.

What is oppression? While the actualization of capacities gives rise to autonomy, their remaining only virtual creates vulnerability. If this claim is interpreted in the light of the feminist analyses of oppression, we can shed some light on the problem of political subjectivity. In radical feminism, the political subject wrestles with gender inequality and sexual oppression. Autonomy is confidence in one's own abilities; it implies the belief and the hope that one can act to change the existing state of affairs. This confidence is supported by past and present performances, capacities that have already been actualized, and recognition of the deeds by others as significant. Self-doubt impedes the capacity for action by way of speech. Doubt can be overcome by encouragement coming from the others and in trusting interpersonal relationships. In a similar way, the affirmation of our capacity to act by the interpersonal and institutional relations pave the way for us to become subjects. This helps us understand how gender works: if female children are supported in using their capacities for subjectivity, they become self-confident and extroverted subjects who are not scared to challenge the world. If their capacities are impeded, they turn out too shy to become visible in the public space as who they are. The norms that constitute and regulate the public sphere do not empower women as acting subjects; on the contrary, they make it difficult for them to be speaking, acting, and narrating subjects. Such norms reproduce the patriarchal culture in which there are unquestioned inert practices that reserve the subject position for men.

Feminism interprets the impeding of a possibility or a capacity as "a specific form of power." This power makes it impossible for the subject to relate to reality through her own language and action. It establishes domination over the subject by disregarding the various possibilities in terms of which the situation in which the action takes place can be spoken of; it makes the reality of the situation non-displaceable and closes it to resignification. The asymmetry of power opens the door for the intimidation and manipulation of possible agents in a situation and facilitates their instrumentalization (Ricoeur 2007, 77). Thus, systematic oppression is the institutional paralyzing of the possibilities and capacities to do something, to act. "People do not simply lack power, they are deprived of it" (Ricoeur 2007, 77).

If women are not autonomous this is because they have been imposed a set of "this cannot be done" or "you cannot do that." Gendering processes function to prevent women from empowering themselves and others, to become autonomous; and to keep them as vulnerable and fragile beings. Comparably, the suspension of the law by the sovereign amounts to the loss of the status of the subject of rights. That loss implies the destruction of the possibility of the realization of the subject's capacities such as speech, action, and narration. In dictatorships, totalitarianism, and fascism the creation of an environment of social and political pressure to interrupt free speech and action aims at the annihilation of ethical, political, and legal subjectivity. If there is no longer a position for legal subjectivity, the whole process of subjectivation must either fade away, submerge in apathy or take a revolutionary turn. Iris Marion Young, in her 1998 essay, "Five Faces of Oppression," says that "oppression is the inhibition of a group through a vast network of everyday practices, attitudes, assumptions, behaviors, and institutional rules. Oppression is structural or systemic. The systemic character of oppression implies that an oppressed group need not have a correlate oppressing group" (Young 2004, 94).[2] If we tie that with women's oppression, we can say that for women to be oppressed, they do not have to be mistreated by some concrete men; the constitution of the public space is sufficient to oppress them. Norms and procedures that organize the public realm could erect obstacles on the way to women's autonomy. When the bourgeois male subject was fighting for his autonomy and rights, women were confined to the private sphere. They have been advised not to speak even in interpersonal relations, and they are expected not to challenge the existing order. They are not supposed to defend themselves by arguments in the presence of the keepers of the patriarchal law of the family. Moreover, these gender norms are legitimated by an appeal to nature. In "Oppression," an essay that dates from 1983, Marilyn Frye inquires into what it means for a way to be closed for someone who would like to achieve a certain end. It does not simply mean that this person encounters obstacles on her way. In fact, being in an aporia, the absence of ways out, being in a no-exit situation without alternatives tells more about the situation of the oppressed (Frye 1983, 4). The cloture of the way to do something is explained to the oppressed in a persuasive way. If there is no way out, the reason for that is the individual's lack of ability, unfitness, and absence of liability for what she desires to do. Putting the blame on the individual hides that the real cause of finding oneself in an aporia is to be classified as the member of a group by being constructed as the carrier of some natural, physical, psychical, and moral qualities. Frye argues that "women are oppressed, as *women*" (Frye 1983, 16). When women are forbidden to speak for themselves and forced to play gender roles that are strictly delimited, they are driven to believe that they are not good speakers; they are intimidated to express themselves in public. Consequently, they start contributing to the system that effaces them (Frye 1983, 16). This process begins at home, continues at school, and reaches its peak with women's lack of affirmation and authorization as subjects in the public space. In a wide range of discourses, including those that pervade professional life and media, a sexist way of articulating the matters at hand, unfold as to support women's loss of confidence so that it becomes more difficult for them to become subjects. Cudd and Jones argue that "sexism" is not just the creation of ungrounded, illegitimate, unjustifiable differences among people. It is a general name for women's institutional and systematic oppression.

> In the widest sense "sexism" can be referred to anything that creates, constitutes, promotes, sustains, or exploits an unjustifiable distinction between the sexes (Frye 1983, 18). In this wide sense the term "sexism" can be used to refer to any purported though mistaken difference between the sexes. This neutral descriptive use of the term, however, is deeply unsatisfactory. [. . .] Sexism refers to a historically and globally pervasive form of oppression against women. (Cudd and Jones 2003, 103–4)

Ricoeur rejects an important postulate of the liberal theory when he theorizes about the connection between autonomy and vulnerability. Liberal theory claims that people are separate beings pursuing their own interests, and each individual person is entitled to be a bearer of rights on equal terms with others. In this model, which understands people as individuals or as separate and indivisible atoms, autonomy in the abstract sense is presupposed. It disregards the fact that people have to go through practical processes in which they exercise their specific capacities to make themselves autonomous and be recognized as such. Even when liberalism sees autonomy as a task to achieve, it conceives the individual as an atom that cannot separate itself from the configuration it entered with other atoms. Hence, the individual could be absorbed into a community that imposes some good to it, and from which it might fail to liberate itself. Ricoeur borrows from Heidegger's existential ontology in *Being and Time*, according to which being-in-the-world is the fundamental state of *Dasein*, which implies being-with-the-others (*Mit-Dasein*) as its existential component. Thus, we are not separate individuals to begin with. Heidegger contests the Cartesian tradition of metaphysics of subjectivity with the new ontological plane he opens up in *Being and Time*. Ricoeur, on the other hand, takes up the question of subjectivity by means of a phenomenological-hermeneutical methodology. The subject is not given to itself as a separate presence; it comes into being as speaking, acting, narrating, imputable, legal, and political subject in a relational manner.

This is a relational ontology because we become, for example, a speaking subject by actualizing our capacity for speech in the relation with the other and the third. These constitute the topography of agency. The "I" enters the dialectic process of identity and ipseity by narrating its life story. My life story constitutes me as "I" by situating me in various encounters, promises, engagements, relations I have formed with others and various public figures of the third. Autonomy is not the capacity to stand alone; it is accomplished in a relational manner, rather than being based on separation from the social and institutional relations or bonds.

RESISTANCE

We have addressed the ordeal of autonomy by coupling it with the question of oppression. We can now tie our analysis with the possibility of resistance: If systemic oppression impedes autonomy, personal and organized resistance may facilitate and enable it. Resistance is the designation for the action to contest unjust power. Even when we are not yet and no longer subjects of rights, resistance is the way for continuing to demand that position of subjectivity in political contexts in which there is an intensification of pressure, and the increase of vulnerability, understood ontologically, in its relation to the exercise of all our aforesaid capacities. The acts of resistance can be imagined as organized by certain general principles or as constructed as a result of an analysis, interpretation, and response to the existing relations of power in specific social and political contexts. Resistance in this second sense is spontaneous assembling or association of people as a response to a situation. However, this way of resisting has also its own dangers. For example, in a state of emergency people may not very well understand changes in institutional behavior, inadequately anticipate the consequences of possible actions, and fail to avoid simple oppositions or a narrow framing of the conceptual framework of action. An urgency to act may contribute to the closing of the public space to democratic criticism. A bad choice of action may, instead of bringing forth more resistance in the future, lead to lesser resistance and cynicism. It can create despair that brings closure in private lives and deepens social silence.

The process that leads to the autonomy of the subject is the actualization of the subjective capacities. Mere citizenship of a lawful state or the state's guaranteeing of rights to its citizens does not make human beings subjects of rights. To fully enjoy one's rights in a lawful state requires an autonomous subject. In dictatorships and totalitarian regimes, we see that people experience loss of rights; citizens are deprived of their human rights by the state. It is even possible to say that the position of subject of rights is barred. People are excluded from the public space; white collars are expulsed from their professional positions. In accordance with that we can speak of dispossession, devaluation, confiscation of property, and condemnation to civil death, a way of inciting people to end their lives. These experiences force the subjects who conceive themselves as citizens, the founders of a political unity, to give up their autonomy and evacuate the position of political subjectivity. Perhaps this is generally true for the era of neoliberal capitalism, in which Marx Fisher sees "the crisis of capitalism" (Fisher 2009, 71) that involves political operations that force the subject to leave the position of subjectivity.

What kind of life is left to us when the crisis of capitalism evolves into a process of autoimmunity that perpetuates its existence in arbitrarily renewed states of emergency? In contrast to the comprehension of the ethical life in ancient philosophy and the modern theories that are inspired by it, by "good life" is now meant the life that does not involve any political activity. And even this life is considered as a grace of the State because it gives itself the right to decide over the living and the dead. A citizen can be among those that are chosen dead because of a reason she may not even be aware of, and which might remain unknown to her. She can be deprived of her job, property, and the resources for survival by an arbitrary government decree. Given that situation, the only constituents of good life that are left are consumption and socialization, which is for the most part only virtual: if the affective condition of the person is *depressive hedonia* lived by strolling through signifiers that are liberated from symbolic structures, her mental condition and memory undergo an increasing fragmentation (Fisher 2009). If this "good life" consists of the dissociation of the subject, can it really be good?

With the collapse of the liberal framework, people's relation to the state is construed in a similar way to people's relation to God—through the effect of fear. Just as God is self-authorized, the state does not get its authority from people, its authority is derived from the violence it exercises. However, if a government can produce the people who benefit from and support it, even its excessive violence would be in its own eyes democratically legitimized power. Once the division of powers breaks down, democracies turn into dictatorships and totalitarian regimes. In such a political situation citizenship is a position that can easily be lost. Subjection and obedience are the conditions for the individual to live like a "human being," which now means the satisfaction of needs and desires. This is clearly depersonalization—a form of biopower. Nonetheless, personalization is a form of modern bio-power as well. In personalism, however, the person is conceived as the bearer of ethical, legal, and political values. According to personalism, which in certain respects echoes Aristotle's conception of human being, what makes human human is not the satisfaction of natural needs and desires; it is the capacity to socially and politically organize to create a human world thanks to which higher capacities can be actualized. In Roman culture person is a legal status and transcends the living body, which can be sold as a thing to slavery. When political organization cannot even be envisaged because of the risk it poses to biological life, politics disappears as a world-building activity. Autonomy based on imputability and self-respect built throughout experiences of subjectivation is displaced by power-centered underclass culture.

In this political scene, the majority to which the political power refers to legitimize itself finds it unnecessary to use reason in a normative way, in accordance with epistemic norms and ethical values. It interprets life situations via the opposition between strength and weakness. In any occasion, the underclass mentality cares a lot less about values than the balance of powers. It aims at being always on the winning side and sees weakness and inflexibility as the major vices. The configuration of various forces being always at the center of its attention, it knows in advance the price that it will pay if it ends up being on the wrong side of the power conflict. Anyway, as long as it can make pragmatic alliances and achieve its ends through the channels of power, it does not care for self-realization to attain autonomy. It sees subjectivation that leads to being subject or rights, as only a different sort of power game in a culture that effectively masks its reality in this way. Most people, who already gave up the hope for subjectivation in Ricoeur's sense have come to that precisely because they have sensed that the system in which they have to live does not support subjectivity beyond subjection. They are realists who do not suffer as much as the subjects who suffer the experience of desubjectivation. Those who tolerate not being subjects of rights and the lack of possibility of realizing their capacities as subjects would certainly hate those who support and perpetuate this culture. In those places in which the political power interrupts subjectivation, nihilist masses proliferate as a consequence of despair. Such a community substitutes actions based on reasoning and axiology with religious formalisms, rituals, and gender rules and norms. These gender rules and norms remain in effect even though they fail the test of ethical validity. The loss of the conditions of possibility for subjectivation lies at the heart of a nihilistic age in which human beings become useless and dispensable living material.

In a country where the sovereign controls the law and turns it as a weapon against his opponents who happen to be politicians, intellectuals, and activists who raise the consciousness of reclaiming rights and freedoms, the amount of anxiety about one's fragility and vulnerability is certainly on the rise. The sovereign can use our fragility and vulnerability against us to displace us from the position of subjects of rights. If rights no longer work to protect people, the only way of resisting is to turn our own fragility and vulnerability against the existing system of oppression. There is a paradoxical situation here: because fragility and vulnerability disappear at the limit of death, performing with the resources of fragility and vulnerability only marks the empty place of a subject of rights. The real gain is to fill that place by a subject who survives and is capable of building social bonds, alliances, and networks.

Resistance has two options available: either to end life for the sake of life or to survive assault. The factors that determine the choice of one alternative over the other have to do with our previous experiences, the inherited ways of resistance, our psychological dependencies and traumas. When a historical trauma starts repeating itself in the present, the gate is opened for the frozen images, ancient credos, and engagements that compete for the determination of the will. Resistance is not struggle for power, the effort for a power to outdo another power that confronts it. It is not a "heroism," which pushes the body to appear before disproportionate violence. To resist is to create social bonds and relations. These bonds and relations fulfill the task of letting people live and making them flourish so that they can reproduce themselves as subjects of rights. They constitute the spaces for subjectivation. Resistance is the activity in which fragile subjects come together to empower themselves to make their voices heard. This is to participate in the building of a future for the society. This is why resistance, rather than adopting a strategy of sacrifice, should be a commitment to defend life and to survive. Resilience is the capacity to build a new life when some possibilities are closed. If the state is no longer a fair institution, we must spend all our efforts to make it regain fairness. For that, we need to be resilient survivors who never give up rational discourse, solidarity, and patience.

REFERENCES

Anderson, Pamela Sue. 2016. "Ricoeur in Dialogue with Feminist Philosophy of Religion: Hermeneutic Hospitality in Contemporary Practice." In *Feminist Explorations of Paul Ricoeur's Philosophy*, edited by Annemie Halsema and Fernanda Henriques, 199–220. Lanham, MD: Lexington Books.

Arel, Stephanie N. 2016. "Paul Ricoeur, Mary Daly, Attestation, and the Dis-covery of Feminine Religious Symbols." In *Feminist Explorations of Paul Ricoeur's Philosophy*, edited by Annemie Halsema and Fernanda Henriques, 221–38. Lanham, MD: Lexington Books.

Arendt, Hannah. 1962. *The Origins of Totalitarianism*. Cleveland and New York: Meridian Books.

Benhabib, Seyla. 1992. *Situating the Self: Gender, Community and Postmodernism in Contemporary Ethics*. Cambridge: Polity Press.

Cudd, A. E., and Jones, L. E. Jones. 2003. "Sexism." In *A Companion to Applied Ethics*, edited by R. G. Frey and C. H. Wellman, 102–17. Oxford: Wiley Blackwell.

Derrida, Jacques. 2009. *The Beast and the Sovereign*. Vol 1. Edited by Michel Lisse, Marie-Louise Mallet, and Ginette Michaud. Translated by Geoffrey Bennington. Chicago and London: The University of Chicago Press.

———. 2011. *The Beast and the Sovereign*. Vol 2. Edited by Michel Lisse, Marie-Louise Mallet, and Ginette Michaud. Translated by Geoffrey Bennington. Chicago and London: The University of Chicago Press.

Esposito, Roberto. 2008. *Biopolitics and Philosophy*. Translated by Timothy Campbell. Minneapolis and London: University of Minnesota Press.

Fisher, Marc. 2009. *Capitalist Realism: Is There No Alternative?* Winchester: Zero Books.

Frye, Marilyn. 1983. *The Politics of Reality: Essay in Feminist Theory*. New York: Crossing Press.

Hegel, Georg Wilhelm Friedrich. 2010. *The Science of Logic*. Translated and edited by George Di Giovanni. New York: Cambidge University Press.

Heidegger, Martin. *Being and Time*. 2001. Translated by John Macquarrie and Edward Robinson. Oxford and Cambridge: Basic Blackwell.

Jean, Grégori. 2018. "On Habit." In *A Companion to Ricoeur's* Freedom and Nature, edited by Scott Davidson, 135–56. Lanham, MD: Lexington Books.

Kant, Immanuel. 1964. *Groundwork of the Metaphysics of Morals*. Translated by H. J. Paton. New York: Harper Torchbooks.

Ricoeur, Paul. 1966. *Freedom and Nature: The Voluntary and the Involuntary*. Translated by Erazim V. Kohák. Evanston, IL: Northwestern University Press.

———. 1970. *Freud and Philosophy: An Essay on Interpretation*. Translated by Denis Savage. New Haven and London: Yale University Press.

———. 1972. *The Symbolism of Evil*. Translated by Emerson Buchanan. Boston: Beacon Press.

———. 2000. *The Just*. Translated by David Pellauer. Chicago: University of Chicago Press.

———. 2005. *The Course of Recognition*. Translated by David Pellauer. Cambridge, MA: Harvard University Press.

———. 2007. *Reflections on the Just*. Translated by David Pellauer. Chicago: University of Chicago Press.

Spinoza, Benedict de. 1955. *On the Improvement of the Understanding: The Ethics; Correspondence*. Translated by R. H. M. Elmas. New York: Dover Publications.

Young, Iris Marion. 1990. *Justice and the Politics of Difference*. Princeton, NJ: Princeton University Press.

———. 2004. "Five Faces of Oppression." In *Oppression, Privilege, and Resistance: Theoretical Perspectives on Racism, Sexism, and Heterosexism*, edited by Lisa M. Heldke and Peg O'Connor, 37–63. Boston: McGraw-Hill.

NOTES

1. Reinforced on September 2nd, 1981, CEDAW has been ratified by 189 countries.
2. My quote comes from the second version of the essay. The first version is in Iris Marion Young, *Justice and the Politics of Difference* (Princeton, NJ: Princeton University Press, 1990).

Conclusion

Ontology of sex is a philosophical account of sex and sexuation (in the sense of being/becoming sexed in human reality or being-in-the-world). Throughout my six chapters, I considered ontologies of sex in feminist as well as non-feminist philosophies that belong to the continental philosophical tradition. In six chapters, I addressed the main concepts and problems of ten ontologies. My book dealt with the great theories in this philosophical domain, by explaining their differences in approaching the same phenomena. It brings together the existentialist-phenomenological, psychoanalytical, queer performativist, and naturalist ontologies of sex with the ontological accounts of sex that are inspired by Heidegger and Ricoeur's capacity approach for the constitution of embodied subjectivity as subject of rights and site of resistance to sexual oppression. This book does not talk about the ontological role of technology in fashioning gender and leaves out the debate on sex as a post-human question. I think these are questions that all ontologies of sex have to face. What I have done in this book can be considered as a preliminary step that lays the ground for ulterior research on these issues.

The ontological question about sex is the primary question for it shapes how we think about sex in the first place. There can be no sexual politics and ethics of Eros without a more or less articulate ontology of sex. That does not of course mean that ethical questions should come after the ontological conceptions. Because they are not secondary, it makes more sense perhaps to speak of onto-ethics as Elizabeth Grosz does. In this book I was much more concerned with the ontological questions in the domain of sex than with the questions of the ethics of Eros or sexual ethics.

Although the philosophical domain I work may be perceived as the battleground of different approaches, I do not think that alternative ontologies should be represented as necessarily exclusive of one another. More precisely, the plurality of the ontological perspectives is not a historical situation of crisis that should be overcome. These ontologies can learn a lot from each other in their ongoing discussion. What we learn from different theories may come and work together in making sense of our experience. Which ontology gives a better account of what it means to be sexed for different groups and offers a better sexual politics? We cannot answer this question without judging the strengths and weaknesses of alternative ontologies, in their actual and virtual dialogue with each other.

All the theories that I have been engaged here contributed to my own reflection on what it means to be sexuated. In dealing with the existential and political problem of sex, it is wise to have different interlocutors. Different perspectives of seeing a phenomenon improve our understanding of it. I did not start writing this book to defend a pre-determined position in mind. Nonetheless, the engagement enabled me to develop my own theoretical tendencies in the course of writing.

My book has the novelty to bring together ontologies of sex that focus on sexual difference with ontologies of sex that focus on erotic experience. I read Simone de Beauvoir, Luce Irigaray, Judith Butler, Elizabeth Grosz, and Jacques Derrida as offering ontologies of sex, which are organized around the question of sexual difference. Although Judith Butler repudiates the question of sexual difference and offers an ontology of gender, this is an attempt to reassess the ontological status of sex. In Georges Bataille and Jean-Luc Nancy, there are ontologies of sex, which are organized around the notion of erotic experience. In my chapter on Paul Ricoeur, I offer a feminist interpretation of his ontology of embodied subjectivity in its vulnerable engagement to fulfill the concrete possibilities of political and legal subjectivity.

In ontologies of sex as erotic experience, at issue is being sexed in corporeal, affective encounters such as relation, communication, expression, signification, being-together, intimacy, coexistence, and separation. These ontologies rest on the awareness that Eros is not just a social and psychological phenomenon of human life, it has existential and ontological significance. In Eros our being as a whole is in question. Bataille holds that sexuality must be included in the ontological analysis of our being-in-the-world. The existential significance of Eros in human life as a problem of ipseity, truth in the existential sense, sovereignty, and violence requires that we grapple with concepts such as law, prohibitions, death, abjection, subjectivity, engagement, intimacy, enjoyment, love, care, incarnated freedom, etc. Ontologies of sex that focus on erotic experience should be part of the ontologies of sex because we need to reflect on ourselves as desiring, relational beings, that have to set limits to sexual violence, of which so many women, children, and nongender-conforming people are victims all over the world. I have only dealt with the erotic experience in the second and fifth chapters, as I commented on Bataille's and Nancy's ontological views. My last chapter sprung from my attempt to overcome the incongruence between ontologies of embodiment and ethics and politics based on the notion of personhood.

Debates on gender and sexual difference constitute a complex field in feminist philosophy. Although the philosophical literature on Beauvoir, Irigaray, and Butler is very rich, their different approaches to sexual difference have not been interpreted as ontologies of sex. These great thinkers of sex/sexual difference/gender have, by thinking through the body as sexed, opened new ontological planes that give us very different ontological perspectives. In my focus to the ontological question, I adopted the continental philosophical strategy of explaining concepts in their relations to philosophical/psychoanalytical approaches that have been major influences on them.

My chapter on Simone de Beauvoir pursues the leading philosophical problem (freedom) that brought her to her own philosophical undertaking, which is, as I see it, an existentialist and phenomenological ontology of sex. I situated Beauvoir's argument in a philosophical debate over freedom, which involves Sartre, Merleau-Ponty, Camus, and Hegel in order to highlight that Beauvoir is the first feminist ontologist of sex. I highlighted first what she originally contributed to the debate on the discussion within existentialism of ontological freedom and the existentialist theory of action. Sartre's philosophy of freedom in *Being and Nothingness* and Merleau-Ponty's critique of it leads Beauvoir to rethink the ambiguity of the embodied situation from the ontological and ethical perspectives. This reflection culminated in the philosophical problematization of sexual oppression in *The Second Sex*. I also see *The Second Sex* as a response to Hegel for whom sexual oppression was not a problem. *The Second Sex* defends the ontological thesis that sexual oppression is grounded in the historical constitution of sexual difference. Beauvoir made explicit the materialist dialectic, which produced the historical sense of radical alterity that grounded sexual relations as sites for oppression of women by men. In other words, sexual violence, women's deprivation of their ontological possibility of freedom, is naturalized by the historical constitution of sexual difference. This ontology of sex is the ground on which feminist theories of oppression have flourished.

We can only read *The Second Sex* superficially, if we lose from sight that Beauvoir's existentialist ontology is an account of the lived experience of the body. For Simone de Beauvoir there is a female biology, even though corporeality in its psychological and physiological expressions is lived by woman in history. The material conditions of history, the tension between the forces of production and reproduction that traverse that history, that is to say patriarchy, confer meaning on how the female body is lived. Biology acknowledged though biological determinism is rejected; in one and the same gesture historical determinism is negated and the history of sense constituted by the domination of men over women is recognized. Beauvoir would reject the metaphysical idea that being a woman has to do with an original feeling that indicates having being born woman. That women can rewrite their corporeal history as they wish manifests an idealist notion of freedom from which she distanced herself. Although women are not born women, they are gendered by the norms society associates with those biological properties. This is still an important lesson to remember today.

Beauvoir is not a voluntarist philosopher as Judith Butler wrongly represented her in *Gender Trouble*. She is always thinking at the intersection between the voluntary and the involuntary material reality. Although existentialism may look like an outdated ontology after structuralism, poststructuralism, deleuzianism, and after many critical readings of *The Second Sex*, I think Beauvoir's phenomenological existentialism is still very inspiring in our task to resolve the disturbing clashes in feminist thought by going back to the tradition of feminist philosophy. Beauvoir starts with the concrete problems of existence and comes back to the lived experience to ask the question how it is structured in its multiple axis of power. Her phenomenology provides great resources to rethink intersectionality. A phenomenological existentialist ontology is definitely needed to understand the unicity and singularity of the experiences of oppression.

My chapter on Beauvoir did not address the question of ethics of Eros, because I fundamentally agree with the feminist readings of Beauvoir's *The Second Sex* as offering an ethics of Eros. She makes gender equality and reciprocity a condition of erotic generosity, the possibility that erotic experience brings with it corporeal, affective, liberating, flourishing, and rewarding love. Beauvoir understands erotic experience as a site of struggle against the colonizing and dehumanizing patriarchal oppression. She argues that we need to fight sexual oppression to live erotic relations in ethical ways.

Lastly, Beauvoir is a thinker of subjectivation, and her sexual politics imply the commitment to working for the freedom of others. And in this struggle, women should not forget that it is the male power that defined what being woman meant. The way women live their lives conform to some patriarchal stereotypes that are constructed and challenge others; and it is in this ambiguity that women struggle to redefine themselves.

In my second chapter, I argued that Bataille, whom, I think, is guilty for failing to problematize sexual oppression, opened a new plane to consider erotic experience. Bataille's ontology of sex rejects that we can understand sex by just looking at how specific types of power shape human bodies in accordance with the economic and political systems they create. In contrast to Foucault and Butler who refuse to begin with nature, Bataille insists we need to begin not with nature as a determinable object of science, but as involving a general economy. He defines the erotic experience as an experience of desire, as the expenditure of life energy, as sovereignty. The flow of life energy in desire brings us into contact with a corporeal Self, which is inseparable from the global energy, the movement of life as a whole. This energy contests the restricted economy and cannot be accommodated by it. The sovereign Self, which Bataille encounters in inner experience is best understood as negating separation, identity, and resists reduction to concerns about utility and survival. Bataille's subject is a relational and generous subject in communion; a subject that affirms violence that destroys the restricted economy of the profane order. This violence is less than the violence suffered because of the enslavement of life for the sake of the accumulation of the surplus value. Bataille has no ethics of Eros, beyond this economy of violence; no means of normatively regulating the boundaries between intimate bodies. He has not clarified how an ethics based on general economy is possible. His atheistic view, which affirms that the sacred realm comes into being by a transposition of the immanence to a transcendent realm, posits that the sacred realm is not simply life denying non-sense. Bataille's thought presents a challenge to the oppressive sexual ontology of theological politics because it keeps the door open for the inquiry into the relation between the religious and the erotic.

In the third chapter, I discussed how Irigaray understands phallocentrism by focusing on her criticism of the imaginary and the symbolic at work in Freud's and Lacan's articulation of sexual difference. Irigaray's reading of Lacan is so brief and so puzzling in so many ways that it takes an immense effort to spell out why she thinks Lacan's approach to sexual difference is similar to Freud's in its phallocentrism. For her, Lacan symbolically enhances the phallocentric universe in which sexual difference cannot appear. This is the claim that in the phallocentric economy of signification female alterity is repressed. This is an ontology of the unapparent, because the phallocentric economy of signification prevents the real feminine alterity from appearing. The question arose if this is an ontological essentialism. According to naturalist essentialism, sexual difference, which is given by nature, attains expressions in the cultural realm. The natural sexual differences display what they have in reserve when they pass in the cultural realm. This view is complicated if we take into account the possibility that the manifestation of a difference can be obstructed. The cultural manifestation of an alterity can be suppressed with the destruction of the conditions of its self-expression. In that case, we are left with a non-apparent alterity, along with the symptoms of its disappearance or absence. And assuming the non-appearing essence is not reducible to one; the realm of expression is even more complicated. This approximates Luce Irigaray's position in *This Sex Which Is Not One*. On this view the continuity and discontinuity between nature and culture is susceptible to the contingencies of power relations. According to the naturalist readers of Irigaray, one cannot deny that nature involves an evolutionary dynamism, which could not be expressed in the form of static differences. There are possibilities and virtualities, which multiply sexual differences and therefore their sexual expressions. Elizabeth Grosz's Darwinian feminism prefers this theoretical thread. I argue that the best strategy to show why Irigaray is not essentialist, is to focus on the role she gives to the imaginary, which paves the way for the creation of a new symbolism, which is the condition of possibility for the real to appear and to attain self-expression.

In the fourth chapter, I turn to the naturalist philosophical feminist/queer understanding of nature as life force or energy. My discussion of the naturalist and the non-naturalist versions of queer theories show how these versions are grounded in different ontologies. This is, indeed, an ongoing philosophical debate in contemporary queer theory. In Bataille, too, Eros is grounded on life's energy. The fourth chapter begins with Judith Butler's gender ontology and explains the major terms of its theory of embodiment as materialization in relation to the performativity of power. Then I turn to the naturalist understandings of sexual difference in Elizabeth Grosz and Claire Colebrook. This post-Kantian dynamic notion of nature that goes back to Nietzsche, Darwin, and Deleuze is conceived as expressing itself in the social and political realm. In general, I do not agree with the view that culture is an expression of nature, even though I value Irigaray's insight that nature can be an inspiring source to artistically create a new culture. I think Bataille's account is richer than Deleuzian feminist theories, because it includes a nonteleological dialectic, which allows for leaps, interruptions, and transposition of desire and significations that help us understand the complexity of nature's relation to the profane and the sacred.

In the fourth chapter, I wondered if a dynamic understanding of sexual difference could be complemented with a Butlerian analysis of gender identity. In my interpretation, naturalism is a metaphysical theory, which assumes that there are natural forces that express themselves in culture. I think naturalism fails to give a good account of power and relies on affirming nature for political change. Just like studies on race show that the scientific argument that race is not real proves to be ineffective to change people's racist attitudes, an argument about the reality of sex is not sufficient to fight sexual discrimination. Sexism is systematic oppression, and, to resist it, we need to inquire how power regimes function.

If naturalism gets rid of normativity, it is unclear how it can have an ethics of Eros at all. To have an ethics of Eros we need to provide naturalism with a political phenomenology and axiology that it misses. Seeing culture as an expression of the natural forces is incongruent with the experience that reveals the effect of power on our bodies. How can naturalism explain, on its own ontological grounds, power/discourse regimes that form bodies? That the affirmation of nature shall emancipate everybody is a dangerous idea, because there will be people who impose their nature on others and force us to act in accordance with our own nature. In the last analysis, I have more sympathy for Butler than for naïve formulations of naturalism, even though I disagree with her idea that sex is reducible to gender and that female and male biology are just theoretical constructions with no basis in reality. Sex is important for women to have sexed rights, but woman as gender can be expanded to include people who desire to live as women. And as an intersectional concept, gender is complex.

It seems to me that in a world that turns toward fascism and authoritarianism, naturalism is more dangerous than in times of liberal democracies. The idea that if something passes as natural, it will be more easily accepted is naïve. History shows that power subverts naturalism and makes use of it to justify its discriminative policies. Sovereign power determines what is and what is not natural. Naturalism has no normative basis beyond natural norms; it can neither offer an ethics nor politics except affirmation and mobilization. The idea that beings with already existing fixed or fluid natural essences can pass in the cultural realm by self-affirmation and political mobilization, invites a politics of war instead of peaceful transformation through dialogue. That violence can change reality and impose a new order is a male idea, even if is a use of power that subverts the oppressed people's arguments and instrumentalizes them for political and economical power. As feminism opposed the ontotheological logic of patriarchy that assigned natural essences to the sexes and instituted the regime of heterosexuality to preserve its power. The re-naturalization of the sexual differentiation and its politicization as identification for emancipatory ends should be seen as suspect as the assignment of natural essences to the sexes.

In contrast to naturalism, Butler's queer theory was developed as a critique of heteronormativity and paved the way for a philosophical reflection on normativity. Norms in our lives regulate and make possible communication between bodies that relate to each other and separate. More significantly, they set some bodies as intelligible and capable of meaningful speech, while others are excluded from the position of subjectivity. Judith Butler's own way of thinking normativity is nourished by Foucauldian and Lacanian approaches. According to Butler, the norms that indicate the place of the speaking subject in Lacan's symbolic system are just as historical, cultural, and constructed by power relations as the norms relating to sexuality of which Foucault has spoken. Butler's significant contribution to this framework is her theory of performativity, in which norms are conceived as rules of behavior that could be assumed or subverted by the bodies, which regulate and produce them. In Lacan the body does not have a role in its taking a position in the symbolic system. At least in the first volume of *The History of Sexuality* bodies are passive beings that are determined by discourses. In Butler, however, the body comes back as capable of behaving, adopting, repeating, appropriating, or ex-appropriating a certain style; it can assume and play with the gender norms. Butler explains how the body encounters cultural norms and is gendered through acts of assumption and transgression. This explains more for me than the naturalist approach. There is a tension and constant struggle with the norms with which the body is forced by language to comply. The norms that we have internalized as children, and the symbolic positions we were forced to take, can create pain and suffering as they assign advantages and disadvantages. To substitute free play with norms to solve gender trouble is to miss the whole argument.

In my fifth chapter, I explain Jean-Luc Nancy's ontology of sex by comparing it mainly with Derrida's ontology of sex. In their attempt to think sex ontologically, both Derrida and Nancy take their main inspiration from Heidegger's *Being and Time*. Although Derrida offers an ontology of sexual difference, Nancy thinks of sexistence with a focus on erotic experience. I argue that Nancy understands sexual differentiation as a function of the erotic experience. For Nancy there is return of sex to philosophy and he conceives his ontological account of sexuation within this return. In Nancy's relational ontology, sex is a force that transforms our existence and puts us in relationship. Bodies become sexed in relations; they differ and defer in the in-between of the relation. To discuss the question of erotic signification in Nancy make us go back to Bataille, and to articulate what Nancy means by *jouissance*, I needed to go into his exchange with Lacan. For Nancy, erotic relation is a site of truth in the sense of self-disclosure in the relation to the other, in the possibility of infinite intimacy. The sexual relation is something to think about in its "there." In this ontology of Eros, reproduction is not the telos of sexuality: Nancy is close to Irigaray in his argument that Eros opens a space for self-relation as much as for the relation to the other. He also sees Eros as the force and site of sexual differentiation. This positive characterization should not make us forget that erotic experience in the impossibility of enjoyment can also be considered as risk, confusion, despair, destruction, loss, and even death. Philosophy can certainly teach us to value erotic encounters as ways of flourishing, as an experience in which we learn about the other, the world, and ourselves and perhaps cope with the destructive consequences of our investments of desire.

My last chapter on Ricoeur, where I talk about the constitution of political subjectivity, can be seen as an attempt to revive philosophy of subjectivity and freedom. This new attempt to come back to freedom and subjectivity is well informed by the critique of subjectivity made in structuralism, psychoanalysis, Foucault's reflection on power, and Butlerian gender theory. We must give sufficient weight to the idea that subject as a sexed/gendered being is produced by the juridical systems of power and that oppression should be thought of as a system of compulsory cis-heterosexuality. Nonetheless, I also think that there is a way of negotiating the thesis that the subject is produced by power with the possibility of a process of subjectivation in which freedom can manifest itself not only as resistance, but also, as in Ricoeur, as a striving to become a subject of rights. This subject is a vulnerable subject, and has to achieve autonomy by exercising the capacities that transform and empower it, even in contexts where vulnerability can never be completely superseded. In fact, this is close to Butler's political phenomenological position in *Dispossessions*. I like Ricoeur's account of subjectivation because it gives me a glimpse of how a phenomenological existentialism could be revived after structuralism, poststructuralism, and even Deleuzian naturalisms.

In times of authoritarianism and fascism it is necessary to come back to existentialism, because individual efforts of resistance and appreciation of personal responsibility mean a lot to struggle with political oppression. The new phenomenological existentialism that I think we should reinvent, should be an ethical and political response to the obliteration of truth and meaning in the public realm, and the consequential collapse of the society into nonsense.

Bibliography

Althusser, Louis. 2014. *Ideology and the Ideological State Apparatuses*. Translated by G. M. Goshgarian. London: Verso.

Anderson, Pamela Sue. 2016. "Ricoeur in Dialogue with Feminist Philosophy of Religion: Hermeneutic Hospitality in Contemporary Practice." In *Feminist Explorations of Paul Ricoeur's Philosophy*, edited by Annemie Halsema and Fernanda Henriques, 199–220. Lanham, MD: Lexington Books.

Arendt, Hannah. 1962. *The Origins of Totalitarianism*. Cleveland and New York: Meridian Books.

Augustine, Saint. 1993. *Confessions*. Books I-XIII. Translated by F. J. Sheed. Indianapolis, Cambridge: Hackett Publishing Company, Inc.

Bachelard, Gaston. 1943. *L'Air et les songes*. Librairie José Corti.

Bataille, Georges. 1970. *Œuvres Complètes I*. Paris: Gallimard.

———. 1974. "Théorie de la religion." *Œuvres Complètes VII*. Paris: Gallimard.

———. 1978. *L'Expérience Intérieure*. Paris: Editions Tel Gallimard.

———. 1986. *Erotism: Death and Sensuality*. Translated by Mary Dalwood. San Francisco: City Lights.

———. 1987. *Story of the Eye*. Translated by Joachim Neugroschel. San Francisco: City Lights Books. (Georges Bataille. 1970. *Œuvres Complètes I*, 12–78. Paris: Gallimard.)

———. 1988. *Inner Experience*. Translated by Leslie Anne Boldt. Albany: State University of New York Press.

———. 1991a. *The Accursed Share*. Vol. 1. Translated by Robert Hurley. New York: Zone Books.

———. 1991b. *The Accursed Share*. Vols. 2–3. Translated by Robert Hurley. New York: Zone Books.

———. 1992. *The Theory of Religion*. Translated by Robert Hurley. New York: Zone Books.

———. 1995. *My Mother, Madame Edwarda, The Dead Man*. Translated by Austryn Wainhouse. New York: Marion Boyars.

———. 2011. *Guilty*. Translated by Stuart Kendall. Albany: State University of New York Press.

Bauer, Nancy. 2001. *Simone de Beauvoir, Philosophy and Feminism*. New York: Columbia University Press.

———. 2011. "Beauvoir on the Allure of Self-Objectification." In *Feminist Metaphysics: Explorations in the Ontology of Sex, Gender and the Self*, edited by Charlotte Witt, 117–29. New York: Springer.

Beauvoir, Simone de. 1944. *Pyrrhus et Cinéas*. Paris: Gallimard.

————. 1945. "La phénoménologie de la perception de Maurice Merleau-Ponty." *Les Temps Modernes*1, no. 2: 363–67.

————. 1966. "Must We Burn Sade?" In *Marquis de Sade*. Translated by A. Michelson. New York: Grove.

————. 1972. *The Coming of Age*. Translated by P. O'Brian. New York: Putnam.

————. 1975. *Force of Circumstance*. The third volume of her autobiography. Translated by Richard Howard. London: Penguin Boooks. Originally published as *La Force des Choses* (Paris: Gallimard, 1963).

————. 1976. *The Ethics of Ambiguity*. Translated by Bernard Frechtman. New York: Citadel Press.

————. 2010. *The Second Sex*. Translated by Constance Borde and Sheila Malovany-Chevallier. New York: Alfred A. Knopf.

Benhabib, Seyla. 1992. *Situating the Self: Gender, Community and Postmodernism in Contemporary Ethics*. Cambridge: Polity Press.

Bergoffen, Debra B. 1997. *The Philosophy of Simone de Beauvoir: Gendered Phenomenologies, Erotic Generosities*. Albany: State University of New York Press.

————. 2000. "From Husserl to Beauvoir: Gendering the Perceiving Subject." In *Feminist Phenomenology*, edited by Linda Fisher and Lester Embree, 187–203. Dordrecht, Boston, London: Kluwer Academic Publishers.

Butler, Judith. 1988. "Performative Acts and Gender Constitution: An Essay in Phenomenology and Feminist Theory." *Theatre Journal* 40, no. 4: 519–31.

————. 1992. "Gendering the Body: Beauvoir's Philosophical Contribution." In *Women, Knowledge and Reality: Explorations in Feminist Philosophy*, edited by Ann Garry and Marilyn Pearsall. Routledge, London and New York. First published 1989.

————. 1993. *Bodies That Matter: On the Discursive Limits of Sex*, London and New York: Routledge.

————. 1994. "Variations on Sex and Gender: Beauvoir, Wittig and Foucault." *Feminism as Critique: Essays on the Politics of Gender in Late Capitalist Societies*, edited by Seyla Benhabib and Drucilla Cornell, 128–42. Cambridge: Polity Press.

————. 1997a. *Excitable Speech: A Politics of the Performative*. New York: Routledge.

————. 1997b. *The Psychic Life of Power, Theories in Subjection*. Stanford, CA: Stanford University Press.

————. 1998. "Sex and Gender in Simone de Beauvoir's *Second Sex*." In *Simone de Beauvoir: A Critical Reader*, edited by Elizabeth Fallaize, 29–42. New York: Routledge. Originally published in *Yale French Studies* 72 (1986).

————. 2008. *Gender Trouble: Feminism and the Subversion of Identity*. London and New York: Routledge.

Camus, Albert. 1955. *The Myth of Sisyphus and Other Essays*. Translated by Justin O'Brien. New York: Alfred A. Knopf.

Cheah, Pheng. 1996. "Mattering (Review Essay of *Bodies That Matter* and Elizabeth Grosz's *Volatile Bodies*)." *Diacritics*, 26, no. 1: 116–18. http://muse.jhu.edu/demo/diacritics/26.1er_butler.html.

Cheah, Pheng, Elizabeth Grosz, and Judith Butler. 1998. "Irigaray and the Political Future of Sexual Difference." *Diacritics* 28, no. 1 (Spring): 19–42.

Colebrook, Claire. 2000. "From Radical Representations to Corporeal Becomings: The Feminist Philosophy of Llyod, Grosz, and Gatens." *Hypatia* 15, no. 2 (Spring): 76–93.

————. 2002. *Gilles Deleuze*. New York: Routledge.

————. 2010. "Queer Vitalism." *New Formations* 1(March): 77–92.

Cudd, A. E., and L. E. Jones. 2003. "Sexism." In *A Companion to Applied Ethics*, edited by R. G. Frey and C. H. Wellman, 102–17. Oxford: Wiley Blackwell.

Deleuze, Gilles, and Félix Guattari. 1983. *Anti-Oedipus: Capitalism and Schizophrenia*. Translated by Robert Hurley, Mark Seem, and Helen R. Lane. Minneapolis: University of Minnesota Press.

————. 1987. *A Thousand Plateaus: Capitalism and Schizophrenia*. Translated by Brian Massumi. Minnesota: University of Minnesota Press.

Derrida, Jacques. 1974. *Glas*. Paris: Éditions Galilée.

———. 1981. *Spurs: Nietzsche's Styles*. Translated by Barbara Harlow. Chicago: University of Chicago Press.

———. 1983. "Geschlecht: Sexual Difference, Ontological Difference." *Research in Phenomenology* XIII: 65–83.

———. 1986. *Glas*. Translated by John. P. Leavey Jr. and Richard Rand. Lincoln: University of Nebraska Press.

———. 1997. *Of Grammatology*. Translated by Gayatri Spivak. Baltimore, MD: Johns Hopkins University Press.

———. 2005. *On Touching—Jean Luc Nancy*. Translated by Christine Irizarry. Stanford, California: Stanford University Press.

———. 2009. *The Beast and the Sovereign*. Vol 1. Edited by Michel Lisse, Marie-Louise Mallet, and Ginette Michaud. Translated by Geoffrey Bennington. Chicago and London: The University of Chicago Press.

———. 2011. *The Beast and the Sovereign*. Vol 2. Edited by Michel Lisse, Marie-Louise Mallet, and Ginette Michaud. Translated by Geoffrey Bennington. Chicago and London: The University of Chicago Press.

Direk, Zeynep. 2011. "Immanence and Abjection in Simone De Beauvoir." *Southern Journal of Philosophy* 49, no. 1 (March 2011): 49–72.

———. 2015. "Kristeva and Bataille: On Religion." In *Negative Ecstasies: Georges Bataille and the Study of Religion*, edited by Kent Brintnall and Jeremy Biles, 182–201. New York: Fordham University Press.

Dworkin, Andrea. 1981. *Pornography: Men Possessing Women*. New York: Perigee.

Esposito, Roberto. 2008. *Biopolitics and Philosophy*. Translated by Timothy Campbell. Minneapolis and London: University of Minnesota Press.

Feder, Ellen K. and Emily Zarkin. 1997. "Flirting with the Truth: Derrida's Discourse with 'Woman' and Wenches." In *Derrida and Feminism: Recasting the Question of Woman*, edited by Ellen K. Feder, Mary C. Rawlinson, and Emily Zarkin, 21–52. New York and London: Routledge.

Fisher, Marc. 2009. *Capitalist Realism: Is There No Alternative*. Winchester: Zero Books.

Flaubert, Gustav. 1965. *Madame Bovary*. Translated by Paul de Man. New York: W.W. Norton & Company.

Foucault, Michel. 1977. *Discipline and Punish: The Birth of Prison*. Translated by Alan Sheridan. New York: Vintage Books.

———. 1980. *The History of Sexuality: An Introduction*. Vol. 1. Translated by Robert Hurley. New York: Vintage Books.

———. 1985. *The History of Sexuality: The Use of Pleasure*. Vol. 2. Translated by Robert Hurley. New York: Vintage Books.

Freud, Sigmund. 2001a. "Totem and Taboo: Resemblances Between the Psychic Lives of Savages and Neurotics." In *Standard Edition of the Complete Psychological Works of Sigmund Freud*. Vol. 13. Translated by James Strachey. London: Hogarth Press and the Institute of Psycho-Analysis.

———. 2001b. "Female Sexuality." In *Standard Edition of the Complete Psychological Works of Sigmund Freud*. Vol. 21. Translated by James Strachey. London: Hogarth Press and the Institute of Psycho-Analysis.

———. 2001c. "The Taboo of Virginity." In *Standard Edition of the Complete Psychological Works of Sigmund Freud*. Vol. 11. Translated by James Strachey. London: Hogarth Press and the Institute of Psycho-Analysis.

———. 2001d. "Femininity." In *Standard Edition of the Complete Psychological Works of Sigmund Freud*. Vol. 24. Translated by James Strachey. London: Hogarth Press and the Institute of Psycho-Analysis.

Frye, Marilyn. 1983. *The Politics of Reality: Essay in Feminist Theory*. New York: Crossing Press.

Gallop, Jane. 1997. "'Women' in *Spurs* and Nineties Feminism." In *Derrida and Feminism: Recasting the Question of Woman*, edited by Ellen K. Feder, Mary C. Rawlinson, and Emily Zarkin, 7–20. New York and London: Routledge.

Grosz, Elizabeth. 1989. *Sexual Subversions. Three French Feminists*. Sydney: Allen & Unwin.

————. 1990. *Jacques Lacan: A Feminist Introduction*. London and New York: Routledge.
————. 1994. *Volatile Bodies: Towards a Corporeal Feminism*. Bloomington and Indianapolis: Indiana University Press.
————. 2012. "The Nature of Sexual Difference: Irigaray and Darwin." *Angelaki* 17, no. 2 (July): 69–93.
————. 2017a. *The Incorporeal: Ontology, Ethics and the Limits of Materialism*. New York: Columbia University Press.
————. 2017b. "Irigaray, the Untimely, and the Constitution of an Onto-Ethics." *Australian Feminist Law* 43, no. 1.
Grosz, Elizabeth, and Rebecca Hill. 2017. "Onto-Ethics and Difference: An Interview with Elizabeth Grosz." *Australian Feminist Law Journal* 43, no. 1: 5–14.
Hartmann, Nadine. 2016. "Eroticism." In *Georges Bataille: Key Concepts*, edited by Mark Hewson and Marcus Coelen, 136–47. London and New York: Routledge.
Hegel, Georg Wilhelm Friedrich. 2010. *The Science of Logic*. Translated and edited by George Di Giovanni. New York: Cambidge University Press.
————. 2018. *The Phenomenology of Spirit*. Translated by Michael Inwood. Oxford: Oxford University Press.
Heidegger, Martin. 1991. *Nietzsche*. Vols. 3 and 4. Translated by Joan Stambaugh, David Farell Krell, and Frank A. Capuzzi. San Francisco: Harper.
Heinämaa, Sara. 1997. "What Is a Woman? Butler and de Beauvoir on the Foundations of Sexual Difference." *Hypatia* 12, no. 1 (Winter).
Irigaray, Luce. 1985a. *Speculum of the Other Woman*. Ithaca, NY: Cornell University Press.
————. 1985b. *This Sex Which Is Not One*. Translated by Catherine Porter with Carolyn Burke. Ithaca, NY: Cornell University Press.
————. 1993. *An Ethics of Sexual Difference*. Translated by Carolyn Burke and Gillian C. Gill. Ithaca, NY: Cornell University Press.
————. 2000. *Why Different? A Culture of Two Subjects: Interviews with Luce Irigaray*. Edited S. Lotringer. Translated by C. Collins. New York: Semiotext(e).
————. 2001. *To Be Two*. New York. Routledge.
Jean, Grégori. 2018. "On Habit." In *A Companion to Ricoeur's* Freedom and Nature, edited by Scott Davidson, 135–56. Lanham, MD: Lexington Books.
Johnstone, Maxine Sheets. 2016. "The Roots of Power." *Google Books*. N.p., n.d. Web. Dec. 3, 2016.
Kant, Immanuel. 1964. *Groundwork of the Metaphysics of Morals*. Translated by H. J. Paton. New York: Harper Torchbooks.
————. 1997. *Critique of Practical Reason*. Translated and edited by Mary Gregor. Cambridge: Cambridge University Press.
————. 1998. *Critique of Pure Reason*. Translated and edited by Paul Guyer and Allen W. Wood. Cambridge: Cambridge University Press.
Kontturi, Katve Kaisa, and Milla Tiainen. 2007. "Feminism, Art, Deleuze, and Darwin: An Interview with Elizabeth Grosz." *Nora Nordic Journal of Women's Studies* 15, no. 4 (November): 246–56.
Kristeva, Julia. 1987. *Tales of Love*. Translated by Leon S. Roudiez. New York: Columbia University Press.
Kruks, Sonia. 1990. *Situation and Human Existence: Freedom, Subjectivity, and Society*. New York: Routledge.
————. 1995. "Teaching Sartre about Freedom." In *Feminist Interpretations of Simone de Beauvoir*, edited by Margaret A. Simons, 79–95. University Park: Pennsylvania State University Press.
Lacan, Jacques. 1999. *Encore: The Seminar of Jacques Lacan: On Feminine Sexuality, the Limits of Love and Knowledge, 1972–1973*. Book 20. Edited by Jacques-Alain Miller. Translated with notes by Bruce Fink. New York and London: W.W. Norton & Company. Originally published as *Le Séminaire, Livre XX, Encore* (Paris: Éditions du Seuil, 1975).
————. 2006. *Écrits*. Translated by Bruce Fink. New York and London: W.W. Norton & Company.

————. 2008. *The Seminar of Jacques Lacan: The Ethics of Psychoanalysis*. Book VIII. Edited by Jacques-Alain Miller. Translated with notes by Dennis Porter. New York and London: W.W. Norton & Company.

Langer, Monica. 2003. "Beauvoir and Merleau-Ponty on Ambiguity." In *The Cambridge Companion to Simone de Beauvoir*, edited by Claudia Card, 87–106. Cambridge University Press.

Levi-Strauss, Claude. 1969. *The Elementary Structures of Kinship*. Translated by James Harle Bell and John Richard von Sturmer. Edited by Rodney Needham. Boston: Beacon Press.

Levinas, Emmanuel. 2009. *Carnets de captivité et autres inédits. Œuvres*, Vol 1. Edited by Rodolphe Calin and Catherine Chalier. Paris: IMEC /Grasset.

Lundren-Gothlin, Eva. 1998. "The Master-Slave Dialectic in *The Second Sex*." In *Simone de Beauvoir: A Critical Reader*, edited by Elizabeth Fallaize, 93–108. London: Routledge.

Manjali, Franson, and Marc Crépon. 2018. *Philosophy, Language, and the Political: Post-Structuralism in Perspective*. Translated by C. Cordova, edited by Franson Manjali and Marc Crépon. Delhi: Aakar Books.

Merleau-Ponty, Maurice. 1973. *Adventures of the Dialectic*. Translated by Hugh J. Silverman and Joseph J. Bien. Evanston, IL: Northwestern University Press.

————. 1990. *Humanism and Terror: An Essay on the Communist Problem*. Translated by John O'Neill. Boston: Beacon Press.

————. 2012. *Phenomenology of Perception*. Translated by Donald A. Landes. London: Routledge Classics.

Moi, Toril. 1999. *What Is a Woman? And Other Essays*. New York: Oxford University Press.

Nancy, Jean-Luc. 2001. *L' "il y a" du rapport sexuel*. Paris: Éditions Galilée.

————. 2013. *Corpus II: Writings on Sexuality*. New York: Fordham University Press.

————. 2017a. *Sexistence*. Accompagné d'un Frontispice de Miquel Barceló. Paris: Éditions Galilée.

————. 2017b. "Jouis Anniversaire," *L'Entretien no. 3: Jacques Derrida*, edited by Laure Adler and Alain Veinstein. Paris: Seuil/Éditions du sous-sol.

Nancy, Jean-Luc and Lacou-Labarthe Philippe. 1992. *The Title of the Letter: A Reading of Lacan*. Translated by François Raffoul and David Pettigrew. Albany: State University of New York Press.

Nietzsche, Friedrich. 1999. *Philosophy and Truth: Selections from Nietzsche's Notebooks of the Early 1870s*. Translated by Daniel Breazeale. New York: Humanity Books.

Noddings, Nell. 2012. *Peace Eduation: How We Come to Love and Hate War*. Cambridge: Cambridge University Press.

Ong-Van-Cung, Kim Sang. 2011. "Critique et subjectivation. Foucault et Butler sur le sujet." *Actuel Marx* 1, no. 49: 148–61.

Plato. 1984. "The Symposium." *The Dialogues of Plato*. Translated by Reginald E. Allen. New Haven: Yale University Press.

————. *Gorgias*. Translated by Robin Waterfield. Clarendon: Oxford University Press.

————. *Phaedrus*. Translated by Robin Waterfield. Clarendon: Oxford University Press.

Ricoeur, Paul. 1966. *Freedom and Nature: The Voluntary and The Involuntary*. Translated by Erazim V. Kohák. Evanston, IL: Northwestern University Press.

————. 1970. *Freud and Philosophy: An Essay on Interpretation*. Translated by Denis Savage. New Haven and London: Yale University Press.

————. 1972. *The Symbolism of Evil*. Translated by Emerson Buchanan. Boston: Beacon Press.

————. 2000. *The Just*. Translated by David Pellauer. Chicago: University of Chicago Press.

————. 2005. *The Course of Recognition*. Translated by David Pellauer. Cambridge, MA: Harvard University Press.

————. 2007. *Reflections on the Just*. Translated by David Pellauer. Chicago: University of Chicago Press.

Rose, Jacqueline. 1985. "Introduction II." *Feminine Sexuality: Jacques Lacan and the écol freudienne*, edited by Juliet Mitchell and Jacqueline Rose, 27–58. Translated by Jacqueline Rose. New York and London: W.W. Norton and Pantheon Books.

Sandford, Stella. 1999. "Contingent Ontologies, Sex, Gender and 'Woman' in Simone de Beauvoir and Judith Butler." *Radical Philosophy* 97: 18–29.

———. 2006. *How to Read Beauvoir*. London: Granta Books.

Sartre, Jean-Paul. 1940. *L'imaginaire*. Paris: Gallimard.

———. 1987. *The Family Idiot: Gustave Flaubert 1821–1857*. Translated by Carol Cosman. Chicago: The University of Chicago Press.

———. 2003. *Being and Nothingness*. Translated by Hazel E. Barnes. London: Routledge Classics.

———. 2004. *Critique of Dialectical Reason*. Vol. 1. Translated by Alan Sheridan Smith. Edited by Jonathan Rée. London New York: Verso.

Sontag, Susan. 1969. *Styles of Radical Will*. New York: Vintage.

Spinoza, Benedict de. 1955. *On the Improvement of the Understanding: The Ethics; Correspondence*. Translated by R. H. M. Elmas. New York: Dover Publications.

Stoetzler, Marcel. 2005. "Subject Trouble: Judith Butler and Dialectics." *Philosophy Social Criticism* 31: 343–68.

Stoller, Silvia. 2010. "Expressivity and Performativity: Merleau-Ponty and Butler." *Continental Philosophical Review* 43, no. 1 (April): 97–110.

Stone, Alison. 2003. "Irigaray and Hölderlin on the Relation between Nature and Culture." *Continental Philosophy Review* 36: 415–32.

———. 2004a. "From Political to Realist Essentialism: Re-Reading Luce Irigaray." *Feminist Theory* 5, no. 1: 5–23.

———. 2004b. "The Way of Love, by Luce Irigaray, translated by Heidi Bostic and Stephen Pluháček." *Journal of the British Society for Phenomenology* 35, no. 3: 318–20.

Suleiman, Rubin Susan. 1995a. "Transgression and the Avant-Garde: Bataille's Histoire de 'Oeil." In *On Bataille: Critical Essays*, edited by Leslie Anne Boldt-Irons, 313–34. Albany: State University of New York Press.

———. 1995b. "Bataille in the Street: The Search for Virility in 1930s." In *Bataille: Writing the Sacred*, edited by Carolyn Bailey Gill, 26–45. London and New York: Routledge.

Sullivan, Ellie Raglan. 1986. *Jacques Lacan and the Philosophy of Psychoanalysis*. Chicago: University of Illinois Press.

Tidd, Ursula. 2004. *Simone de Beauvoir: Gender and Testimony*. Cambridge: Cambridge University Press.

Ward, Julie K. 1995. "Beauvoir's Two Senses of 'Body' in *The Second Sex*." In *Feminist Interpretations of Simone de Beauvoir*, edited by Margaret A. Simons, 223–42. University Park: Pennsylvania State University Press.

Whitford, Margaret. 1986. "Luce Irigaray and the Female Imaginary: Speaking as a Woman." *Radical Philosophy* 43, no. 4: 3–8.

———. 1991a. "Irigaray's Body Symbolic." *Hypatia* 6, no. 3: 97–110.

———. 1991b. *Philosophy in the Feminine*. London and New York: Routledge.

Wilkerson, William. 2017. *A Companion to Simone de Beauvoir*. Edited by Nancy Bauer and Laura Hengehold, 224–35. Hoboken, NJ: Wiley-Blackwell.

Winnubst, Shannon. 2007. "Bataille's Queer Pleasures: The Universe as Spider or Spit." In *Reading Bataille Now*, edited by Shannon Winnubst, 75–93. Bloomington and Indianapolis: Indiana University Press.

Wright, Elizabeth. 1992. *Feminism and Psychoanalysis: A Critical Dictionary*. Oxford and Cambridge: Basil Blackwell.

Young, Iris Marion. 1990. *Justice and the Politics of Difference*. Princeton, NJ: Princeton University Press.

———. 2004. "Five Faces of Oppression." *Oppression, Privilege, and Resistance: Theoretical Perspectives on Racism, Sexism, and Heterosexism*, edited by Lisa M. Heldke and Peg O'Connor, 37–63. Boston: McGraw-Hill.

Index

117, 118, 135, 141, 142, 153, 171, 179,
182, 188, 192, 194, 200, 201, 206, 207,
208–209, 211
vulnerability, xiii, xiv, 126, 177, 178, 179,
180, 183, 191, 195, 197, 199, 201, 213

Ward, Julie K., 27, 43, 220
Whitford, Margareth, 84, 93, 99, 100, 101,
106, 107, 109, 110, 220

Wilkerson, William, 13, 43, 220
Winnubst, Shannon, 65, 78, 220
Wright, Elizabeth, 93, 110, 220

Young, Iris Marion, xiv, 196, 197, 202,
203n2, 220

Zarkin, Emily, 156, 175, 217

About the Author

Zeynep Direk obtained her PhD from the University of Memphis in 1998. She is professor in the Department of Philosophy at Koç University, in Istanbul, Turkey. She publishes on contemporary French philosophy, ethics, political philosophy, feminism, and the history of Turkish philosophy. Her research on feminism focuses on feminist thinkers' interpretations of the fundamental problems and concepts of Western philosophy. She has co-edited, with Leonard Lawlor, *A Companion to Derrida* (2014), and is the author of three books in Turkish.

www.ingramcontent.com/pod-product-compliance
Lightning Source LLC
Chambersburg PA
CBHW021814270326
41932CB00007B/179